Learn OpenCV 4 by Building Projects
Second Edition

Build real-world computer vision and image processing
applications with OpenCV and C++

David Millán Escrivá
Vinícius G. Mendonça
Prateek Joshi

BIRMINGHAM - MUMBAI

Learn OpenCV 4 by Building Projects
Second Edition

Commissioning Editor: Aaron Lazar
Acquisition Editor: Sandeep Mishra
Content Development Editor: Pooja Parvatkar
Technical Editor: Abin Sebastian
Copy Editor: Safis Editing
Project Coordinator: Ulhas Kambali
Proofreader: Safis Editing
Indexer: Pratik Shirodkar
Graphics: Tom Scaria
Production Coordinator: Nilesh Mohite

First published: January 2016
Second edition: November 2018

Production reference: 1301118

Published by Packt Publishing Ltd.
Livery Place
35 Livery Street
Birmingham
B3 2PB, UK.

ISBN 978-1-78934-122-5

www.packtpub.com

`mapt.io`

Mapt is an online digital library that gives you full access to over 5,000 books and videos, as well as industry leading tools to help you plan your personal development and advance your career. For more information, please visit our website.

Why subscribe?

- Spend less time learning and more time coding with practical eBooks and Videos from over 4,000 industry professionals

- Improve your learning with Skill Plans built especially for you

- Get a free eBook or video every month

- Mapt is fully searchable

- Copy and paste, print, and bookmark content

Packt.com

Did you know that Packt offers eBook versions of every book published, with PDF and ePub files available? You can upgrade to the eBook version at `www.packt.com` and as a print book customer, you are entitled to a discount on the eBook copy. Get in touch with us at `customercare@packtpub.com` for more details.

At `www.packt.com`, you can also read a collection of free technical articles, sign up for a range of free newsletters, and receive exclusive discounts and offers on Packt books and eBooks.

Contributors

About the authors

David Millán Escrivá was eight years old when he wrote his first program on an 8086 PC using the BASIC language. He completed his studies in IT from the Universitat Politécnica de Valencia with honors in human-computer interaction supported by computer vision with OpenCV (v0.96). He has a master's degree in artificial intelligence, computer graphics, and pattern recognition, focusing on pattern recognition and computer vision. He also has more than nine years' experience in computer vision, computer graphics, and pattern recognition. He is the author of the Damiles Blog, where he publishes articles and tutorials on OpenCV, computer vision in general, and optical character recognition algorithms.

I would like thank to my wife, Izaskun, my daughter, Eider, and my son, Pau, for their unlimited patience and support at all times. They have changed my life and made it awesome every day. I love you all.

I would like to thank the OpenCV team and community that gives us this wonderful library. I would also like to thank my co-authors and Packt Publishing for supporting me and helping me to complete this book.

Vinícius G. Mendonça is a computer graphics university professor at Pontifical Catholic University of Paraná (PUCPR). He started programming with C++ back in 1998, and ventured into the field of computer gaming and computer graphics back in 2006. He is currently a mentor at the Apple Developer Academy in Brazil, working with, and teaching, metal, machine learning and computer vision for mobile devices. He has served as a reviewer on other Pack books, including *OpenNI Cookbook*, and *Mastering OpenCV and Computer Vision with OpenCV 3 and Qt5*. In his research, he has used Kinect, OpenNI, and OpenCV to recognize Brazilian sign language gestures. His areas of interest include mobile, OpenGL, image processing, computer vision, and project management.

I would like to thank my wife, Thais A. L. Mendonça, for the support she gave me while writing this book. I also dedicate this work to my four girls, Laura, Helena, Alice, and Mariana, and to my stepson, Bruno.

My life and work would have no meaning without this great family. I would also like to thank Fabio Binder – my teacher, boss, and mentor – who introduced me to computer graphics and gaming fields, and who has helped me greatly throughout my career.

Prateek Joshi is an artificial intelligence researcher, an author of eight published books, and a TEDx speaker. He has been featured in Forbes 30 Under 30, CNBC, TechCrunch, Silicon Valley Business Journal, and many more publications. He is the founder of Pluto AI, a venture-funded Silicon Valley start-up building an intelligence platform for water facilities. He graduated from the University of Southern California with a Master's degree specializing in Artificial Intelligence. He has previously worked at NVIDIA and Microsoft Research.

About the reviewers

Marc Amberg is an experienced machine learning and computer vision engineer with a proven history of working in the IT and service industries. He is skilled in Python, C/C++, OpenGL, 3D Reconstruction, and Java. He is a strong engineering professional with a master's degree focused on computer science (Image, Vision, and Interactions) from Université des Sciences et Technologies de Lille (Lille I).

Vincent Kok currently works as a software platform application engineer with Intel in the transportation industry sector. He graduated from the University Sains Malaysia (USM) with a degree in electronic engineering. Currently, he is pursuing his master's degree in embedded system engineering at USM. Vincent actively involves himself with the developer community and regularly participates in the Maker Faire, which is held in different parts of the world. He likes to design electronic hardware kits and gives soldering/arduino classes for beginners during his spare time.

Packt is searching for authors like you

If you're interested in becoming an author for Packt, please visit `authors.packtpub.com` and apply today. We have worked with thousands of developers and tech professionals, just like you, to help them share their insight with the global tech community. You can make a general application, apply for a specific hot topic that we are recruiting an author for, or submit your own idea.

Table of Contents

Preface

OpenCV is one of the most popular libraries used to develop computer vision applications. It enables us to run many different computer vision algorithms in real time. It has been around for many years, and it has become the standard library in this field. One of the main advantages of OpenCV is that it is highly optimized and available on almost all platforms.

This book starts off by giving a brief introduction to the various fields in computer vision and the associated OpenCV functionalities in C++. Each chapter contains real-world examples and code samples to demonstrate the use cases. This helps you to easily grasp the topics and understand how they can be applied in real life. To sum up, this is a practical guide on how to use OpenCV in C++ and build various applications using this library.

Who this book is for

This book is for developers who are new to OpenCV and want to develop computer vision applications with OpenCV in C++. A basic knowledge of C++ would be helpful in understanding this book. This book is also useful for people who want to get started with computer vision and understand the underlying concepts. They should be aware of basic mathematical concepts, such as vectors, matrices, and matrix multiplication, in order to get the most out of this book. During the course of this book, you will learn how to build various computer vision applications from scratch using OpenCV.

What this book covers

Chapter 1, *Getting Started with OpenCV*, covers installation steps on various operating systems and provides an introduction to the human visual system, as well as various topics in computer vision.

Chapter 2, *Introduction to OpenCV Basics*, discusses how to read/write images and videos in OpenCV, and also explains how to build a project using CMake.

Chapter 3, *Learning Graphical User Interface and Basic Filtering*, covers how to build a graphical user interface and mouse event detector to build interactive applications.

Chapter 4, *Delving into Histograms and Filters*, explores histograms and filters and also shows how we can cartoonize an image.

Chapter 5, *Automated Optical Inspection, Object Segmentation, and Detection*, describes various image pre-processing techniques, such as noise removal, thresholding, and contour analysis.

Chapter 6, *Learning Object Classification*, deals with object recognition and machine learning, and how to use support vector machines to build an object classification system.

Chapter 7, *Detecting Face Parts and Overlaying Masks*, discusses face detection and Haar Cascades, and then explains how these methods can be used to detect various parts of the human face.

Chapter 8, *Video Surveillance, Background Modeling, and Morphological Operations*, explores background subtraction, video surveillance, and morphological image processing, and describes how they are connected to one another.

Chapter 9, *Learning Object Tracking*, covers how to track objects in a live video using different techniques, such as color-based and feature-based tracking.

Chapter 10, *Developing Segmentation Algorithms for Text Recognition*, covers optical character recognition, text segmentation, and provides an introduction to the Tesseract OCR engine.

Chapter 11, *Text Recognition with Tesseract*, delves deeper into the Tesseract OCR engine to explain how it can be used for text detection, extraction, and recognition.

Chapter 12, *Deep Learning with OpenCV*, explores how to apply deep learning in OpenCV with two commonly used deep learning architectures: YOLO v3 for object detection, and Single Shot Detector for face detection.

To get the most out of this book

A basic knowledge of C++ would be helpful in understanding this book. The examples are built using the following technologies: OpenCV 4.0; CMake 3.3.x or newer; Tesseract; Leptonica (a dependency of Tesseract); Qt (optional); and OpenGL (optional).

Detailed installation instructions are provided in the relevant chapters.

Download the example code files

You can download the example code files for this book from your account at www.packt.com. If you purchased this book elsewhere, you can visit www.packt.com/support and register to have the files emailed directly to you.

You can download the code files by following these steps:

1. Log in or register at `www.packt.com`.
2. Select the **SUPPORT** tab.
3. Click on **Code Downloads & Errata**.
4. Enter the name of the book in the **Search** box and follow the onscreen instructions.

Once the file is downloaded, please make sure that you unzip or extract the folder using the latest version of:

- WinRAR/7-Zip for Windows
- Zipeg/iZip/UnRarX for Mac
- 7-Zip/PeaZip for Linux

The code bundle for the book is also hosted on GitHub at `https://github.com/PacktPublishing/Learn-OpenCV-4-By-Building-Projects-Second-Edition`. In case there's an update to the code, it will be updated on the existing GitHub repository.

We also have other code bundles from our rich catalog of books and videos available at `https://github.com/PacktPublishing/`. Check them out!

Download the color images

We also provide a PDF file that has color images of the screenshots/diagrams used in this book. You can download it here: `https://www.packtpub.com/sites/default/files/downloads/9781789341225_ColorImages.pdf`.

Code in Action

Visit the following link to check out videos of the code being run:
`http://bit.ly/2Sfrxgu`

Conventions used

There are a number of text conventions used throughout this book.

`CodeInText`: Indicates code words in text, database table names, folder names, filenames, file extensions, pathnames, dummy URLs, user input, and Twitter handles. Here is an example: "Also, installing this package is optional. OpenCV will work just fine if you don't install `opencv_contrib`."

A block of code is set as follows:

```
// Load image to process
  Mat img= imread(img_file, 0);
  if(img.data==NULL){
    cout << "Error loading image "<< img_file << endl;
    return 0;
  }
```

When we wish to draw your attention to a particular part of a code block, the relevant lines or items are set in bold:

```
for(auto i=1; i<num_objects; i++){
    cout << "Object "<< i << " with pos: " << centroids.at<Point2d>(i) << "
with area " << stats.at<int>(i, CC_STAT_AREA) << endl;
```

Any command-line input or output is written as follows:

```
C:> setx -m OPENCV_DIR D:OpenCVBuildx64vc14
```

Bold: Indicates a new term, an important word, or words that you see on screen. For example, words in menus or dialog boxes appear in the text like this. Here is an example: "Select **System info** from the **Administration** panel."

Warnings or important notes appear like this.

Tips and tricks appear like this.

Get in touch

Feedback from our readers is always welcome.

General feedback: If you have questions about any aspect of this book, mention the book title in the subject of your message and email us at customercare@packtpub.com.

Errata: Although we have taken every care to ensure the accuracy of our content, mistakes do happen. If you have found a mistake in this book, we would be grateful if you would report this to us. Please visit `www.packt.com/submit-errata`, selecting your book, clicking on the Errata Submission Form link, and entering the details.

Piracy: If you come across any illegal copies of our works in any form on the internet, we would be grateful if you would provide us with the location address or website name. Please contact us at `copyright@packt.com` with a link to the material.

If you are interested in becoming an author: If there is a topic that you have expertise in, and you are interested in either writing or contributing to a book, please visit `authors.packtpub.com`.

Reviews

Please leave a review. Once you have read and used this book, why not leave a review on the site that you purchased it from? Potential readers can then see and use your unbiased opinion to make purchase decisions, we at Packt can understand what you think about our products, and our authors can see your feedback on their book. Thank you!

For more information about Packt, please visit `packt.com`.

Getting Started with OpenCV 1

Computer vision applications are interesting and useful, but the underlying algorithms are computationally intensive. With the advent of cloud computing, we are getting more processing power to work with.

The OpenCV library enables us to run computer vision algorithms efficiently in real time. It has been around for many years, and has become the standard library in this field. One of the main advantages of OpenCV is that it is highly optimized, and available on almost all platforms.

This book will cover the various algorithms we will be using, why we are using them, and how to implement them in OpenCV.

In this chapter, we are going to learn how to install OpenCV on various operating systems. We will discuss what OpenCV offers out of the box, and the various things that we can do using the inbuilt functions.

By the end of this chapter, you will be able to answer the following questions:

- How do humans process visual data, and how do they understand image content?
- What can we do with OpenCV, and what are the various modules available in OpenCV that can be used to achieve those things?
- How do we install OpenCV on Windows, Linux, and Mac OS X?

Understanding the human visual system

Before we jump into OpenCV functionalities, we need to understand why those functions were built in the first place. It's important to understand how the human visual system works, so that you can develop the right algorithms.

The goal of computer vision algorithms is to understand the content of images and videos. Humans seem to do it effortlessly! So, how do we get machines to do it with the same accuracy?

Let's consider the following diagram:

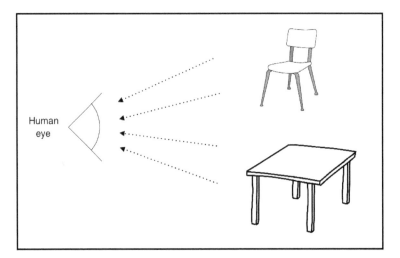

The human eye captures all the information that comes along the way, such as color, shape, brightness, and so on. In the preceding image, the human eye captures all the information about the two main objects and stores it in a certain way. Once we understand how our system works, we can take advantage of it to achieve what we want.

For example, here are a few things we need to know:

- Our visual system is more sensitive to low-frequency content than high-frequency content. Low-frequency content refers to planar regions where pixel values don't change rapidly, and high-frequency content refers to regions with corners and edges where pixel values fluctuate a lot. We can easily see if there are blotches on a planar surface, but it's difficult to spot something like that on a highly-textured surface.
- The human eye is more sensitive to changes in brightness than to changes in color.

- Our visual system is sensitive to motion. We can quickly recognize if something is moving in our field of vision, even though we are not directly looking at it.

- We tend to make a mental note of salient points in our field of vision. Let's say you look at a white table with four black legs, and a red dot at one of the corners of the table surface. When you look at this table, you'll immediately make a mental note that the surface and legs have opposing colors, and that there is a red dot on one of the corners. Our brain is really smart that way! We do this automatically so that we can immediately recognize an object if we encounter it again.

To get an idea of our field of view, let's look at the top view of a human, and the angles at which we see various things:

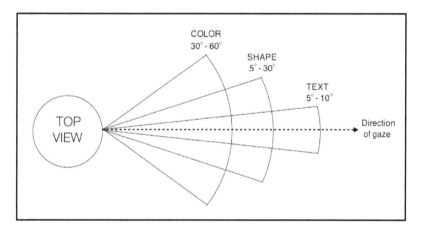

Our visual system is actually capable of a lot more, but this should be good enough to get us started. You can explore further by reading up on **Human Visual System** (**HVS**) models on the web.

How do humans understand image content?

If you look around, you will see a lot of objects. You encounter many different objects every day, and you recognize them almost instantaneously without any effort. When you see a chair, you don't wait for a few minutes before realizing that it is in fact a chair. You just know that it's a chair right away.

Computers, on the other hand, find it very difficult to do this task. Researchers have been working for many years to find out why computers are not as good as we are at this.

To get an answer to that question, we need to understand how humans do it. The visual data processing happens in the ventral visual stream. This ventral visual stream refers to the pathway in our visual system that is associated with object recognition. It is basically a hierarchy of areas in our brain that helps us recognize objects.

Humans can recognize different objects effortlessly, and can cluster similar objects together. We can do this because we have developed some sort of invariance toward objects of the same class. When we look at an object, our brain extracts the salient points in such a way that factors such as orientation, size, perspective, and illumination don't matter.

A chair that is double the normal size and rotated by 45 degrees is still a chair. We can recognize it easily because of the way we process it. Machines cannot do that so easily. Humans tend to remember an object based on its shape and important features. Regardless of how the object is placed, we can still recognize it.

In our visual system, we build up these hierarchical invariances with respect to position, scale, and viewpoint that help us to be very robust. If you look deeper into our system, you will see that humans have cells in their visual cortex that can respond to shapes such as curves and lines.

As we move further along our ventral stream, we will see more complex cells that are trained to respond to more complex objects such as trees, gates, and so on. The neurons along our ventral stream tend to show an increase in the size of the receptive field. This is coupled with the fact that the complexity of their preferred stimuli increases as well.

Why is it difficult for machines to understand image content?

We now understand how visual data enters the human visual system, and how our system processes it. The issue is that we still don't fully understand how our brain recognizes and organizes this visual data. In machine learning, we just extract some features from images, and ask the computers to learn them using algorithms. We still have these variations, such as shape, size, perspective, angle, illumination, occlusion, and so on.

For example, the same chair looks very different to a machine when you look at it from the profile view. Humans can easily recognize that it's a chair, regardless of how it's presented to us. So, how do we explain this to our machines?

One way to do this would be to store all the different variations of an object, including sizes, angles, perspectives, and so on. But this process is cumbersome and time-consuming. Also, it's actually not possible to gather data that can encompass every single variation. The machines would consume a huge amount of memory and a lot of time to build a model that can recognize these objects.

Even with all this, if an object is partially occluded, computers still won't recognize it. This is because they think this is a new object. So when we build a computer vision library, we need to build the underlying functional blocks that can be combined in many different ways to formulate complex algorithms.

OpenCV provides a lot of these functions, and they are highly optimized. So once we understand what OpenCV is capable of, we can use it effectively to build interesting applications.

Let's go ahead and explore that in the next section.

What can you do with OpenCV?

Using OpenCV, you can pretty much do every computer vision task you can think of. Real-life problems require you to use many computer vision algorithms and modules together to achieve the desired result. So, you just need to understand which OpenCV modules and functions to use, in order to get what you want.

Let's look at what OpenCV can do out of the box.

Inbuilt data structures and input/output

One of the best things about OpenCV is that it provides a lot of in-built primitives to handle operations related to image processing and computer vision. If you have to write something from scratch, you will have to define `Image`, `Point`, `Rectangle`, and so on. These are fundamental to almost any computer vision algorithm.

OpenCV comes with all these basic structures out of the box, contained in the core module. Another advantage is that these structures have already been optimized for speed and memory, and so you don't have to worry about the implementation details.

The `imgcodecs` module handles reading and writing of image files. When you operate on an input image and create an output image, you can save it as a `.jpg` or a `.png` file with a simple command.

You will be dealing with a lot of video files when you work with cameras. The `videoio` module handles everything related to the input and output of video files. You can easily capture a video from the webcam or read a video file in many different formats. You can even save a bunch of frames as a video file by setting properties such as frames per second, frame size, and so on.

Image processing operations

When you write a computer vision algorithm, there are a lot of basic image processing operations that you will use over and over again. Most of these functions are present in the `imgproc` module. You can do things such as image filtering, morphological operations, geometric transformations, color conversions, drawing on images, histograms, shape analysis, motion analysis, feature detection, and more.

Let's consider the following photo:

The right image is a rotated version of the one on the left. We can carry out this transformation with a single line in OpenCV.

There is another module, called `ximgproc`, which contains advanced image processing algorithms such as structured forests for edge detection, domain transform filter, adaptive manifold filter, and so on.

GUI

OpenCV provides a module called highgui that handles all the high-level user interface operations. Let's say you are working on a problem, and you want to check what the image looks like before you proceed to the next step. This module has functions that can be used to create windows to display images and/or videos.

There is a waiting function that will wait until you hit a key on your keyboard before it goes on to the next step. There is also a function that can detect mouse events. This is very useful in developing interactive applications.

Using this functionality, you can draw rectangles on those input windows, and then proceed based on the selected region. Consider the following screenshot:

As you can see, we drew a green rectangle on top of the window. Once we have the coordinates of that rectangle, we can operate only on that region.

Video analysis

Video analysis includes tasks such as analyzing the motion between successive frames in a video, tracking different objects in a video, creating models for video surveillance, and so on. OpenCV provides a module called `video` that can handle all of this.

There is also a module called `videostab` that deals with video stabilization. Video stabilization is important, as when you are capturing videos by holding the camera in your hands, there's usually a lot of shake that needs correcting. All modern devices use video stabilization to process the video before it's presented to the end user.

3D reconstruction

3D reconstruction is an important topic in computer vision. Given a set of 2D images, we can reconstruct the 3D scene using relevant algorithms. OpenCV provides algorithms that can find the relationship between various objects in those 2D images to compute their 3D positions in its `calib3d` module.

This module can also handle camera calibration, which is essential for estimating the parameters of the camera. These parameters define how the camera sees the scene in front of it. We need to know these parameters to design algorithms, or else we might get unexpected results.

Let's consider the following diagram:

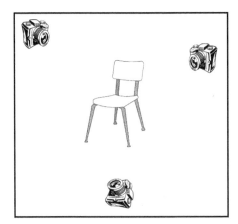

As we can see here, the same object is captured from multiple positions. Our job is to reconstruct the original object using these 2D images.

Feature extraction

As we discussed earlier, the human visual system tends to extract the salient features from a given scene to remember it for retrieval later. To mimic this, people started designing various feature extractors that can extract these salient points from a given image. Popular algorithms include **Scale Invariant Feature Transform (SIFT)**, **Speeded Up Robust Features (SURF)**, and **Features From Accelerated Segment Test (FAST)**.

An OpenCV module called `features2d` provides functions to detect and extract all these features. Another module called `xfeatures2d` provides a few more feature extractors, some of which are still in the experimental phase. You can play around with these if you get the chance.

There is also a module called `bioinspired` that provides algorithms for biologically-inspired computer vision models.

Object detection

Object detection refers to detecting the location of an object in a given image. This process is not concerned with the type of object. If you design a chair detector, it will not tell you whether the chair in a given image is red with a high back, or blue with a low back—it will just tell you the location of the chair.

Detecting the location of objects is a critical step in many computer vision systems. Consider the following photo:

If you run a chair detector on this image, it will put a green box around all the chairs—but it won't tell you what kind of chair it is.

Object detection used to be a computationally-intensive task because of the number of calculations required to perform the detection at various scales. To solve this, Paul Viola and Michael Jones came up with a great algorithm in their seminal 2001 paper, which you can read at the following link:
`https://www.cs.cmu.edu/~efros/courses/LBMV07/Papers/viola-cvpr-01.pdf`. They provided a fast way to design an object detector for any object.

OpenCV has modules called `objdetect` and `xobjdetect` that provide the framework to design an object detector. You can use it to develop detectors for random items such as sunglasses, boots, and so on.

Machine learning

Machine learning algorithms are used extensively to build computer vision systems for object recognition, image classification, face detection, visual search, and so on.

OpenCV provides a module called `ml`, which has many machine learning algorithms bundled into it, including a **Bayes classifier**, **k-nearest neighbors** (**KNN**), **support vector machines** (**SVM**), **decision trees**, **neural networks**, and more.

It also has a module called **Fast Approximate Nearest Neighbor Search Library** (**FLANN**), which contains algorithms for fast nearest neighbor searches in large datasets.

Computational photography

Computational photography refers to using advanced image processing techniques to improve the images captured by cameras. Instead of focusing on optical processes and image capture methods, computational photography uses software to manipulate visual data. Applications include high dynamic range imaging, panoramic images, image relighting, and light field cameras.

Let's look at the following image:

Look at those vivid colors! This is an example of a high dynamic range image, and it wouldn't be possible to get this using conventional image capture techniques. To do this, we have to capture the same scene at multiple exposures, register those images with each other, and then blend them nicely to create this image.

The `photo` and `xphoto` modules contain various algorithms that provide algorithms pertaining to computational photography. There is also a module called `stitching` that provides algorithms to create panoramic images.

 The image shown can be found here: `https://pixabay.com/en/hdr-high-dynamic-range-landscape-806260/`.

Shape analysis

The notion of shape is crucial in computer vision. We analyze visual data by recognizing various different shapes in the image. This is actually an important step in many algorithms.

Let's say you are trying to identify a particular logo in an image. You know that it can appear in various shapes, orientations, and sizes. One good way to get started is to quantify the characteristics of the shape of the object.

The `shape` module provides all the algorithms required to extract different shapes, measure similarity between them, transform the shapes of objects, and more.

Optical flow algorithms

Optical flow algorithms are used in videos to track features across successive frames. Let's say you want to track a particular object in a video. Running a feature extractor on each frame would be computationally expensive; hence, the process would be slow. So, you just extract the features from the current frame, and then track those features in successive frames.

Optical flow algorithms are heavily used in video-based applications in computer vision. The `optflow` module contains all the algorithms required to perform optical flow. There is also a module called `tracking` that contains more algorithms that can be used to track features.

Face and object recognition

Face recognition refers to identifying the person in a given image. This is not the same as face detection, where you simply identify the location of a face in the given image.

If you want to build a practical biometric system that can recognize the person in front of the camera, you first need to run a face detector to identify the location of the face, and then run a separate face recognizer to identify who the person is. There is an OpenCV module called `face` that deals with face recognition.

As we discussed earlier, computer vision tries to model algorithms based on how humans perceive visual data. So, it would be helpful to find salient regions and objects in the images that can help with different applications such as object recognition, object detection and tracking, and so on. There is a module called `saliency` that's designed for this purpose. It provides algorithms that can detect salient regions in static images and videos.

Surface matching

We are increasingly interacting with devices that can capture the 3D structure of the objects around us. These devices essentially capture depth information, along with the regular 2D color images. So, it's important for us to build algorithms that can understand and process 3D objects.

Kinect is a good example of a device that captures depth information along with the visual data. The task at hand is to recognize the input 3D object, by matching it to one of the models in our database. If we have a system that can recognize and locate objects, then it can be used for many different applications.

There is a module called `surface_matching` that contains algorithms for 3D object recognition and a pose estimation algorithm using 3D features.

Text detection and recognition

Identifying text in a given scene and recognizing the content is becoming increasingly important. Applications include number plate recognition, recognizing road signs for self-driving cars, book scanning to digitize content, and more.

There is a module called `text` that contains various algorithms to handle text detection and recognition.

Deep learning

Deep learning has a big impact on computer vision and image recognition, and achieves a higher level of accuracy than other machine learning and artificially intelligent algorithms. Deep learning is not a new concept; it was introduced to the community around 1986, but it started a revolution around 2012 when new GPU hardware was optimized for parallel computing and **Convolutional Neural Network** (**CNN**) implementations and other techniques allowed the training of complex neural network architectures in reasonable times.

Deep learning can be applied to multiple use cases such as image recognition, object detection, voice recognition, and natural language processing. Since version 3.4, OpenCV has been implementing deep learning algorithms—in the latest version, multiple importers for important frameworks such as **TensorFlow** and **Caffe** have been added.

Installing OpenCV

Let's see how to get OpenCV up and running on various operating systems.

Windows

To keep things easy, let's install OpenCV using pre-built libraries. Go to opencv.org and download the latest version for Windows. The current version is 4.0.0, and you can get the download link from the OpenCV homepage. You should make sure you have admin rights before you proceed.

The downloaded file will be an executable file, so just double-click on it to start the installation. The installer expands the content into a folder. You will be able to choose the installation path, and check the installation by inspecting the files.

Once you are done with the previous step, we need to set the OpenCV environment variables and add them to the system path to complete the installation. We will set up an environment variable that will hold the build directory of the OpenCV library. We will be using this in our projects.

Open up the Terminal and type the following:

```
C:> setx -m OPENCV_DIR D:OpenCVBuildx64vc14
```

 We are assuming that you have a 64-bit machine with Visual Studio 2015 installed. If you have Visual Studio 2012, replace vc14 with vc11 in the command. The path specified is where we would have our OpenCV binaries, and you should see two folders inside that path called lib and bin. If you are using Visual Studio 2018, you should compile OpenCV from scratch.

Let's go ahead and add a path to the bin folder to our system path. The reason we need to do this is because we will be using the OpenCV library in the form of **dynamic link libraries** (**DLLs**). Essentially, all the OpenCV algorithms are stored here, and our operating system will only load them during runtime.

In order to do that, our operating system needs to know where they are located. The PATH system variable contains a list of all the folders where it can find DLLs. So, naturally, we need to add the path of the OpenCV library to this list.

Why do we need to do all this? Well, the other option is to copy the required DLLs in the same folder as the application's executable file (.exe file). This is an unnecessary overhead, especially when we are working with many different projects.

We need to edit the `PATH` variable to add this folder. You can use software such as Path Editor to do this, which you can download from here: `https://patheditor2.codeplex.com`. Once you install it, start it up and add the following new entry (you can right-click on the path to insert a new item):

```
%OPENCV_DIR%bin
```

Go ahead and save it to the registry. We are done!

Mac OS X

In this section, we will see how to install OpenCV on Mac OS X. Precompiled binaries are not available for Mac OS X, so we need to compile OpenCV from scratch.

Before we proceed, we need to install CMake. If you don't already have CMake installed, you can download it from here: `https://cmake.org/files/v3.12/cmake-3.12.0-rc1-Darwin-x86_64.dmg`. It's a `.dmg` file, so once you download it, just run the installer.

Download the latest version of OpenCV from `opencv.org`. The current version is 4.0.0, and you can download it from here: `https://github.com/opencv/opencv/archive/4.0.0.zip`. Unzip the contents into a folder of your choice.

OpenCV 4.0.0 also has a new package called `opencv_contrib`, containing user contributions that are not yet considered stable, and some algorithms that are not freely available for commercial use in all the latest computer vision algorithms, which is worth keeping in mind. Installing this package is optional—OpenCV will work just fine if you don't install `opencv_contrib`.

Since we are installing OpenCV anyway, it's good to install this package so that you can experiment with it later on (as opposed to going through the whole installation process again). It is a great way to learn and play around with new algorithms. You can download it from the following link: `https://github.com/opencv/opencv_contrib/archive/4.0.0.zip`.

Unzip the contents of the zip file into a folder of your choice. For convenience, unzip it into the same folder as before, so that the `opencv-4.0.0` and `opencv_contrib-4.0.0` folders are in the same main folder.

We are now ready to build OpenCV. Open up your Terminal and navigate to the folder where you unzipped the contents of OpenCV 4.0.0. Run the following commands after substituting the right paths in the commands:

```
$ cd /full/path/to/opencv-4.0.0/
$ mkdir build
$ cd build
$ cmake -D CMAKE_BUILD_TYPE=RELEASE -D
CMAKE_INSTALL_PREFIX=/full/path/to/opencv-4.0.0/build -D
INSTALL_C_EXAMPLES=ON -D BUILD_EXAMPLES=ON -D
OPENCV_EXTRA_MODULES_PATH=/full/path/to/opencv_contrib-4.0.0/modules ../
```

It's time to install OpenCV 4.0.0. Go to the /full/path/to/opencv-4.0.0/build directory, and run the following commands on your Terminal:

```
$ make -j4
$ make install
```

In the preceding command, the -j4 flag indicates that it should be using four cores to install it. It's faster this way! Now, let's set the library path. Open up your ~/.profile file in your Terminal using the vi ~/.profile command, and add the following line:

```
export
DYLD_LIBRARY_PATH=/full/path/to/opencv-4.0.0/build/lib:$DYLD_LIBRARY_PATH
```

We need to copy the pkgconfig file in opencv.pc to /usr/local/lib/pkgconfig and name it opencv4.pc. This way, if you already have an existing OpenCV 3.x.x installation, there will be no conflict. Let's go ahead and do that:

```
$ cp /full/path/to/opencv-4.0.0/build/lib/pkgconfig/opencv.pc
/usr/local/lib/pkgconfig/opencv4.pc
```

We need to update our PKG_CONFIG_PATH variable as well. Open up your ~/.profile file and add the following line:

```
export PKG_CONFIG_PATH=/usr/local/lib/pkgconfig/:$PKG_CONFIG_PATH
```

Reload your ~/.profile file using the following command:

```
$ source ~/.profile
```

We're finished! Let's see if it's working:

```
$ cd /full/path/to/opencv-4.0.0/samples/cpp
$ g++ -ggdb `pkg-config --cflags --libs opencv4` opencv_version.cpp -o
/tmp/opencv_version && /tmp/opencv_version
```

If you see **Welcome to OpenCV 4.0.0** printed on your Terminal, you are good to go. We will be using CMake to build our OpenCV projects throughout this book. We will cover it in more detail in `Chapter 2`, *An Introduction to the Basics of OpenCV*.

Linux

Let's see how to install OpenCV on Ubuntu. We need to install some dependencies before we begin. Let's install them using the package manager by running the following command in your Terminal:

```
$ sudo apt-get -y install libopencv-dev build-essential cmake libdc1394-22
libdc1394-22-dev libjpeg-dev libpng12-dev libtiff5-dev libjasper-dev
libavcodec-dev libavformat-dev libswscale-dev libxine2-dev
libgstreamer0.10-dev libgstreamer-plugins-base0.10-dev libv4l-dev libtbb-
dev libqt4-dev libmp3lame-dev libopencore-amrnb-dev libopencore-amrwb-dev
libtheora-dev libvorbis-dev libxvidcore-dev x264 v4l-utils
```

Now that you have installed the dependencies, let's download, build, and install OpenCV:

```
$ wget "https://github.com/opencv/opencv/archive/4.0.0.tar.gz" -O
opencv.tar.gz
$ wget "https://github.com/opencv/opencv_contrib/archive/4.0.0.tar.gz" -O
opencv_contrib.tar.gz
$ tar -zxvf opencv.tar.gz
$ tar -zxvf opencv_contrib.tar.gz
$ cd opencv-4.0.0
$ mkdir build
$ cd build
$ cmake -D CMAKE_BUILD_TYPE=RELEASE -D
CMAKE_INSTALL_PREFIX=/full/path/to/opencv-4.0.0/build -D
INSTALL_C_EXAMPLES=ON -D BUILD_EXAMPLES=ON -D
OPENCV_EXTRA_MODULES_PATH=/full/path/to/opencv_contrib-4.0.0/modules ../
$ make -j4
$ sudo make install
```

Let's copy the `pkgconfig` file in `opencv.pc` to `/usr/local/lib/pkgconfig`, and name it `opencv4.pc`:

```
$ cp /full/path/to/opencv-4.0.0/build/lib/pkgconfig/opencv.pc
/usr/local/lib/pkgconfig/opencv4.pc
```

We're finished! We will now be able to use it to compile our OpenCV programs from the command line. Also, if you already have an existing OpenCV 3.x.x installation, there will be no conflict.

Let's check the installation is working properly:

```
$ cd /full/path/to/opencv-4.0.0/samples/cpp
$ g++ -ggdb `pkg-config --cflags --libs opencv4` opencv_version.cpp -o
/tmp/opencv_version && /tmp/opencv_version
```

If you see **Welcome to OpenCV 4.0.0** printed on your Terminal, you should be good to go. In the following chapters, we will learn how to use CMake to build our OpenCV projects.

Summary

In this chapter, we discussed the human visual system, and how humans process visual data. We explained why it's difficult for machines to do the same, and what we need to consider when designing a computer vision library.

We learned what could be done using OpenCV, and the various modules that can be used to complete those tasks. Finally, we learned how to install OpenCV in various operating systems.

In the next chapter, we will discuss how to operate on images and how we can manipulate them using various functions. We will also learn about building a project structure for our OpenCV applications.

An Introduction to the Basics of OpenCV

2

After covering OpenCV installation on different operating systems in `Chapter 1`, *Getting Started with OpenCV*, we are going to introduce the basics of OpenCV development in this chapter. It begins with showing how to create our project using CMake. We are going to introduce the basic image data structures and matrices, along with other structures that are required to work in our projects. We are going to introduce how to save our variables and data into files using the XML/YAML persistence OpenCV functions.

In this chapter, we will cover the following topics:

- Configuring projects with CMake
- Reading/writing images from/to disk
- Reading videos and accessing camera devices
- The main image structures (for example, matrices)
- Other important and basic structures (for example, vectors and scalars)
- An introduction to basic matrix operations
- File storage operations with XML/YAML persistence OpenCV API

Technical requirements

This chapter requires familiarity with the basic C++ programming language. All the code used in this chapter can be downloaded from the following GitHub link: `https://github.com/PacktPublishing/Learn-OpenCV-4-By-Building-Projects-Second-Edition/tree/master/Chapter_02`. The code can be executed on any operating system, though it is only tested on Ubuntu.
Check out the following video to see the Code in Action:
`http://bit.ly/2QxhNBa`

Basic CMake configuration file

To configure and check all the requisite dependencies for our project, we are going to use CMake, but it is not the only way that this can be done; we can configure our project in any other tool or IDE, such as **Makefiles** or **Visual Studio**, but CMake is a more portable way to configure multiplatform **C++** projects.

CMake uses configuration files called CMakeLists.txt, where the compilation and dependencies process is defined. For a basic project based on an executable built from a single source code file, a CMakeLists.txt file comprising three lines is all that is required. The file looks as follows:

```
cmake_minimum_required (VERSION 3.0)
project (CMakeTest)
add_executable(${PROJECT_NAME} main.cpp)
```

The first line defines the minimum version of CMake required. This line is mandatory in our CMakeLists.txt file and allows us to use the functionality of CMake defined from a specific version; in our case, we require a minimum of CMake 3.0. The second line defines the project name. This name is saved in a variable called PROJECT_NAME.

The last line creates an executable command (add_executable()) from the main.cpp file, gives it the same name as our project (${PROJECT_NAME}), and compiles our source code into an executable called **CMakeTest** which is the name that we set up as a project name. The ${} expression allows access to any variable defined in our environment. Then, we can use the ${PROJECT_NAME} variable as an executable output name.

Creating a library

CMake allows us to create libraries used by the OpenCV build system. Factorizing shared code among multiple applications is a common and useful practice in software development. In big applications, or common code shared in multiple applications, this practice is very useful. In this case, we do not create a binary executable, but instead we create a compiled file that includes all the functions, classes, and so on. We can then share this library file with other applications without sharing our source code.

CMake includes the add_library function to this end:

```
# Create our hello library
    add_library(Hello hello.cpp hello.h)

# Create our application that uses our new library
```

```
    add_executable(executable main.cpp)

# Link our executable with the new library
    target_link_libraries(executable Hello)
```

The lines starting with # add comments and are ignored by CMake. The
add_library(Hello hello.cpp hello.h) command defines the source files of our
library and its name, where Hello is the library name and hello.cpp and hello.h are the
source files. We add the header file too to allow IDEs such as Visual Studio to link to the
header files. This line is going to generate a shared (.so for Mac OS X, and Unix or .dll for
Windows) or static library (.a for Mac OS X, and Unix or .lib for Windows) file,
depending on whether we add a SHARED or STATIC word between library name and source
files. target_link_libraries(executable Hello) is the function that links our
executable to the desired library, in our case, the Hello library.

Managing dependencies

CMake has the ability to search our dependencies and external libraries, giving us the
ability to build complex projects, depending on the external components in our projects,
and add some requirements.

In this book, the most important dependency is, of course, OpenCV, and we will add it to
all of our projects:

```
    cmake_minimum_required (VERSION 3.0)
    PROJECT(Chapter2)
# Requires OpenCV
    FIND_PACKAGE( OpenCV 4.0.0 REQUIRED )
# Show a message with the opencv version detected
    MESSAGE("OpenCV version : ${OpenCV_VERSION}")
# Add the paths to the include directories/to the header files
    include_directories(${OpenCV_INCLUDE_DIRS})
# Add the paths to the compiled libraries/objects
    link_directories(${OpenCV_LIB_DIR})
# Create a variable called SRC
    SET(SRC main.cpp)
# Create our executable
    ADD_EXECUTABLE(${PROJECT_NAME} ${SRC})
# Link our library
    TARGET_LINK_LIBRARIES(${PROJECT_NAME} ${OpenCV_LIBS})
```

Now, let's understand the working of the script from the following:

```
cmake_minimum_required (VERSION 3.0)
cmake_policy(SET CMP0012 NEW)
PROJECT(Chapter2)
```

The first line defines the minimum CMake version, and the second line tells CMake to use the new behavior of CMake to facilitate recognition of the correct numbers and Boolean constants without dereferencing variables with such names; this policy was introduced in CMake 2.8.0, and CMake warns when the policy is not set from version 3.0.2. Finally, the last line defines the project title. After defining the project name, we have to define the requirements, libraries, and dependencies:

```
# Requires OpenCV
    FIND_PACKAGE( OpenCV 4.0.0 REQUIRED )
# Show a message with the opencv version detected
    MESSAGE("OpenCV version : ${OpenCV_VERSION}")
    include_directories(${OpenCV_INCLUDE_DIRS})
    link_directories(${OpenCV_LIB_DIR})
```

Here is where we search for our OpenCV dependency. `FIND_PACKAGE` is the function that allows us to find our dependencies, the minimum version required, and whether this dependency is required or optional. In this sample script, we look for OpenCV in version 4.0.0 or greater and state that it is a required package.

The `FIND_PACKAGE` command includes all OpenCV submodules, but you can specify the submodules that you want to include in the project by executing your application smaller and faster. For example, if we are only going to work with the basic OpenCV types and core functionality, we can use the following command: `FIND_PACKAGE(OpenCV 4.0.0 REQUIRED core)`.

If CMake does not find it, it returns an error and does not prevent us from compiling our application. The `MESSAGE` function shows a message in the terminal or CMake GUI. In our case, we are showing the OpenCV version as follows:

```
OpenCV version : 4.0.0
```

The ${OpenCV_VERSION} is a variable where CMake stores the OpenCV package version. include_directories() and link_directories() add to our environment the headers and the directory of the specified library. OpenCV CMake's module saves this data in the ${OpenCV_INCLUDE_DIRS} and ${OpenCV_LIB_DIR} variables. These lines are not required in all platforms, such as Linux, because these paths normally are in the environment, but it's recommended to have more than one OpenCV version to choose the correct link and include directories. Now is the time to include our developed sources:

```
# Create a variable called SRC
    SET(SRC main.cpp)
# Create our executable
    ADD_EXECUTABLE(${PROJECT_NAME} ${SRC})
# Link our library
    TARGET_LINK_LIBRARIES(${PROJECT_NAME} ${OpenCV_LIBS})
```

This last line creates the executable and links the executable with the OpenCV library, as we saw in the previous section, *Creating a library*. There is a new function in this piece of code, SET; this function creates a new variable and adds to it any value that we need. In our case, we incorporate the main.cpp value in the SRC variable. We can add more and more values to the same variable, as can be seen in the following script:

```
SET(SRC main.cpp
        utils.cpp
        color.cpp
)
```

Making the script more complex

In this section, we are showing a more complex script that includes subfolders, libraries, and executables; all told, just two files and a few lines, as demonstrated in this script. It's not mandatory to create multiple CMakeLists.txt files, because we can specify everything in the main CMakeLists.txt file. However, it is more common to use different CMakeLists.txt files for each project subfolder, thereby making it more flexible and portable.

This example has a code structure folder, which contains one folder for a utils library and the root folder, which contains the main executable:

```
CMakeLists.txt
main.cpp
utils/
    CMakeLists.txt
    computeTime.cpp
```

```
computeTime.h
logger.cpp
logger.h
plotting.cpp
plotting.h
```

Then, we have to define two CMakeLists.txt files, one in the root folder and the other in the utils folder. The CMakeLists.txt root folder file has the following content:

```
cmake_minimum_required (VERSION 3.0)
project (Chapter2)

# Opencv Package required
FIND_PACKAGE( OpenCV 4.0.0 REQUIRED )

#Add opencv header files to project
include_directories(${OpenCV_INCLUDE_DIR})
link_directories(${OpenCV_LIB_DIR})

# Add a subdirectory to the build.
add_subdirectory(utils)

# Add optional log with a precompiler definition
option(WITH_LOG "Build with output logs and images in tmp" OFF)
if(WITH_LOG)
    add_definitions(-DLOG)
endif(WITH_LOG)

# generate our new executable
add_executable(${PROJECT_NAME} main.cpp)
# link the project with his dependencies
target_link_libraries(${PROJECT_NAME} ${OpenCV_LIBS} Utils)
```

Almost all lines are described in previous sections, except some functions which we will explain. add_subdirectory() tells CMake to analyze CMakeLists.txt of a desired subfolder. Before continuing with the main CMakeLists.txt file explanation, we are going to explain the CMakeLists.txt file in utils.

In the CMakeLists.txt file of the utils folders, we are going to write a new library to include in our main project folder:

```
# Add new variable for src utils lib
    SET(UTILS_LIB_SRC
        computeTime.cpp
        logger.cpp
        plotting.cpp
    )
```

```
# create our new utils lib
    add_library(Utils ${UTILS_LIB_SRC})
# make sure the compiler can find include files for our library
    target_include_directories(Utils PUBLIC ${CMAKE_CURRENT_SOURCE_DIR})
```

This CMake script file defines a variable, UTILS_LIB_SRC, where we add all source files included in our library, generate the library with the add_library function, and use the target_include_directories function to allow our main project to detect all header files. Leaving the utils subfolder and continuing with the root CMake script, the Option function creates a new variable, in our case WITH_LOG, with a small description attached. This variable could be changed through the ccmake command line or CMake GUI interface, where the description appears, and a check that allows users to enable or disable this option. This function is very useful for allowing the user to decide about compile-time features, such as whether we want enabling or disabling logs or not, compiling with Java or Python support, just as OpenCV does, and so on.

In our case, we use this option to enable a logger in our application. To enable the logger, we use a pre-compiler definition in our code, as follows:

```
#ifdef LOG
    logi("Number of iteration %d", i);
#endif
```

This LOG macro can be defined in our CMakeLists.txt through a call to the add_definitions function (-DLOG), which itself can be run or hidden by the CMake variable WITH_LOG with a simple condition:

```
if(WITH_LOG)
    add_definitions(-DLOG)
endif(WITH_LOG)
```

Now we are ready to create our CMake script files to compile our computer vision projects in any operating system. Then, we are going to continue with the OpenCV basics before starting with a sample project.

Images and matrices

The most important structure in computer vision is, without doubt, the images. The image in a computer vision is the representation of the physical world captured with a digital device. This picture is only a sequence of numbers stored in a matrix format (refer to the following diagram). Each number is a measurement of the light intensity for the considered wavelength (for example, red, green, or blue in color images) or for a wavelength range (for panchromatic devices). Every point in an image is called a **pixel** (for a picture element), and each pixel can store one or more values depending on whether it is a black and white image (also referred to as a binary image) that stores only one value, such as 0 or 1, a grayscale-level image that stores two values, or a color image that stores three values. These values are usually between 0 and 255 in an integer number, but you can use other ranges, for example 0 to 1 in floating point numbers, as in **high dynamic range imaging** (**HDRI**) or thermal images:

The image is stored in a matrix format, where each pixel has a position in it and can be referenced by the number of the column and row. OpenCV uses the Mat class for this purpose. In the case of a grayscale image, a single matrix is used, as demonstrated in the following diagram:

159	165	185	187	185	190	189	198	193	197	184	152	123
174	167	186	194	185	196	204	191	200	178	149	129	125
168	184	185	188	195	192	191	195	169	141	116	115	129
178	188	190	195	196	199	195	164	128	120	118	126	135
188	194	189	195	201	196	166	114	113	120	128	131	129
187	200	197	198	190	144	107	106	113	120	125	125	125
198	195	202	183	134	98	97	112	114	115	116	116	118
194	206	178	111	87	99	97	101	107	105	101	97	95
206	168	107	82	80	100	102	91	98	102	104	99	72
160	97	80	86	80	92	80	79	71	74	81	81	64
98	66	76	86	76	83	72	71	55	53	61	61	56
60	76	74	70	67	64	63	60	55	49	54	52	54

In the case of a color image, such as the following diagram, we use a matrix of width x height x the number of color channels:

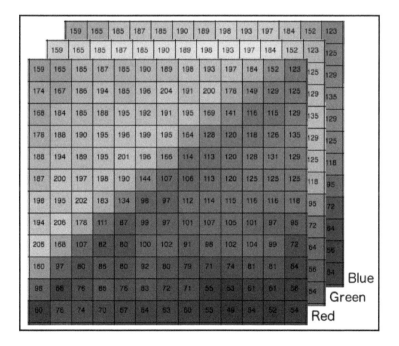

But the `Mat` class is not only for storing images; it also enables you to store any type of matrix and different sizes. You can use it as an algebraic matrix and perform operations with it. In the following sections, we are going to describe the most important matrix operations, such as addition, multiplication, diagonalization. But, before that, it's important to know how the matrix is stored internally in the computer memory, because it is always more efficient to access the memory slots instead of accessing each pixel with the OpenCV functions.

In memory, the matrix is saved as an array or sequence of values ordered by columns and rows. The following table shows the sequence of pixels in **BGR** image format:

Row 0			Row 1			Row 2		
Col 0	Col 1	Col 2	Col 0	Col 1	Col 2	Col 0	Col 1	Col 2
Pixel 1	Pixel 2	Pixel 3	Pixel 4	Pixel 5	Pixel 6	Pixel 7	Pixel 8	Pixel 9
B G R	B G R	B G R	B G R	B G R	B G R	B G R	B G R	B G R

With this order, we can access any pixel by observing the following formula:

```
Value= Row_i*num_cols*num_channels + Col_i + channel_i
```

 OpenCV functions are quite optimized for random access, but sometimes, direct access to the memory (work with pointer arithmetic) is more efficient, for example, when we have to access all pixels in a loop.

Reading/writing images

Following the introduction to matrices, we are going to start with the OpenCV code basics. The first thing that we have to learn is how to read and write images:

```cpp
#include <iostream>
#include <string>
#include <sstream>
using namespace std;

// OpenCV includes
#include "opencv2/core.hpp"
#include "opencv2/highgui.hpp"
using namespace cv;

int main(int argc, const char** argv)
{
    // Read images
    Mat color= imread("../lena.jpg");
    Mat gray= imread("../lena.jpg",CV_LOAD_IMAGE_GRAYSCALE);

  if(! color.data ) // Check for invalid input
  {
 cout << "Could not open or find the image" << std::endl ;
 return -1;
  }
    // Write images
    imwrite("lenaGray.jpg", gray);
    // Get same pixel with opencv function
    int myRow=color.cols-1;
    int myCol=color.rows-1;
    Vec3b pixel= color.at<Vec3b>(myRow, myCol);
    cout << "Pixel value (B,G,R): (" << (int)pixel[0] << "," <<
(int)pixel[1] << "," << (int)pixel[2] << ")" << endl;
    // show images
    imshow("Lena BGR", color);
    imshow("Lena Gray", gray);
    // wait for any key press
    waitKey(0);
    return 0;
}
```

Let's now move on to understanding the code:

```
// OpenCV includes
#include "opencv2/core.hpp"
#include "opencv2/highgui.hpp"
using namespace cv;
```

First, we have to include the declarations of the functions that we need in our sample. These functions come from `core` (basic image data handling) and `highgui` (cross-platform I/O functions provided by OpenCV are `core` and `highui`;; the first includes the basic classes, such as matrices, while the second includes the functions to read, write, and show images with graphical interfaces). Now it is time to read images:

```
// Read images
Mat color= imread("../lena.jpg");
Mat gray= imread("../lena.jpg",CV_LOAD_IMAGE_GRAYSCALE);
```

`imread` is the main function for reading images. This function opens an image and stores it in a matrix format. `imread` accepts two parameters. The first parameter is a string containing the image's path, while the second is optional and, by default, loads the image as a color image. The second parameter allows the following options:

- `cv::IMREAD_UNCHANGED`: If set, this returns a 16-bit/32-bit image when the input has the corresponding depth, otherwise it converts it to 8-bit
- `cv::IMREAD_COLOR`: If set, this always converts an image to a color one (BGR, 8-bit unsigned)
- `cv::IMREAD_GRAYSCALE`: If set, this always converts an image to a grayscale one (8-bit unsigned)

To save images, we can use the `imwrite` function, which stores a matrix image in our computer:

```
// Write images
imwrite("lenaGray.jpg", gray);
```

The first parameter is the path where we want to save the image with the extension format that we desire. The second parameter is the matrix image that we want to save. In our code sample, we create and store a gray version of the image and then save it as a .jpg file. The gray image that we loaded will be stored in the gray variable:

```
// Get same pixel with opencv function
int myRow=color.cols-1;
int myCol=color.rows-1;
```

Using the .cols and .rows attributes of a matrix, we can get access to the number of columns and rows in an image, or, in other words, the width and height:

```
Vec3b pixel= color.at<Vec3b>(myRow, myCol);
cout << "Pixel value (B,G,R): (" << (int)pixel[0] << "," << (int)pixel[1]
<< "," << (int)pixel[2] << ")" << endl;
```

To access one pixel of the image, we use the template function cv::Mat::at<typename t>(row,col) from the Mat OpenCV class. The template parameter is the desired return type. A type name in an 8-bit color image is a Vec3b class that stores three unsigned char data (Vec = vector, 3 = number of components, and b = 1 byte). In the case of the gray image, we can directly use the unsigned character, or any other number format used in the image, such as uchar pixel= color.at<uchar>(myRow, myCol). Finally, in order to show the images, we can use the imshow function, which creates a window with a title as a first parameter and the image matrix as a second parameter:

```
// show images
imshow("Lena BGR", color);
imshow("Lena Gray", gray);
// wait for any key press
waitKey(0);
```

If we want to stop the application from waiting, we can use the OpenCV function waitKey, with a parameter of the number of milliseconds we want to wait for a key press. If we set up the parameter to 0, then the function will wait until a key is pressed.

The result of the preceding code is demonstrated in the following image. The left-hand image is a color image, and the right-hand image is a grayscale image:

Finally, by way of an example for the following samples, we are going to create the CMakeLists.txt file and see how to compile the code using the file.

The following code describes the CMakeLists.txt file:

```
cmake_minimum_required (VERSION 3.0)
cmake_policy(SET CMP0012 NEW)
PROJECT(project)

# Requires OpenCV
FIND_PACKAGE( OpenCV 4.0.0 REQUIRED )
MESSAGE("OpenCV version : ${OpenCV_VERSION}")

include_directories(${OpenCV_INCLUDE_DIRS})
link_directories(${OpenCV_LIB_DIR})

ADD_EXECUTABLE(sample main.cpp)
TARGET_LINK_LIBRARIES(sample ${OpenCV_LIBS})
```

To compile our code using this `CMakeLists.txt` file, we have to carry out the following steps:

1. Create a `build` folder.
2. Inside the `build` folder, execute CMake or open CMake GUI app in Windows, choose the `source` and `build` folders, and press the **Configure** and **Generate** buttons.
3. If you are on Linux or macOS, generate a Makefile as usual, and then compile the project using the `make` command. If you are on Windows, open the project using the editor selected in step 2 and then compile.

Finally, after compiling our application, we will have an executable called `app` in the build folder that we can execute.

Reading videos and cameras

This section introduces you to video and camera reading using this simple example. Before explaining how to read videos or camera input, we want to introduce a new, very useful class that helps us to manage the input command-line parameters. This new class was introduced in OpenCV version 3.0, and is the `CommandLineParser` class:

```
// OpenCV command line parser functions
// Keys accepted by command line parser
const char* keys =
{
    "{help h usage ? | | print this message}"
     "{@video | | Video file, if not defined try to use webcamera}"
};
```

The first thing that we have to do for `CommandLineParser` is define what parameters we need or allow in a constant `char` vector; each line has the following pattern:

```
"{name_param | default_value | description}"
```

`name_param` can be preceded with @, which defines this parameter as a default input. We can use more than one `name_param`:

```
CommandLineParser parser(argc, argv, keys);
```

The constructor will get the inputs of the main function and the key constants defined previously:

```
//If requires help show
if (parser.has("help"))
{
        parser.printMessage();
        return 0;
}
```

The `.has` class method checks the existence of the parameter. In the sample, we check whether the user adds the parameter `help` or `?`, and then use the class function `printMessage` to show all the description parameters:

```
String videoFile= parser.get<String>(0);
```

With the `.get<typename>(parameterName)` function, we can access and read any of input parameters:

```
// Check if params are correctly parsed in his variables
if (!parser.check())
{
    parser.printErrors();
    return 0;
}
```

After obtaining all the requisite parameters, we can check whether these parameters are parsed correctly and show an error message if one of the parameters was not parsed, for example, add a string instead of a number:

```
VideoCapture cap; // open the default camera
if(videoFile != "")
    cap.open(videoFile);
else
    cap.open(0);
if(!cap.isOpened())  // check if we succeeded
    return -1;
```

The class for video reading and camera reading is the same: the `VideoCapture` class that belongs to the `videoio` submodule instead of the `highgui` submodule, as in the previous version of OpenCV. After creating the object, we check whether the input command-line parameter `videoFile` has a path filename. If it's empty, then we try to open a web camera; if it has a filename, then open the video file. To do this, we use the `open` function, giving as a parameter the video filename or the index camera that we want to open. If we have a single camera, we can use 0 as a parameter.

To check whether we can read the video filename or the camera, we use the `isOpened` function:

```
namedWindow("Video",1);
for(;;)
{
    Mat frame;
    cap >> frame; // get a new frame from camera
    if(frame)
        imshow("Video", frame);
    if(waitKey(30) >= 0) break;
}
// Release the camera or video cap
cap.release();
```

Finally, we create a window to show the frames with the `namedWindow` function and, with an infinite loop, we grab each frame using the `>>` operation and show the frame with the `imshow` function if we retrieve the frame correctly. In this case, we don't want to stop the application, but will wait 30 milliseconds to check whether any users want to stop the application execution with any key using `waitKey(30)`.

The time required to wait for the next frame using camera access is calculated from the camera speed and our spent algorithm time. For example, if a camera works at 20 fps, and our algorithm spent 10 milliseconds, a great waiting value is $30 = (1000/20) - 10$ milliseconds. This value is calculated considering a wait of a sufficient amount of time to ensure that the next frame is in the buffer. If our camera takes 40 milliseconds to take each image, and we use 10 milliseconds in our algorithm, then we only need to stop with waitKey 30 milliseconds, because 30 milliseconds of wait time, plus 10 milliseconds of our algorithm, is the same amount of time for which each frame of the camera is accessible.

When the user wants to finish the application, all they have to do is press any key and then we have to release all video resources using the release function.

It is very important to release all resources that we use in a computer vision application. If we do not, we can consume all RAM memory. We can release the matrices using the `release` function.

The result of the previous code is a new window showing a video or web camera in BGR format.

Other basic object types

We have learned about the `Mat` and `Vec3b` classes, but there are many more classes that we have to learn.

In this section, we will learn the most basic object types required in the majority of projects:

- `Vec`
- `Scalar`
- `Point`
- `Size`
- `Rect`
- `RotatedRect`

Vec object type

`Vec` is a template class mainly for numerical vectors. We can define any type of vector and the number of components:

```
Vec<double,19> myVector;
```

We can also use any of the predefined types:

```
typedef Vec<uchar, 2> Vec2b;
typedef Vec<uchar, 3> Vec3b;
typedef Vec<uchar, 4> Vec4b;

typedef Vec<short, 2> Vec2s;
typedef Vec<short, 3> Vec3s;
typedef Vec<short, 4> Vec4s;

typedef Vec<int, 2> Vec2i;
typedef Vec<int, 3> Vec3i;
typedef Vec<int, 4> Vec4i;

typedef Vec<float, 2> Vec2f;
typedef Vec<float, 3> Vec3f;
typedef Vec<float, 4> Vec4f;
typedef Vec<float, 6> Vec6f;

typedef Vec<double, 2> Vec2d;
typedef Vec<double, 3> Vec3d;
```

```
typedef Vec<double, 4> Vec4d;
typedef Vec<double, 6> Vec6d;
```

All the following vector operations are also implemented:
```
v1 = v2 + v3
v1 = v2 - v3
v1 = v2 * scale
v1 = scale * v2
v1 = -v2
v1 += v2
```

Other augmenting operations implemented are the following:
```
v1 == v2, v1 != v2
norm(v1) (euclidean norm).
```

Scalar object type

The `Scalar` object type is a template class derived from `Vec` with four elements. The `Scalar` type is widely used in OpenCV to pass and read pixel values.

To access `Vec` and `Scalar` values, we use the `[]` operator, which can be initialized from another scalar, vector, or value by value, as in the following sample:

```
Scalar s0(0);
Scalar s1(0.0, 1.0, 2.0, 3.0);
Scalar s2(s1);
```

Point object type

Another very common class template is `Point`. This class defines a 2D point specified by its coordinates x and y.

Like `Point`, there is a `Point3` template class for 3D point support.

Like the `Vec` class, OpenCV defines the following `Point` aliases for our convenience:

```
typedef Point_<int> Point2i;
typedef Point2i Point;
typedef Point_<float> Point2f;
```

```
typedef Point_<double> Point2d;
  The following operators are defined for points:
    pt1 = pt2 + pt3;
    pt1 = pt2 - pt3;
    pt1 = pt2 * a;
    pt1 = a * pt2;
    pt1 = pt2 / a;
    pt1 += pt2;
    pt1 -= pt2;
    pt1 *= a;
    pt1 /= a;
    double value = norm(pt); // L2 norm
    pt1 == pt2;
    pt1 != pt2;
```

Size object type

Another template class that is very important and widely used in OpenCV is the template class for specifying the size of an image or rectangle—Size. This class adds two members, width and height, and the useful area() function. In the following sample, we can see a number of ways of using size:

```
Size s(100,100);
Mat img=Mat::zeros(s, CV_8UC1); // 100 by 100 single channel matrix
s.width= 200;
int area= s.area(); returns 100x200
```

Rect object type

Rect is another important template class for defining 2D rectangles defined by the following parameters:

- The coordinates of the upper-left corner

- The width and height of a rectangle

The Rect template class can be used to define a **region of interest** (ROI) of an image, as follows:

```
Mat img=imread("lena.jpg");
Rect rect_roi(0,0,100,100);
Mat img_roi=img(r);
```

RotatedRect object type

The last useful class is a particular rectangle called `RotatedRect`. This class represents a rotated rectangle specified by a center point, the width and height of a rectangle, and the rotation angle in degrees:

```
RotatedRect(const Point2f& center, const Size2f& size, float angle);
```

An interesting function of this class is `boundingBox`. This function returns `Rect`, which contains the rotated rectangle:

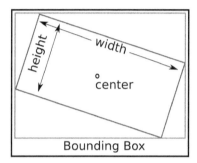

Basic matrix operations

In this section, we will learn a number of basic and important matrix operations that we can apply to images or any matrix data. We learned how to load an image and store it in a `Mat` variable, but we can create `Mat` manually. The most common constructor is giving the matrix a size and type, as follows:

```
Mat  a= Mat(Size(5,5), CV_32F);
```

You can create a new matrix linking with a stored buffer from third-party libraries without copying data using this constructor: `Mat(size, type, pointer_to_buffer)`.

The types supported depend on the type of number you want to store and the number of channels. The most common types are as follows:

```
CV_8UC1
CV_8UC3
CV_8UC4
CV_32FC1
```

```
CV_32FC3
CV_32FC4
```

 You can create any type of matrix using `CV_number_typeC(n)`, where the `number_type` is 8 bits unsigned (8U) to 64 float (64F), and where `(n)` is the number of channels; the number of channels permitted ranges from 1 to `CV_CN_MAX`.

The initialization does not set up the data values, and hence you can get undesirable values. To avoid undesirable values, you can initialize the matrix with 0 or 1 values with their respective functions:

```
Mat mz= Mat::zeros(5,5, CV_32F);
Mat mo= Mat::ones(5,5, CV_32F);
```

The results of the preceding matrix are as follows:

```
[0, 0, 0, 0, 0;    [1, 1, 1, 1, 1;
 0, 0, 0, 0, 0;     1, 1, 1, 1, 1;
 0, 0, 0, 0, 0;     1, 1, 1, 1, 1;
 0, 0, 0, 0, 0;     1, 1, 1, 1, 1;
 0, 0, 0, 0, 0]     1, 1, 1, 1, 1]
```

A special matrix initialization is the eye function that creates an identity matrix with the specified type and size:

```
Mat m= Mat::eye(5,5, CV_32F);
```

The output is as follows:

```
[1, 0, 0, 0, 0;
 0, 1, 0, 0, 0;
 0, 0, 1, 0, 0;
 0, 0, 0, 1, 0;
 0, 0, 0, 0, 1]
```

All matrix operations are allowed in OpenCV's `Mat` class. We can add or subtract two matrices of the same size using the + and – operators, as demonstrated in the following code block:

```
Mat a= Mat::eye(Size(3,2), CV_32F);
Mat b= Mat::ones(Size(3,2), CV_32F);
Mat c= a+b;
Mat d= a-b;
```

The results of the preceding operations are as follows:

$$\begin{bmatrix} 1, 0, 0; \\ 0, 1, 0 \end{bmatrix} + \begin{bmatrix} 1, 1, 1; \\ 1, 1, 1 \end{bmatrix} = \begin{bmatrix} 2, 1, 1; \\ 1, 2, 1 \end{bmatrix}$$

$$\begin{bmatrix} 1, 0, 0; \\ 0, 1, 0 \end{bmatrix} - \begin{bmatrix} 1, 1, 1; \\ 1, 1, 1 \end{bmatrix} = \begin{bmatrix} 0, -1, -1; \\ -1, 0, -1 \end{bmatrix}$$

We can multiply by a scalar using the `*` operator or a matrix per element using the `mul` function, and we can perform matrix multiplication using the `*` operator:

```
Mat m1= Mat::eye(2,3, CV_32F);
Mat m2= Mat::ones(3,2, CV_32F);
// Scalar by matrix
cout << "nm1.*2n" << m1*2 << endl;
// matrix per element multiplication
cout << "n(m1+2).*(m1+3)n" << (m1+1).mul(m1+3) << endl;
// Matrix multiplication
cout << "nm1*m2n" << m1*m2 << endl;
```

The results of the preceding operations are as follows:

$$\begin{bmatrix} 1, 0, 0; \\ 0, 1, 0 \end{bmatrix} * 2 = \begin{bmatrix} 2, 0, 0; \\ 0, 2, 0 \end{bmatrix}$$

$$\begin{bmatrix} 2, 1, 1; \\ 1, 2, 1 \end{bmatrix} * \begin{bmatrix} 4, 3, 3; \\ 3, 4, 3 \end{bmatrix} = \begin{bmatrix} 8, 3, 3; \\ 3, 8, 3 \end{bmatrix}$$

$$\begin{bmatrix} 1, 0, 0; \\ 0, 1, 0 \end{bmatrix} * \begin{bmatrix} 1, 1; \\ 1, 1; \\ 1, 1 \end{bmatrix} = \begin{bmatrix} 1, 1; \\ 1, 1 \end{bmatrix}$$

Other common mathematical matrix operations are **transposition** and **matrix inversion**, defined by the `t()` and `inv()` functions, respectively. Other interesting functions that OpenCV provides are array operations in matrix, for example, counting the nonzero elements. This is useful for counting the pixels or areas of objects:

```
int countNonZero(src);
```

OpenCV provides some statistical functions. Mean and standard deviation by channel can be calculated using the `meanStdDev` function:

```
meanStdDev(src, mean, stddev);
```

Another useful statistical function is `minMaxLoc`. This function finds the minimum and the maximum of a matrix or array, and returns the location and value:

```
minMaxLoc(src, minVal, maxVal, minLoc, maxLoc);
```

Here `src` is the input matrix, `minVal` and `maxVal` are double values detected, and `minLoc` and `maxLoc` are `Point` values detected.

 Other core and useful functions are described in detail at: `http://docs.opencv.org/modules/core/doc/core.html`.

Basic data persistence and storage

Before finishing this chapter, we will explore the OpenCV functions to store and read our data. In many applications, such as calibration or machine learning, when we finish performing a number of calculations, we need to save these results to retrieve them in subsequent operations. OpenCV provides an XML/YAML persistence layer to this end.

Writing to FileStorage

To write a file with some OpenCV or other numeric data, we can use the `FileStorage` class, using a streaming << operator such as STL streaming:

```cpp
#include "opencv2/opencv.hpp"
using namespace cv;

int main(int, char** argv)
{
    // create our writer
    FileStorage fs("test.yml", FileStorage::WRITE);
    // Save an int
    int fps= 5;
    fs << "fps" << fps;
    // Create some mat sample
    Mat m1= Mat::eye(2,3, CV_32F);
    Mat m2= Mat::ones(3,2, CV_32F);
    Mat result= (m1+1).mul(m1+3);
    // write the result
    fs << "Result" << result;
    // release the file
    fs.release();

    FileStorage fs2("test.yml", FileStorage::READ);

    Mat r;
    fs2["Result"] >> r;
```

```
    std::cout << r << std::endl;

    fs2.release();

    return 0;
}
```

To create a file storage where we save the data, we only need to call the constructor, giving a path filename with the extension format desired (XML or YAML), and the second parameter set to write:

```
FileStorage fs("test.yml", FileStorage::WRITE);
```

If we want to save data, we only need to use the stream operator by giving an identifier in the first stage, and later the matrix or value that we want to save. For example, to save an `int` variable, we only have to write the following lines of code:

```
int fps= 5;
fs << "fps" << fps;
```

Otherwise, we can write/save `mat` as shown:

```
Mat m1= Mat::eye(2,3, CV_32F);
Mat m2= Mat::ones(3,2, CV_32F);
Mat result= (m1+1).mul(m1+3);
// write the result
fs << "Result" << result;
```

The result of the preceding code is a YAML format:

```
%YAML:1.0
fps: 5
Result: !!opencv-matrix
    rows: 2
    cols: 3
    dt: f
    data: [ 8., 3., 3., 3., 8., 3. ]
```

Reading from a file storage to read a file saved previously is very similar to the `save` functions:

```
#include "opencv2/opencv.hpp"
using namespace cv;

int main(int, char** argv)
{
    FileStorage fs2("test.yml", FileStorage::READ);
```

```
Mat r;
fs2["Result"] >> r;
std::cout << r << std::endl;

fs2.release();

return 0;
}
```

The first stage is to open a saved file with the `FileStorage` constructor using the appropriate parameters, path, and `FileStorage::READ`:

```
FileStorage fs2("test.yml", FileStorage::READ);
```

To read any stored variable, we only need to use the common stream operator `>>` using our `FileStorage` object and the identifier with the `[]` operator:

```
Mat r;
fs2["Result"] >> r;
```

Summary

In this chapter, we learned the basics and the most important types and operations of OpenCV, access to images and videos, and how they are stored in matrices. We learned the basic matrix operations and other basic OpenCV classes to store pixels, vectors, and so on. Finally, we learned how to save our data in files to allow them to be read in other applications or other executions.

In the next chapter, we are going to learn how to create our first application, learning the basics of graphical user interfaces that OpenCV provides. We will create buttons and sliders, and introduce some image processing basics.

3
Learning Graphical User Interfaces

In `Chapter 2`, *An Introduction to the Basics of OpenCV*, we learned the basic classes and structures of OpenCV and the most important class, called `Mat`. We learned how to read and save images and videos and the internal structure in the memory of images. We are now ready to work with OpenCV, but, in most cases, we need to show our image results and retrieve user interaction with our images using a number of user interfaces. OpenCV provides us with a few basic user interfaces to facilitate the creation of our applications and prototypes. To better understand how the user interface works, we are going to create a small application called **PhotoTool** at the end of this chapter. In this application, we will learn how to use filters and color conversions.

This chapter introduces the following topics:

- The OpenCV basic user interface
- The OpenCV Qt interface
- Sliders and buttons
- An advanced user interface – OpenGL
- Color conversion
- Basic filters

Technical requirements

This chapter requires familiarity with the basic C++ programming language. All the code used in this chapter can be downloaded from the following GitHub link: `https://github.com/PacktPublishing/Learn-OpenCV-4-By-Building-Projects-Second-Edition/tree/master/Chapter_03`. The code can be executed on any operating system, although it has only been tested on Ubuntu.

Check out the following video to see the code in action:
`http://bit.ly/2KH2QXD`

Introducing the OpenCV user interface

OpenCV has its own cross-OS user interface that allows developers to create their own applications without the need to learn complex user interface libraries. The OpenCV user interface is basic, but it gives computer vision developers the basic functions to create and manage their software developments. All of them are native and optimized for real-time use.

OpenCV provides two user interface options:

- A basic interface based on native user interfaces, cocoa or carbon for Mac OS X, and GTK for Linux or Windows user interfaces, selected by default when compiling OpenCV.
- A slightly more advanced interface based on Qt library that is a cross-platform interface. You have to enable the Qt option manually in CMake before compiling OpenCV.

In the following screenshot, you can see the basic user interface window on the left, and the Qt user interface on the right:

Basic graphical user interface with OpenCV

We are going to create a basic user interface with OpenCV. The OpenCV user interface allows us to create windows, add images to it, and move, resize, and destroy it. The user interface is in OpenCV's `highui` module. In the following code, we are going to learn how to create and show two images by pressing a key to display multiple windows with the image moving in the window on our desktop.

Don't worry about reading the full code; we are going to explain it in small chunks:

```cpp
#include <iostream>
#include <string>
#include <sstream>
using namespace std;

// OpenCV includes
#include <opencv2/core.hpp>
#include <opencv2/highgui.hpp>
using namespace cv;

int main(int argc, const char** argv)
{
    // Read images
    Mat lena= imread("../lena.jpg");
    # Checking if Lena image has been loaded
    if (!lena.data) {
cout << "Lena image missing!" << enld;
return -1;
    }
    Mat photo= imread("../photo.jpg");
    # Checking if Lena image has been loaded
    if (!photo.data) {
cout << "Lena image missing!" << enld;
return -1;
}
    // Create windows
    namedWindow("Lena", WINDOW_NORMAL);
    namedWindow("Photo", WINDOW_AUTOSIZE);

    // Move window
    moveWindow("Lena", 10, 10);
    moveWindow("Photo", 520, 10);
    // show images
    imshow("Lena", lena);
    imshow("Photo", photo);

    // Resize window, only non autosize
```

```
resizeWindow("Lena", 512, 512);

// wait for any key press
waitKey(0);

// Destroy the windows
destroyWindow("Lena");
destroyWindow("Photo");

// Create 10 windows
for(int i =0; i< 10; i++)
{
      ostringstream ss;
      ss << "Photo" << i;
      namedWindow(ss.str());
      moveWindow(ss.str(), 20*i, 20*i);
      imshow(ss.str(), photo);
}

waitKey(0);
// Destroy all windows
destroyAllWindows();
return 0;
}
```

Let's understand the code:

1. The first task we have to do in order to facilitate a graphical user interface is to import OpenCV's `highui` module:

   ```
   #include <opencv2/highgui.hpp>
   ```

2. Now that we are prepared to create our new windows, we have to load some images:

   ```
   // Read images
   Mat lena= imread("../lena.jpg");
   Mat photo= imread("../photo.jpg");
   ```

3. To create the windows, we use the `namedWindow` function. This function has two parameters; the first is a constant string with the window's name, and the second is the flags that we require. This second parameter is optional:

   ```
   namedWindow("Lena", WINDOW_NORMAL);
   namedWindow("Photo", WINDOW_AUTOSIZE);
   ```

4. In our case, we create two windows: the first is called `Lena`, and the second is called `Photo`.

   There are three flags by default for Qt and native:

   - `WINDOW_NORMAL`: This flag allows the user to resize the window
   - `WINDOW_AUTOSIZE`: If this flag is set, the window size is automatically adjusted to fit the display image and it is not possible to resize the window
   - `WINDOW_OPENGL`: This flag enables the OpenGL support

   Qt has a number of additional flags:

   - `WINDOW_FREERATIO` or `WINDOW_KEEPRATIO`: If `WINDOW_FREERATIO` is set, the image is adjusted with no respect for its ratio. If `WINDOW_FREERATIO` is set, the image is adjusted with respect to its ratio.
   - `WINDOW_GUI_NORMAL` or `WINDOW_GUI_EXPANDED`: The first flag facilitates a basic interface without the status bar and the toolbar. The second flag facilitates the most advanced graphical user interface, with the status bar and the toolbar.

 If we compile OpenCV with Qt, all the windows that we create are, by default, in the expanded interface, but we can use native interfaces and more basic ones adding the `CV_GUI_NORMAL` flag. By default, the flags are `WINDOW_AUTOSIZE`, `WINDOW_KEEPRATIO`, and `WINDOW_GUI_EXPANDED`.

5. When we create multiple windows, they are superimposed, but we can move the windows to any area of our desktop using the `moveWindow` function, as follows:

```
// Move window
moveWindow("Lena", 10, 10);
moveWindow("Photo", 520, 10);
```

6. In our code, we move the `Lena` window `10` pixels to the left, and `10` pixels up, and the `Photo` window `520` pixels to the left, and `10` pixels up:

```
// show images
imshow("Lena", lena);
imshow("Photo", photo);
// Resize window, only non autosize
resizeWindow("Lena", 512, 512);
```

7. After showing the images that we loaded previously using the `imshow` function, we resize the `Lena` window to `512` pixels, calling the `resizeWindow` function. This function has three parameters: the `window name`, `width`, and `height`.

 The specific window size is for the image area. Toolbars are not counted. Only windows without the `WINDOW_AUTOSIZE` flag enabled can be resized.

8. After waiting for a key press with the `waitKey` function, we are going to remove or delete our windows using the `destroyWindow` function, where the name of the window is the only parameter required:

```
waitKey(0);

// Destroy the windows
destroyWindow("Lena");
destroyWindow("Photo");
```

9. OpenCV has a function to remove all windows that we create in only one call. The function is called `destroyAllWindows`. To demonstrate how this works, we create 10 windows in our sample and await a key press. When the user presses any key, it destroys all the windows:

```
// Create 10 windows
for(int i =0; i< 10; i++)
{
    ostringstream ss;
    ss << "Photo" << i;
    namedWindow(ss.str());
    moveWindow(ss.str(), 20*i, 20*i);
    imshow(ss.str(), photo);
}

waitKey(0);
// Destroy all windows
destroyAllWindows();
```

In any event, OpenCV handles the destruction of all windows automatically when the application is terminated, and it is not necessary to call this function at the end of our application.

The result of all this code can be seen in the following images across two steps. First, it shows two windows:

After pressing any key, the application continues and draws several windows changing their positions:

With a few lines of code, we are able to create and manipulate windows and show images. We are now ready to facilitate user interaction with images and add user interface controls.

Adding slider and mouse events to our interfaces

Mouse events and slider control are very useful in computer vision and OpenCV. Using these control users, we can interact directly with the interface and change the properties of the input images or variables. In this section, we are going to introduce the mouse events and slider controls for basic interactions. To facilitate proper understanding, we have created the following code, by means of which we are going to paint green circles in an image, using mouse events, and blur the image with the slider:

```cpp
// Create a variable to save the position value in track
int blurAmount=15;

// Trackbar call back function
static void onChange(int pos, void* userInput);

//Mouse callback
static void onMouse(int event, int x, int y, int, void* userInput);

int main(int argc, const char** argv)
{
    // Read images
    Mat lena= imread("../lena.jpg");
    // Create windows
    namedWindow("Lena");
    // create a trackbar
    createTrackbar("Lena", "Lena", &blurAmount, 30, onChange, &lena);
    setMouseCallback("Lena", onMouse, &lena);

    // Call to onChange to init
    onChange(blurAmount, &lena);
    // wait app for a key to exit
    waitKey(0);
    // Destroy the windows
    destroyWindow("Lena");
    return 0;
}
```

Let's understand the code!

First, we create a variable to save the slider position. We need to save the slider position for access from other functions:

```cpp
// Create a variable to save the position value in track
int blurAmount=15;
```

Now, we define our callbacks for our slider and mouse event, required for the OpenCV functions setMouseCallback and createTrackbar:

```
// Trackbar call back function
static void onChange(int pos, void* userInput);

//Mouse callback
static void onMouse(int event, int x, int y, int, void* userInput);
```

In the main function, we load an image and create a new window called Lena:

```
int main(int argc, const char** argv)
{
    // Read images
    Mat lena= imread("../lena.jpg");
    // Create windows
    namedWindow("Lena");
```

Now is the time to create the slider. OpenCV has the createTrackbar function to generate a slider with the following parameters in order:

1. Trackbar name.
2. Window name.
3. Integer pointer to use as a value; this parameter is optional. If it is set, the slider attains this position when created.
4. Maximum position on slider.
5. Callback function when the position of the slider changes.
6. User data to send to callback. It can be used to send data to callbacks without using global variables.

To this code, we add trackbar for the Lena window and call the Lena trackbar too in order to blur the image. The value of the trackbar is stored in the blurAmount integer that we pass as a pointer and set the maximum value of the bar to 30. We set up onChange as a callback function and send the lena mat image as user data:

```
// create a trackbar
createTrackbar("Lena", "Lena", &blurAmount, 30, onChange, &lena);
```

After creating the slider, we add the mouse events to paint circles when a user clicks the left button on the mouse. OpenCV has the `setMouseCallback` function. This function has three parameters:

- A window name where we get mouse events.

- A callback function to call when there is any mouse interaction.

- **User data**: this is any data that will be sent to the callback function when it's fired. In our example, we'll send the entire `Lena` image.

Using the following code, we can add a mouse callback to the `Lena` window and set up `onMouse` as a callback function, passing the lena mat image as user data:

```
setMouseCallback("Lena", onMouse, &lena);
```

To finalize the main function only, we need to initialize the image with the same parameter as the slider. To carry out the initialization, we only need to call the `onChange` callback function and wait for events before closing the windows with `destroyWindow`, as can be seen in the following code:

```
// Call to onChange to init
onChange(blurAmount, &lena);
// wait app for a key to exit
waitKey(0);
// Destroy the windows
destroyWindow("Lena");
```

The slider callback applies a basic blur filter to the image using the slider value as a blur quantity:

```
// Trackbar call back function
static void onChange(int pos, void* userData) {
    if(pos <= 0) return;
    // Aux variable for result
    Mat imgBlur;
    // Get the pointer input image
    Mat* img= (Mat*)userInput;
    // Apply a blur filter
    blur(*img, imgBlur, Size(pos, pos));
    // Show the result
    imshow("Lena", imgBlur);
}
```

This function checks whether the slider value is 0 using the variable `pos`. In this case, we do not apply the filter because it generates a bad execution. We cannot apply a 0 pixel blur either. After checking the slider value, we create an empty matrix called `imgBlur` to store the blur result. To retrieve the image sent through user data in the callback function, we have to cast `void* userData` to the correct image type pointer `Mat*`.

Now we have the correct variables to apply the blur filter. The blur function applies a basic median filter to an input image, `*img` in our case; to an output image, the last required parameter is the size of the blur kernel (a kernel is a small matrix used to calculate the means of convolution between the kernel and the image) that we want to apply. In our case, we are using a squared kernel of `pos` size. Finally, we only need to update the image interface using the `imshow` function.

The mouse events callback has five input parameters: the first parameter defines the event type; the second and third define the mouse position; the fourth parameter defines the wheel movement; and the fifth parameter defines the user input data.

The mouse event types are as follows:

Event type	Description
EVENT_MOUSEMOVE	When the user moves the mouse.
EVENT_LBUTTONDOWN	When the user clicks the left mouse button.
EVENT_RBUTTONDOWN	When the user clicks the right mouse button.
EVENT_MBUTTONDOWN	When the user clicks the middle mouse button.
EVENT_LBUTTONUP	When the user releases the left mouse button.
EVENT_RBUTTONUP	When the user releases the right mouse button.
EVENT_MBUTTONUP	When the user releases the middle mouse button.
EVENT_LBUTTONDBLCLK	When the user double-clicks the left mouse button.
EVENT_RBUTTONDBLCLK	When the user double-clicks the right mouse button.
EVENT_MBUTTONDBLCLK	When the user double-clicks the middle mouse button.
EVENTMOUSEWHEEL	When the user executes a vertical scroll with the mousewheel.
EVENT_MOUSEHWHEEL	When the user executes a horizontal scroll with the mousewheel.

In our sample, we only manage events that result from a left-click of the mouse, and any event other than EVENT_LBUTTONDOWN is discarded. After discarding other events, we obtain the input image like that with the slider callback, and with a circle in the image using the circle OpenCV function:

```
//Mouse callback
static void onMouse(int event, int x, int y, int, void* userInput)
{
    if(event != EVENT_LBUTTONDOWN)
            return;

    // Get the pointer input image
    Mat* img= (Mat*)userInput;
    // Draw circle
    circle(*img, Point(x, y), 10, Scalar(0,255,0), 3);

    // Call on change to get blurred image
    onChange(blurAmount, img);

}
```

Graphic user interface with Qt

The Qt user interface gives us more control and options to work with our images.

The interface is divided into the following three main areas:

- Toolbar
- Image area
- Status bar

We can see these three areas in the following picture. At the top of the image is the toolbar, the image is the main area, and the status bar can be seen at the bottom of the image:

The toolbar has the following buttons from left to right:

- Four buttons for panning
- Zoom x1
- Zoom x30, show labels
- Zoom in
- Zoom out
- Save current image
- Show properties

These options can be seen clearly in the following image:

The image area shows an image and a contextual menu when we push the right mouse button over the image. This area can show an overlay message at the top of the area using the `displayOverlay` function. This function accepts three parameters: the window name, the text that we want to show, and the period in milliseconds for which the overlay text is displayed. If this time is set to 0, the text never disappears:

```
// Display Overlay
displayOverlay("Lena", "Overlay 5secs", 5000);
```

We can see the result of the preceding code in the following image. You can see a small black box at the top of the image with the sentence **Overlay 5secs**:

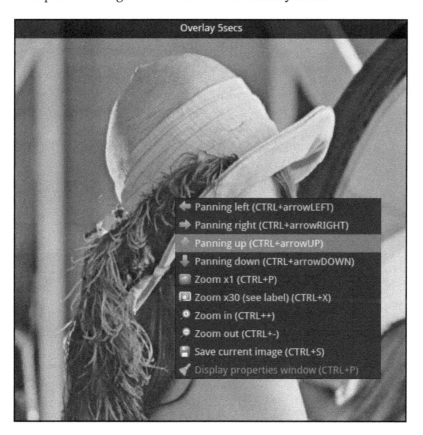

Finally, the status bar shows the bottom part of the window and shows the pixel value and position of the coordinates in the image:

We can use the status bar to show messages like an overlay. The function that can change the status bar message is `displayStatusBar`. This function has the same parameters as those of the overlay functions: the window name, the text to show, and the period of time for which to show it:

Adding buttons to the user interface

In the previous sections, we learned how to create normal or Qt interfaces and interact with them using the mouse and sliders, but we can create different types of buttons too.

Buttons are only supported in Qt windows.

The types of buttons supported by OpenCV Qt are as follows:

- Push button
- Checkbox
- RadioBox

The buttons only appear in the control panel. The control panel is an independent window per program where we can attach buttons and trackbars. To show the control panel, we can push the last toolbar button, right-click in any part of the Qt window and select the **Display properties** window, or use the *Ctrl + P* shortcut. Let's create a basic sample with buttons. The code is extensive, and we are going to explain the main function first and later each callback separately so as to understand everything better. The following code shows us the main code function that generates the user interface:

```
Mat img;
bool applyGray=false;
bool applyBlur=false;
bool applySobel=false;
...
int main(int argc, const char** argv)
{
    // Read images
    img= imread("../lena.jpg");
    // Create windows
    namedWindow("Lena");
    // create Buttons
    createButton("Blur", blurCallback, NULL, QT_CHECKBOX, 0);

    createButton("Gray",grayCallback,NULL,QT_RADIOBOX, 0);
    createButton("RGB",bgrCallback,NULL,QT_RADIOBOX, 1);

    createButton("Sobel",sobelCallback,NULL,QT_PUSH_BUTTON, 0);
    // wait app for a key to exit
    waitKey(0);
    // Destroy the windows
    destroyWindow("Lena");
    return 0;
}
```

We are going to apply thee types of filters: blur, a sobel filter, and a color conversion to gray. All these are optional and the user can choose each one using the buttons that we are going to create. Then, to get the status of each filter, we create three global Boolean variables:

```
bool applyGray=false;
bool applyBlur=false;
bool applySobel=false;
```

In the main function, after loading the image and creating the window, we have to use the `createButton` function to create each button.

There are three button types defined in OpenCV:

- QT_CHECKBOX
- QT_RADIOBOX
- QT_PUSH_BUTTON

Each button has five parameters with the following order:

1. The button name
2. A callback function
3. A pointer to user variable data passed to callback
4. The button type
5. The default initialized state used for the checkbox and RadioBox button types

Then, we create a blur checkbox button, two radio buttons for color conversion, and a push button for a sobel filter, as you can see in the following code:

```
// create Buttons
createButton("Blur", blurCallback, NULL, QT_CHECKBOX, 0);

createButton("Gray",grayCallback,NULL,QT_RADIOBOX, 0);
createButton("RGB",bgrCallback,NULL,QT_RADIOBOX, 1);

createButton("Sobel",sobelCallback,NULL,QT_PUSH_BUTTON, 0);
```

These are the most important parts of the main function. We are going to explore the `Callback` functions. Each `Callback` changes its status variable to call another function called `applyFilters` in order to add the filters activated to the input image:

```
void grayCallback(int state, void* userData)
{
    applyGray= true;
    applyFilters();
```

```
}
void bgrCallback(int state, void* userData)
{
    applyGray= false;
    applyFilters();
}

void blurCallback(int state, void* userData)
{
    applyBlur= (bool)state;
    applyFilters();
}

void sobelCallback(int state, void* userData)
{
    applySobel= !applySobel;
    applyFilters();
}
```

The `applyFilters` function checks the status variable for each filter:

```
void applyFilters(){
    Mat result;
    img.copyTo(result);
    if(applyGray){
        cvtColor(result, result, COLOR_BGR2GRAY);
    }
    if(applyBlur){
        blur(result, result, Size(5,5));
    }
    if(applySobel){
        Sobel(result, result, CV_8U, 1, 1);
    }
    imshow("Lena", result);
}
```

To change the color to gray, we use the `cvtColor` function which accepts three parameters: input image, output image, and the color conversion type.

The most useful color space conversions are as follows:

- RGB or BGR to gray (COLOR_RGB2GRAY, COLOR_BGR2GRAY)
- RGB or BGR to YcrCb (or YCC) (COLOR_RGB2YCrCb, COLOR_BGR2YCrCb)
- RGB or BGR to HSV (COLOR_RGB2HSV, COLOR_BGR2HSV)
- RGB or BGR to Luv (COLOR_RGB2Luv, COLOR_BGR2Luv)
- Gray to RGB or BGR (COLOR_GRAY2RGB, COLOR_GRAY2BGR)

We can see that the codes are easy to memorize.

 OpenCV works by default with the BGR format, and the color conversion is different for RGB and BGR, even when converted to gray. Some developers think that $R+G+B/3$ is true for gray, but the optimal gray value is called **luminosity** and has the formula $0,21*R + 0,72*G + 0,07*B$.

The blur filter was described in the previous section, and finally, if the `applySobel` variable is true, we apply the sobel filter. The sobel filter is an image derivate obtained using the sobel operator, commonly used to detect edges. OpenCV allows us to generate different derivates with kernel size, but the most common is a 3x3 kernel to calculate the x derivates or y derivate.

The most important sobel parameters are the following:

- Input image
- Output image
- Output image depth (`CV_8U`, `CV_16U`, `CV_32F`, `CV_64F`)
- Order of the derivate x
- Order of the derivate y
- Kernel size (a value of 3 by default)

To generate a 3 x 3 kernel and a first x order derivate, we have to use the following parameters:

```
Sobel(input, output, CV_8U, 1, 0);
```

The following parameters are used for y order derivates:

```
Sobel(input, output, CV_8U, 0, 1);
```

In our example, we use the x and y derivate simultaneously, overwriting the input. The following snippet shows how to generate the x and y derivates simultaneously, adding 1 in the fourth and fifth parameters:

```
Sobel(result, result, CV_8U, 1, 1);
```

The result of applying x and y derivatives simultaneously looks like following image applied to the **Lena** picture:

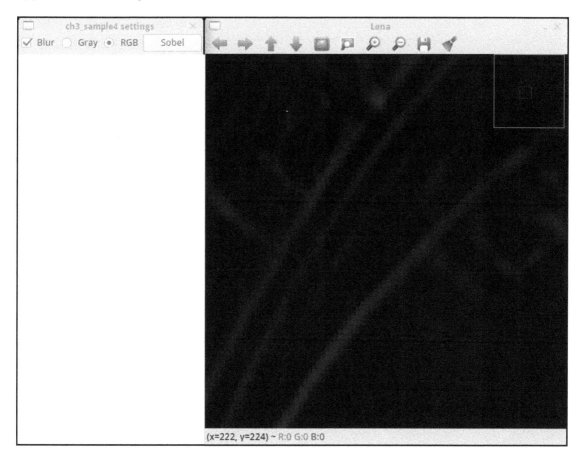

OpenGL support

OpenCV includes OpenGL support. OpenGL is a graphical library integrated in almost all graphical cards as a standard. OpenGL allows us to draw 2D up to complex 3D scenes. OpenCV includes OpenGL support due to the importance of representing 3D spaces in a number of tasks. To allow window support in OpenGL, we have to set up the WINDOW_OPENGL flag when we create the window using the namedWindow call.

The following code creates a window with OpenGL support and draws a rotate plane where we are going to show the web camera frames:

```cpp
Mat frame;
GLfloat angle= 0.0;
GLuint texture;
VideoCapture camera;

int loadTexture() {

    if (frame.data==NULL) return -1;

    glBindTexture(GL_TEXTURE_2D, texture);
    glTexParameteri(GL_TEXTURE_2D,GL_TEXTURE_MAG_FILTER,GL_LINEAR);
    glTexParameteri(GL_TEXTURE_2D,GL_TEXTURE_MIN_FILTER,GL_LINEAR);
    glPixelStorei(GL_UNPACK_ALIGNMENT, 1);

    glTexImage2D(GL_TEXTURE_2D, 0, GL_RGB, frame.cols, frame.rows,0, GL_BGR,
GL_UNSIGNED_BYTE, frame.data);
    return 0;

}

void on_opengl(void* param)
{
    glLoadIdentity();
    // Load frame Texture
    glBindTexture(GL_TEXTURE_2D, texture);
    // Rotate plane before draw
    glRotatef(angle, 1.0f, 1.0f, 1.0f);
    // Create the plane and set the texture coordinates
    glBegin (GL_QUADS);
        // first point and coordinate texture
      glTexCoord2d(0.0,0.0);
      glVertex2d(-1.0,-1.0);
        // second point and coordinate texture
      glTexCoord2d(1.0,0.0);
      glVertex2d(+1.0,-1.0);
        // third point and coordinate texture
      glTexCoord2d(1.0,1.0);
      glVertex2d(+1.0,+1.0);
        // last point and coordinate texture
      glTexCoord2d(0.0,1.0);
      glVertex2d(-1.0,+1.0);
    glEnd();

}
```

```
int main(int argc, const char** argv)
{
    // Open WebCam
    camera.open(0);
    if(!camera.isOpened())
        return -1;

    // Create new windows
    namedWindow("OpenGL Camera", WINDOW_OPENGL);
    // Enable texture
    glEnable( GL_TEXTURE_2D );
    glGenTextures(1, &texture);
    setOpenGlDrawCallback("OpenGL Camera", on_opengl);
    while(waitKey(30)!='q'){
        camera >> frame;
        // Create first texture
        loadTexture();
        updateWindow("OpenGL Camera");
        angle =angle+4;
    }
    // Destroy the windows
    destroyWindow("OpenGL Camera");
    return 0;
}
```

Let's understand the code!

The first task is to create the required global variables, where we store the video capture, save the frames, and control the animation angle plane and the OpenGL texture:

```
Mat frame;
GLfloat angle= 0.0;
GLuint texture;
VideoCapture camera;
```

In our main function, we have to create the video camera capture to retrieve the camera frames:

```
camera.open(0);
    if(!camera.isOpened())
        return -1;
```

If the camera is opened correctly, we can create our window with OpenGL support using the WINDOW_OPENGL flag:

```
// Create new windows
namedWindow("OpenGL Camera", WINDOW_OPENGL);
```

In our example, we want to draw the images that come from the web camera in a plane; then, we need to enable the OpenGL textures:

```
// Enable texture
glEnable(GL_TEXTURE_2D);
```

Now we are ready to draw with OpenGL in our window, but we need to set up a draw OpenGL callback like a typical OpenGL application. OpenCV gives us the setOpenGLDrawCallback function which has two parameters – the window name and the callback function:

```
setOpenGlDrawCallback("OpenGL Camera", on_opengl);
```

With the OpenCV window and callback function defined, we need to create a loop to load the texture, update the window content calling the OpenGL draw callback, and finally update the angle position. To update the window content, we use the OpenCV function update window with the window name as a parameter:

```
while(waitKey(30)!='q'){
        camera >> frame;
        // Create first texture
        loadTexture();
        updateWindow("OpenGL Camera");
        angle =angle+4;
    }
```

We are in the loop when the user presses the *Q* key. Before compiling our application sample, we need to define the loadTexture function and our on_opengl callback draw function. The loadTexture function converts our Mat frame to an OpenGL texture image ready to load and use in each callback drawing. Before loading the image as a texture, we have to ensure that we have data in our frame matrix, checking that the data variable object is not empty:

```
if (frame.data==NULL) return -1;
```

If we have data in our matrix frame, then we can create the OpenGL texture binding and set the OpenGL texture parameter as a linear interpolation:

```
glGenTextures(1, &texture);

glBindTexture(GL_TEXTURE_2D, texture);
    glTexParameteri(GL_TEXTURE_2D,GL_TEXTURE_MAG_FILTER,GL_LINEAR);
    glTexParameteri(GL_TEXTURE_2D,GL_TEXTURE_MIN_FILTER,GL_LINEAR);
```

Now, we have to define how the pixels are stored in our matrix and generate the pixels with the OpenGL `glTexImage2D` function. It's very important to note that OpenGL uses the RGB format, and OpenCV the BGR format, by default, and we have to set up the correct format in this function:

```
glPixelStorei(GL_UNPACK_ALIGNMENT, 1);
glTexImage2D(GL_TEXTURE_2D, 0, GL_RGB, frame.cols, frame.rows,0, GL_BGR,
GL_UNSIGNED_BYTE, frame.data);
    return 0;
```

Now, we only need to finish drawing our plane on every callback when we call `updateWindow` in the main loop. We use the common OpenGL functions, and then we load the identity OpenGL matrix to reset all our previous changes:

```
glLoadIdentity();
```

We also have to bring the frame texture to memory:

```
    // Load Texture
    glBindTexture(GL_TEXTURE_2D, texture);
```

Before drawing our plane, we apply all transformations to our scene. In our case, we are going to rotate our plane in the `1,1,1` axis:

```
    // Rotate plane
    glRotatef(angle, 1.0f, 1.0f, 1.0f);
```

Now that we have the scene correctly set to draw our plane, we are going to draw quads faces (faces with four vertices) and use `glBegin (GL_QUADS)` for this purpose:

```
// Create the plane and set the texture coordinates
    glBegin (GL_QUADS);
```

Next, we will draw a plane centered in the `0,0` position, which is 2 units in size. Then, we have to define the texture coordinate to use and the vertex position using the `glTextCoord2D` and `glVertex2D` functions:

```
    // first point and coordinate texture
glTexCoord2d(0.0,0.0);
glVertex2d(-1.0,-1.0);
    // seccond point and coordinate texture
glTexCoord2d(1.0,0.0);
glVertex2d(+1.0,-1.0);
    // third point and coordinate texture
glTexCoord2d(1.0,1.0);
glVertex2d(+1.0,+1.0);
    // last point and coordinate texture
```

```
glTexCoord2d(0.0,1.0);
glVertex2d(-1.0,+1.0);
    glEnd();
```

 This OpenGL code becomes obsolete, but it is appropriated to understand better the OpenCV and OpenGL integration without complex OpenGL code. By way of an introduction to modern OpenGL, read *Introduction to Modern OpenGL*, from *Packt Publishing*.

We can see the result in the following image:

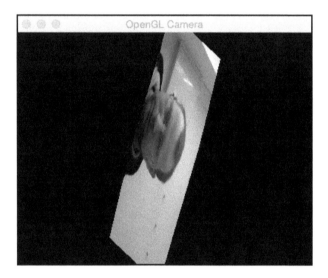

Summary

In this chapter, we learned how to create different types of user interfaces to show images or 3D interfaces using OpenGL. We learned how to create sliders and buttons or draw in 3D. We learned some basic image processing filters too with native OpenCV, but there are new open source alternatives that allow us to add more functionalities, such as cvui (https://dovyski.github.io/cvui/) or OpenCVGUI (https://damiles.github.io/OpenCVGUI/).

In the next chapter, we are going to construct a complete photo tool application where we will be applying all the knowledge that we have learned thus far. With the graphical user interface, we are going to learn how to apply multiple filters to an input image.

Delving into Histogram and Filters

4

In the last chapter, we learned the basics of user interfaces in OpenCV, using Qt libraries or native ones; we also learned how to use advanced OpenGL user interfaces. We learned about basic color conversions, and filters that allow us to create our first application. This chapter will introduce you to the following concepts:

- Histogram and histogram equalization
- Look-up tables
- Blur and median blur
- Canny filter
- Image-color equalization
- Understanding the conversion between image types

After we learn the basics of OpenCV and user interfaces, we are going to create our first complete application in this chapter, a basic photo tool, and cover the following topics:

- Generating a CMake script file
- Creating the graphical user interface
- Calculating and drawing a histogram
- Histogram equalization
- The lomography camera effect
- The cartoonize effect

This application will help us to understand how to create an entire project from scratch and understand the histogram concept. We will see how to equalize the histogram of the color image and create two effects, using a combination of filters and the use of look-up tables.

Technical requirements

This chapter requires familiarity with the basics of the C++ programming language. All the code used in this chapter can be downloaded from the following GitHub link: `https://github.com/PacktPublishing/Learn-OpenCV-4-By-Building-Projects-Second-Edition/tree/master/Chapter_04`. The code can be executed on any operating system, though it is only tested on Ubuntu.

Check out the following video to see the Code in Action:
`http://bit.ly/2Sid17y`

Generating a CMake script file

Before we start creating our source file, we are going to generate the `CMakeLists.txt` file to allow us to compile our project, structure it, and execute it. The following CMake script is simple and basic but enough to compile and generate the executable:

```
cmake_minimum_required (VERSION 3.0)

PROJECT(Chapter4_Phototool)

set (CMAKE_CXX_STANDARD 11)

# Requires OpenCV
FIND_PACKAGE( OpenCV 4.0.0 REQUIRED )
MESSAGE("OpenCV version : ${OpenCV_VERSION}")

include_directories(${OpenCV_INCLUDE_DIRS})
link_directories(${OpenCV_LIB_DIR})

ADD_EXECUTABLE(${PROJECT_NAME} main.cpp)
TARGET_LINK_LIBRARIES(${PROJECT_NAME} ${OpenCV_LIBS})
```

The first line indicates the minimum CMake version required to generate our project, the second one sets the project name that we can use as the ${PROJECT_NAME} variable, and the third one sets the required C++ version; in our case, we require the **C++11** version, as we can see in the next snippet:

```
cmake_minimum_required (VERSION 3.0)

PROJECT(Chapter4_Phototool)

set (CMAKE_CXX_STANDARD 11)
```

Moreover, we require the OpenCV library. First, we need to find the library, and then we'll show a message on the OpenCV library version found with the MESSAGE function:

```
# Requires OpenCV
FIND_PACKAGE( OpenCV 4.0.0 REQUIRED )
MESSAGE("OpenCV version : ${OpenCV_VERSION}")
```

If the library, with a minimum version of 4.0, is found, then we include the headers and library files in our project:

```
include_directories(${OpenCV_INCLUDE_DIRS})
link_directories(${OpenCV_LIB_DIR})
```

Now, we only need to add the source files to compile and link with the OpenCV library. The project name variable is used as the executable name, and we use only a single source file, called main.cpp:

```
ADD_EXECUTABLE(${PROJECT_NAME} main.cpp)
TARGET_LINK_LIBRARIES(${PROJECT_NAME} ${OpenCV_LIBS})
```

Creating the graphical user interface

Before we start with the image processing algorithms, we create the main user interface for our application. We are going to use the Qt-based user interface to allow us to create single buttons. The application receives one input parameter to load the image to process, and we are going to create four buttons, as follows:

- **Show histogram**
- **Equalize histogram**
- **Lomography effect**
- **Cartoonize effect**

We can see the four results in the following screenshot:

Let's begin developing our project. First of all, we are going to include the OpenCV – required headers, define an image matrix to store the input image, and create a constant string to use the new command-line parser already available from OpenCV 3.0; in this constant, we allow only two input parameters, `help` and the required image input:

```
// OpenCV includes
#include "opencv2/core/utility.hpp"
#include "opencv2/imgproc.hpp"
#include "opencv2/highgui.hpp"
using namespace cv;
// OpenCV command line parser functions
// Keys accepted by command line parser
const char* keys =
{
    "{help h usage ? | | print this message}"
     "{@image | | Image to process}"      -
};
```

The main function starts with the command-line parser variable; next, we set the about instruction and print the help message. This line sets up the help instructions of our final executable:

```
int main(int argc, const char** argv)
{
    CommandLineParser parser(argc, argv, keys);
     parser.about("Chapter 4. PhotoTool v1.0.0");
     //If requires help show
     if (parser.has("help"))
    {
        parser.printMessage();
        return 0;
    }
```

If the user doesn't require help, then we have to get the file path image in the `imgFile` variable string and check that all required parameters are added with the `parser.check()` function:

```
String imgFile= parser.get<String>(0);

// Check if params are correctly parsed in his variables
if (!parser.check())
{
    parser.printErrors();
    return 0;
}
```

Now, we can read the image file with the `imread` function, and then create the window in which the input image will be shown later with the `namedWindow` function:

```
// Load image to process
Mat img= imread(imgFile);

// Create window
namedWindow("Input");
```

With the image loaded and the window created, we only need to create the buttons for our interface and link them with the callback functions; each callback function is defined in the source code and we are going to explain these functions later in this chapter. We are going to create the buttons with the `createButton` function with the `QT_PUSH_BUTTON` constant to button style:

```
// Create UI buttons
createButton("Show histogram", showHistoCallback, NULL, QT_PUSH_BUTTON, 0);
createButton("Equalize histogram", equalizeCallback, NULL, QT_PUSH_BUTTON, 0);
createButton("Lomography effect", lomoCallback, NULL, QT_PUSH_BUTTON, 0);
createButton("Cartoonize effect", cartoonCallback, NULL, QT_PUSH_BUTTON, 0);
```

To finish our main function, we show the input image and wait for a key press to finish our application:

```
// Show image
imshow("Input", img);

waitKey(0);
return 0;
```

Now, we only have to define each callback function, and in the next sections, we are going to do just that.

Drawing a histogram

A histogram is a statistical graphic representation of variable distribution that allows us to understand the density estimation and probability distribution of data. A histogram is created by dividing the entire range of variable values into a small range of values, and then counting how many values fall into each interval.

If we apply this histogram concept to an image, it seems to be difficult to understand but, in fact, it is very simple. In a gray image, our variable values' ranges are each possible gray value (from 0 to 255), and the density is the number of pixels of the image that have this value. This means that we have to count the number of pixels of the image that have a value of 0, the number of pixels with a value of 1, and so on.

The callback function that shows the histogram of the input image is showHistoCallback ; this function calculates the histogram of each channel image and shows the result of each histogram channel in a new image.

Now, check the following code:

```
void showHistoCallback(int state, void* userData)
{
    // Separate image in BRG
    vector<Mat> bgr;
    split(img, bgr);

    // Create the histogram for 256 bins
    // The number of possibles values [0..255]
    int numbins= 256;

    /// Set the ranges for B,G,R last is not included
    float range[] = { 0, 256 } ;
    const float* histRange = { range };

    Mat b_hist, g_hist, r_hist;

    calcHist(&bgr[0], 1, 0, Mat(), b_hist, 1, &numbins, &histRange);
    calcHist(&bgr[1], 1, 0, Mat(), g_hist, 1, &numbins, &histRange);
    calcHist(&bgr[2], 1, 0, Mat(), r_hist, 1, &numbins, &histRange);

    // Draw the histogram
    // We go to draw lines for each channel
    int width= 512;
    int height= 300;
    // Create image with gray base
    Mat histImage(height, width, CV_8UC3, Scalar(20,20,20));

    // Normalize the histograms to height of image
    normalize(b_hist, b_hist, 0, height, NORM_MINMAX);
    normalize(g_hist, g_hist, 0, height, NORM_MINMAX);
    normalize(r_hist, r_hist, 0, height, NORM_MINMAX);

    int binStep= cvRound((float)width/(float)numbins);
    for(int i=1; i< numbins; i++)
    {
```

```
            line(histImage,
                    Point( binStep*(i-1), height-cvRound(b_hist.at<float>(i-1)
 )),
                    Point( binStep*(i), height-cvRound(b_hist.at<float>(i) )),
                    Scalar(255,0,0)
                );
            line(histImage,
                    Point(binStep*(i-1), height-
cvRound(g_hist.at<float>(i-1))),
                    Point(binStep*(i), height-cvRound(g_hist.at<float>(i))),
                    Scalar(0,255,0)
                );
            line(histImage,
                    Point(binStep*(i-1), height-
cvRound(r_hist.at<float>(i-1))),
                    Point(binStep*(i), height-cvRound(r_hist.at<float>(i))),
                    Scalar(0,0,255)
                );
    }

    imshow("Histogram", histImage);

}
```

Let's understand how to extract each channel histogram and how to draw it. First, we need to create three matrices to process each input image channel. We use a vector-type variable to store each one and use the `split` OpenCV function to divide the input image among these three channels:

```
// Separate image in BRG
    vector<Mat> bgr;
    split(img, bgr);
```

Now, we are going to define the number of bins of our histogram, in our case, one per possible pixel value:

```
int numbins= 256;
```

Let's define our range of variables and create three matrices to store each histogram:

```
/// Set the ranges for B,G,R
float range[] = {0, 256} ;
const float* histRange = {range};

Mat b_hist, g_hist, r_hist;
```

We can calculate the histograms using the `calcHist` OpenCV function. This function has several parameters with this order:

- **The input image**: In our case, we use one image channel stored in the `bgr` vector
- **The number of images in the input to calculate the histogram**: In our case, we only use 1 image
- **The number channel dimensions used to compute the histogram**: We use 0 in our case
- The optional mask matrix.
- The variable to store the calculated histogram.
- **Histogram dimensionality**: This is the dimension of the space where the image (here, a gray plane) is taking its values, in our case 1
- **Number of bins to calculate**: In our case 256 bins, one per pixel value
- **Range of input variables**: In our case, from 0 to 255 possible pixels values

Our `calcHist` function for each channel looks as follows:

```
calcHist(&bgr[0], 1, 0, Mat(), b_hist, 1, &numbins, &histRange );
calcHist(&bgr[1], 1, 0, Mat(), g_hist, 1, &numbins, &histRange );
calcHist(&bgr[2], 1, 0, Mat(), r_hist, 1, &numbins, &histRange );
```

Now that we have calculated each channel histogram, we have to draw each one and show it to the user. To do this, we are going to create a color image that is 512 by 300 pixels in size:

```
// Draw the histogram
// We go to draw lines for each channel
int width= 512;
int height= 300;
// Create image with gray base
Mat histImage(height, width, CV_8UC3, Scalar(20,20,20));
```

Before we draw the histogram values into our image, we are going to normalize the histogram matrices between the minimum value, 0, and a maximum value; the maximum value is the same as the height of our output histogram image:

```
// Normalize the histograms to height of image
normalize(b_hist, b_hist, 0, height, NORM_MINMAX);
normalize(g_hist, g_hist, 0, height, NORM_MINMAX);
normalize(r_hist, r_hist, 0, height, NORM_MINMAX);
```

Now we have to draw a line from bin 0 to bin 1, and so on. Between each bin, we have to calculate how many pixels there are; then, a `binStep` variable is calculated by dividing the width by the number of bins. Each small line is drawn from horizontal position i-1 to i; the vertical position is the histogram value in the corresponding i, and it is drawn with the color channel representation:

```
int binStep= cvRound((float)width/(float)numbins);
    for(int i=1; i< numbins; i++)
    {
        line(histImage,
                Point(binStep*(i-1), height-
cvRound(b_hist.at<float>(i-1))),
                Point(binStep*(i), height-cvRound(b_hist.at<float>(i))),
                Scalar(255,0,0)
            );
        line(histImage,
                Point(binStep*(i-1), height-
cvRound(g_hist.at<float>(i-1))),
                Point( binStep*(i), height-cvRound(g_hist.at<float>(i))),
                Scalar(0,255,0)
            );
        line(histImage,
                Point(binStep*(i-1), height-
cvRound(r_hist.at<float>(i-1))),
                Point( binStep*(i), height-cvRound(r_hist.at<float>(i))),
                Scalar(0,0,255)
            );
    }
```

Finally, we show the histogram image with the `imshow` function:

```
imshow("Histogram", histImage);
```

This is the result for the `lena.png` image:

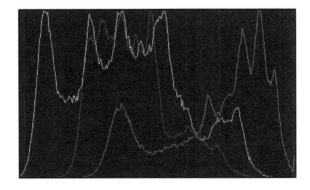

Image color equalization

In this section, we are going to learn how to equalize a color image. Image equalization, or histogram equalization, tries to obtain a histogram with a uniform distribution of values. The result of equalization is an increase in the contrast of an image. Equalization allows lower local contrast areas to gain high contrast, spreading out the most frequent intensities. This method is very useful when the image is extremely dark or bright and there is a very small difference between the background and foreground. Using histogram equalization, we increase the contrast and the details that are over- or under-exposed. This technique is very useful in medical images, such as X-rays.

However, there are two main disadvantages to this method: the increase in background noise and a consequent decrease in useful signals. We can see the effect of equalization in the following photograph, and the histogram changes and spreads when increasing the image contrast:

Let's implement our equalization histogram; we are going to implement it in the `Callback` function defined in the user interface's code:

```
void equalizeCallback(int state, void* userData)
{
    Mat result;
    // Convert BGR image to YCbCr
    Mat ycrcb;
```

```
cvtColor(img, ycrcb, COLOR_BGR2YCrCb);

// Split image into channels
vector<Mat> channels;
split(ycrcb, channels);
// Equalize the Y channel only
equalizeHist(channels[0], channels[0]);

// Merge the result channels
merge(channels, ycrcb);

// Convert color ycrcb to BGR
cvtColor(ycrcb, result, COLOR_YCrCb2BGR);

// Show image
imshow("Equalized", result);
}
```

To equalize a color image, we only have to equalize the luminance channel. We can do this with each color channel but the result is not usable. Alternatively, we can use any other color image format, such as **HSV** or **YCrCb**, that separates the luminance component in an individual channel. Thus, we choose **YCrCb** and use the Y channel (luminance) to equalize. Then, we follow these steps:

1. Convert or input the **BGR** image into **YCrCb** using the cvtColor function:

   ```
   Mat result;
   // Convert BGR image to YCbCr
   Mat ycrcb;
   cvtColor(img, ycrcb, COLOR_BGR2YCrCb);
   ```

2. Split the **YCrCb** image into different channels matrix:

   ```
   // Split image into channels
   vector<Mat> channels;
   split(ycrcb, channels);
   ```

3. Equalize the histogram only in the Y channel, using the equalizeHist function which has only two parameters, the input and output matrices:

   ```
   // Equalize the Y channel only
   equalizeHist(channels[0], channels[0]);
   ```

4. Merge the resulting channels and convert them into the **BGR** format to show the user the result:

   ```
   // Merge the result channels
   merge(channels, ycrcb);
   ```

```
// Convert color ycrcb to BGR
cvtColor(ycrcb, result, COLOR_YCrCb2BGR);

// Show image
imshow("Equalized", result);
```

The process applied to a low-contrast `Lena` image will have the following result:

Lomography effect

In this section, we are going to create another image effect, which is a photograph effect that is very common in different mobile applications, such as Google Camera or Instagram. We are going to discover how to use a **look-up table** (**LUT**). We will go through LUTs later in this same section. We are going to learn how to add an over image, in this case a dark halo, to create our desired effect. The function that implements this effect is the `lomoCallback` callback and it has the following code:

```
void lomoCallback(int state, void* userData)
{
    Mat result;
```

```
const double exponential_e = std::exp(1.0);
// Create Look-up table for color curve effect
Mat lut(1, 256, CV_8UC1);
for (int i=0; i<256; i++)
{
    float x= (float)i/256.0;
    lut.at<uchar>(i)= cvRound( 256 * (1/(1 + pow(exponential_e, -
((x-0.5)/0.1)) )) );
}
// Split the image channels and apply curve transform only to red
channel
vector<Mat> bgr;
split(img, bgr);
LUT(bgr[2], lut, bgr[2]);
// merge result
merge(bgr, result);
// Create image for halo dark
Mat halo(img.rows, img.cols, CV_32FC3, Scalar(0.3,0.3,0.3) );
// Create circle
circle(halo, Point(img.cols/2, img.rows/2), img.cols/3, Scalar(1,1,1),
-1);
blur(halo, halo, Size(img.cols/3, img.cols/3));
// Convert the result to float to allow multiply by 1 factor
Mat resultf;
result.convertTo(resultf, CV_32FC3);
// Multiply our result with halo
multiply(resultf, halo, resultf);
// convert to 8 bits
resultf.convertTo(result, CV_8UC3);

// show result
imshow("Lomography", result);
}
```

Let's look at how the lomography effect works and how to implement it. The lomography effect is divided into different steps, but in our example, we did a very simple lomography effect with two steps:

1. A color manipulation effect by using a look-up table to apply a curve to the red channel
2. A vintage effect by applying a dark halo to the image

The first step was to manipulate the red color with a curve transform by applying the following function:

$$\frac{1}{1 + e^{-\frac{x-0.5}{s}}}$$

This formula generates a curve that makes the dark values darker and the light values lighter, where **x** is the possible pixels value (0 to 255) and **s** is a constant that we set to 0.1 in our example. A lower constant value that generates pixels with values lower than 128 is very dark, and over 128 is very bright. Values near to 1 convert the curve into a line and do not generate our desired effect:

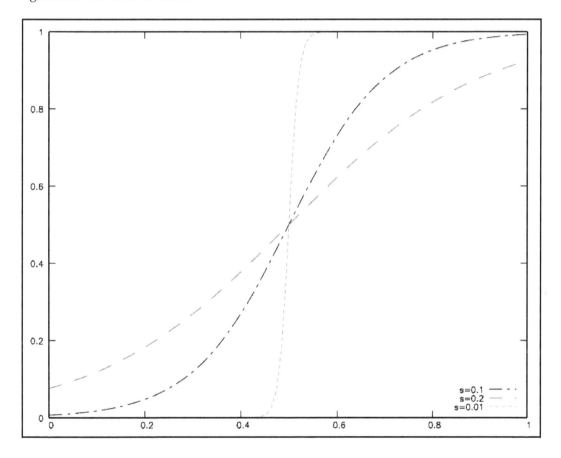

This function is very easy to implement by applying an LUT. An LUT is a vector or table that returns a preprocessed value for a given value to perform computation in the memory. An LUT is a common technique used to spare CPU cycles by avoiding performing costly computations repeatedly. Instead of calling the `exponential/divide` function for each pixel, we perform it only once for each possible pixel value (`256` times) and store the result in a table. Thus, we have saved CPU time at the cost of a bit of memory. While this may not make a great difference on a standard PC with small image sizes, this makes a huge one for CPU-limited hardware, such as Raspberry Pi.

For example, in our case, if we want to apply a function for every pixel in our image, then we have to make *width* x *height* operations; for example, in 100 x 100 pixels, there will be 10,000 calculations. If we can pre-calculate all possible results for all possible inputs, we can create the LUT table. In an image, there are only **256** possible values as a pixel value. If we want to change the color by applying a function, we can pre-calculate the 256 values and save them in an LUT vector. In our sample code, we define the E variable and create an `lut` matrix of `1` row and `256` columns. Then, we do a loop over all possible pixel values by applying our formula and saving it into an `lut` variable:

```
const double exponential_e = std::exp(1.0);
// Create look-up table for color curve effect
Mat lut(1, 256, CV_8UC1);
Uchar* plut= lut.data;
for (int i=0; i<256; i++)
{
    double x= (double)i/256.0;
    plut[i]= cvRound( 256.0 * (1.0/(1.0 + pow(exponential_e, -
((x-0.5)/0.1)) )) );
}
```

As we mentioned earlier in this section, we don't apply the function to all channels; thus, we need to split our input image by channels using the `split` function:

```
// Split the image channels and apply curve transform only to red channel
vector<Mat> bgr;
split(img, bgr);
```

We then apply our `lut` table variable to the red channel. OpenCV gives us the LUT function, which has three parameters:

- Input image
- Matrix of look-up table
- Output image

Then, our call to the LUT function and red channel looks like this:

```
LUT(bgr[2], lut, bgr[2]);
```

Now, we only have to merge our computed channels:

```
// merge result
merge(bgr, result);
```

The first step is done and we only have to create the dark halo to finish our effect. Then, we create a gray image with a white circle inside, with the same input image size:

```
// Create image for halo dark
Mat halo(img.rows, img.cols, CV_32FC3, Scalar(0.3,0.3,0.3));
// Create circle
circle(halo, Point(img.cols/2, img.rows/2), img.cols/3, Scalar(1,1,1),
-1);
```

Check out the following screenshot:

If we apply this image to our input image, we will get a strong change from dark to white; thus, we can apply a big blur using the blur filter function to our circle halo image to get a smooth effect:

```
blur(halo, halo, Size(img.cols/3, img.cols/3));
```

The image will be altered to give us the following result:

Now, if we have to apply this halo to our image from step 1, an easy way to do this is to multiply both images. However, we will have to convert our input image from an 8-bit image to a 32-bit float, because we need to multiply our blurred image, which has values in the 0 to 1 range, with our input image, which has integer values. The following code will do it for us:

```
// Convert the result to float to allow multiply by 1 factor
Mat resultf;
result.convertTo(resultf, CV_32FC3);
```

After converting our image, we only need to multiply each matrix per element:

```
// Multiply our result with halo
multiply(resultf, halo, resultf);
```

Finally, we will convert the float image matrix result to an 8-bit image matrix:

```
// convert to 8 bits
resultf.convertTo(result, CV_8UC3);

// show result
imshow("Lomograpy", result);
```

This will be the result:

Cartoonize effect

The last section of this chapter is dedicated to creating another effect, called **cartoonize**; the purpose of this effect is to create an image that looks like a cartoon. To do this, we divide the algorithm into two steps: **edge detection** and **color filtering**.

The `cartoonCallback` function defines this effect, which has the following code:

```
void cartoonCallback(int state, void* userData)
{
    /** EDGES **/
    // Apply median filter to remove possible noise
    Mat imgMedian;
    medianBlur(img, imgMedian, 7);

    // Detect edges with canny
    Mat imgCanny;
    Canny(imgMedian, imgCanny, 50, 150);
    // Dilate the edges
    Mat kernel= getStructuringElement(MORPH_RECT, Size(2,2));
    dilate(imgCanny, imgCanny, kernel);

    // Scale edges values to 1 and invert values
    imgCanny= imgCanny/255;
    imgCanny= 1-imgCanny;
    // Use float values to allow multiply between 0 and 1
    Mat imgCannyf;
    imgCanny.convertTo(imgCannyf, CV_32FC3);

    // Blur the edgest to do smooth effect
    blur(imgCannyf, imgCannyf, Size(5,5));

    /** COLOR **/
    // Apply bilateral filter to homogenizes color
    Mat imgBF;
    bilateralFilter(img, imgBF, 9, 150.0, 150.0);

    // truncate colors
    Mat result= imgBF/25;
    result= result*25;

    /** MERGES COLOR + EDGES **/
    // Create a 3 channnles for edges
    Mat imgCanny3c;
    Mat cannyChannels[]={ imgCannyf, imgCannyf, imgCannyf};
    merge(cannyChannels, 3, imgCanny3c);
```

```
// Convert color result to float
Mat resultf;
result.convertTo(resultf, CV_32FC3);

// Multiply color and edges matrices
multiply(resultf, imgCanny3c, resultf);

// convert to 8 bits color
resultf.convertTo(result, CV_8UC3);

// Show image
imshow("Result", result);

}
```

The first step is to detect the most important *edges* of the image. We need to remove noise from the input image before detecting the edges. There are several ways to do it. We are going to use a median filter to remove all possible small noise, but we can use other methods, such as Gaussian blur. The OpenCV function is medianBlur, which accepts three parameters: input image, output image, and the kernel size (a kernel is a small matrix used to apply some mathematical operation, such as convolutional means, to an image):

```
Mat imgMedian;
medianBlur(img, imgMedian, 7);
```

After removing any possible noise, we detect the strong edges with the Canny filter:

```
// Detect edges with canny
Mat imgCanny;
Canny(imgMedian, imgCanny, 50, 150);
```

The Canny filter accepts the following parameters:

- Input image
- Output image
- First threshold
- Second threshold
- Sobel size aperture
- Boolean value to indicate whether we need to use a more accurate image gradient magnitude

The smallest value between the first threshold and the second threshold is used for edge linking. The largest value is used to find initial segments of strong edges. The sobel size aperture is the kernel size for the sobel filter that will be used in the algorithm. After detecting edges, we are going to apply a small dilation to join broken edges:

```
// Dilate the edges
Mat kernel= getStructuringElement(MORPH_RECT, Size(2,2));
dilate(imgCanny, imgCanny, kernel);
```

Similar to what we did in the lomography effect, if we need to multiply our edges' result image with the color image, then we require the pixel values to be in the 0 and 1 range. For this, we will divide the canny result by 256 and invert the edges to black:

```
// Scale edges values to 1 and invert values
imgCanny= imgCanny/255;
imgCanny= 1-imgCanny;
```

We will also transform the canny 8 unsigned bit pixel format to a float matrix:

```
// Use float values to allow multiply between 0 and 1
Mat imgCannyf;
imgCanny.convertTo(imgCannyf, CV_32FC3);
```

To give a cool result, we can blur the edges, and to give smooth result lines, we can apply a `blur` filter:

```
// Blur the edgest to do smooth effect
blur(imgCannyf, imgCannyf, Size(5,5));
```

The first step of the algorithm is finished, and now we are going to work with the color. To get a cartoon look, we are going to use the `bilateral` filter:

```
// Apply bilateral filter to homogenizes color
Mat imgBF;
bilateralFilter(img, imgBF, 9, 150.0, 150.0);
```

The `bilateral` filter is a filter that reduces the noise of an image while keeping the edges. With appropriate parameters, which we will explore later, we can get a cartoonish effect.

The `bilateral` filter's parameters are as follows:

- Input image
- Output image
- Diameter of pixel neighborhood; if it's set to negative, it is computed from a sigma space value

- Sigma color value
- Sigma coordinate space

 With a diameter greater than five, the `bilateral` filter starts to become slow. With sigma values greater than 150, a cartoonish effect appears.

To create a stronger cartoonish effect, we truncate the possible color values to 10 by multiplying and dividing the pixels values:

```
// truncate colors
Mat result= imgBF/25;
result= result*25;
```

Finally, we have to merge the color and edges results. Then, we have to create a three-channel image as follows:

```
// Create a 3 channles for edges
Mat imgCanny3c;
Mat cannyChannels[]={ imgCannyf, imgCannyf, imgCannyf};
merge(cannyChannels, 3, imgCanny3c);
```

We can convert our color result image to a 32-bit float image and then multiply both images per element:

```
// Convert color result to float
Mat resultf;
result.convertTo(resultf, CV_32FC3);

// Multiply color and edges matrices
multiply(resultf, imgCanny3c, resultf);
```

Finally, we only need to convert our image to 8 bits and then show the resulting image to the user:

```
// convert to 8 bits color
resultf.convertTo(result, CV_8UC3);

// Show image
imshow("Result", result);
```

In the next screenshot, we can see the input image (left image) and the result of applying the cartoonize effect (right image):

Summary

In this chapter, we saw how to create a complete project that manipulates images by applying different effects. We also split a color image into multiple matrices to apply effects to only one channel. We saw how to create look-up tables, merge multiple matrices into one, use the `Canny` and `bilateral` filters, draw circles, and multiply images to get halo effects.

In the next chapter, we will learn how to do object inspection, and how to segment an image into different parts and detect those parts.

5
Automated Optical Inspection, Object Segmentation, and Detection

In Chapter 4, *Delving into Histogram and Filters*, we learned about histograms and filters, which allow us to understand image manipulation and create a photo application.

In this chapter, we are going to introduce the basic concepts of object segmentation and detection. This means isolating the objects that appear in an image for future processing and analysis.

This chapter introduces the following topics:

- Noise removal
- Light/background removal basics
- Thresholding
- Connected components for object segmentation
- Finding contours for object segmentation

Many industries use complex computer vision systems and hardware. Computer vision tries to detect problems and minimize errors produced in the production process, improving the quality of final products.

In this sector, the name for this computer vision task is **Automated Optical Inspection** (**AOI**). This name appears in the inspection of printed circuit board manufacturers, where one or more cameras scan each circuit to detect critical failures and quality defects. This nomenclature was used in other manufacturing industries so that they could use optical camera systems and computer vision algorithms to increase product quality. Nowadays, optical inspection using different camera types (infrared or 3D cameras), depending on the requirements, and complex algorithms are used in thousands of industries for different purposes such as defect detection, classification, and so on.

Technical requirements

This chapter requires familiarity with the basic C++ programming language. All of the code that's used in this chapter can be downloaded from the following GitHub link: `https://github.com/PacktPublishing/Learn-OpenCV-4-By-Building-Projects-Second-Edition/tree/master/Chapter_05`. The code can be executed on any operating system, though it is only tested on Ubuntu.

Check out the following video to see the Code in Action:
`http://bit.ly/2DRbMbz`

Isolating objects in a scene

In this chapter, we are going to introduce the first step in an AOI algorithm and try to isolate different parts or objects in a scene. We are going to take the example of the object detection and classification of three object types (screw, packing ring, and nut) and develop them in this chapter and `Chapter 6`, *Learning Object Classification*.

Imagine that we are in a company that produces these three objects. All of them are in the same carrier tape. Our objective is to detect each object in the carrier tape and classify each one to allow a robot to put each object on the correct shelf:

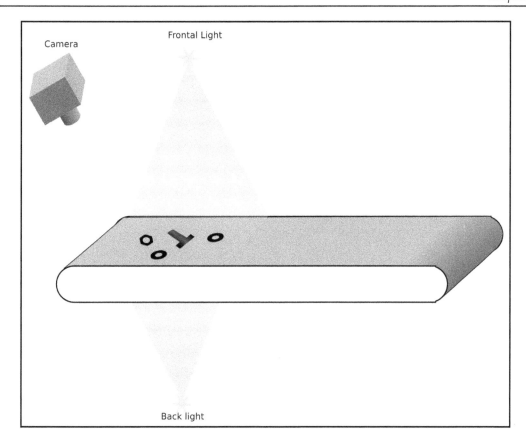

In this chapter, we are going to learn how to isolate each object and detect its position in the image in pixels. In the next chapter, we are going to learn how to classify each isolated object to recognize if it is a nut, screw, or a packing ring.

In the following screenshot, we show our desired result, where there are a few objects in the left image. In the right image, we have drawn each one in a different color, showing different features such as area, height, width, and contour size:

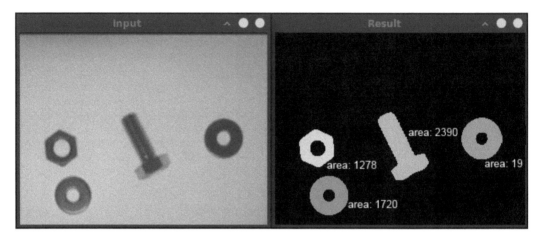

To reach this result, we are going to follow different steps that allow us to understand and organize our algorithms better. We can see these steps in the following diagram:

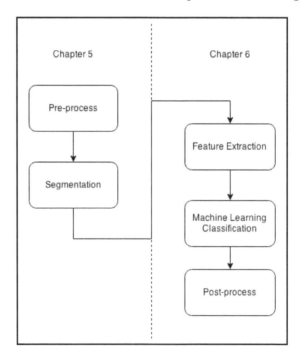

Our application will be divided into two chapters. In this chapter, we are going to develop and understand the preprocessing and segmentation steps. In Chapter 6, *Learning Object Classification*, we are going to extract the characteristics of each segmented object and train our machine learning system/algorithm on how to recognize each object class.

Our preprocessing steps will be divided into three more subsets:

- **Noise Removal**
- **Light Removal**
- **Binarization**

In the segmentation step, we are going to use two different algorithms:

- Contour detection
- **Connected components** extraction (labeling)

We can see these steps and the application flow in the following diagram:

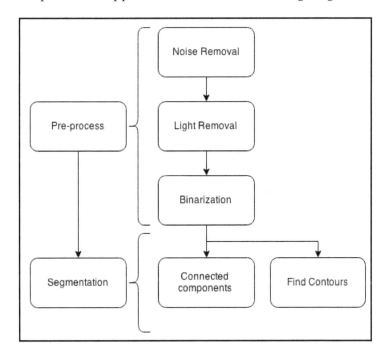

Now, it's time to start the preprocessing step so that we can get the best **Binarization** image by removing the noise and lighting effects. This minimizes any possible detection errors.

Creating an application for AOI

To create our new application, we require a few input parameters. When a user executes the application, all of them are optional, excluding the input image to process. The input parameters are as follows:

- Input image to process
- Light image pattern
- Light operation, where a user can choose between difference or divide operations
- If the user sets 0 as a value, the difference operation is applied
- If the user set 1 as a value, the division operation is applied
- Segmentation, where the user can choose between connected components with or without statistics and find contour methods
- If the user sets 1 as the input value, the connected components method for segment is applied
- If the user sets 2 as the input value, the connected components method with the statistics area is applied
- If the user sets 3 as the input value, the find contours method is applied for Segmentation

To enable this user selection, we are going to use the command line parser class with the following keys:

```
// OpenCV command line parser functions
// Keys accepted by command line parser
const char* keys =
{
    "{help h usage ? | | print this message}"
    "{@image || Image to process}"
    "{@lightPattern || Image light pattern to apply to image input}"
    "{lightMethod | 1 | Method to remove background light, 0 difference, 1
div }"
    "{segMethod | 1 | Method to segment: 1 connected Components, 2 connected
components with stats, 3 find Contours }"
};
```

We are going to use the command line parser class in the main function by checking the parameters. The CommandLineParser is explained in Chapter 2, *An Introduction to the Basics of OpenCV*, in the *Reading videos and cameras* section:

```
int main(int argc, const char** argv)
{
    CommandLineParser parser(argc, argv, keys);
```

```
parser.about("Chapter 5. PhotoTool v1.0.0");
//If requires help show
if (parser.has("help"))
{
    parser.printMessage();
    return 0;
}

String img_file= parser.get<String>(0);
String light_pattern_file= parser.get<String>(1);
auto method_light= parser.get<int>("lightMethod");
auto method_seg= parser.get<int>("segMethod");
// Check if params are correctly parsed in his variables
if (!parser.check())
{
    parser.printErrors();
    return 0;
}
```

After parsing our command-line user data, we need to check the input image has been loaded correctly. We then load the image and check it has data:

```
// Load image to process
Mat img= imread(img_file, 0);
if(img.data==NULL){
  cout << "Error loading image "<< img_file << endl;
  return 0;
}
```

Now, we are ready to create our AOI process of segmentation. We are going to start with the preprocessing task.

Preprocessing the input image

This section introduces some of the most common techniques that we can apply for preprocessing images in the context of object segmentation/detection. The preprocessing is the first change we make to a new image before we start working and extracting the information we require from it. Normally, in the preprocessing step, we try to minimize the image noise, light conditions, or image deformation due to a camera lens. These steps minimize errors while detecting objects or segments in our image.

Noise removal

If we don't remove the noise, we can detect more objects than we expect because noise is normally represented as small points in the image and can be segmented as an object. The sensor and scanner circuit normally produces this noise. This variation of brightness or color can be represented in different types, such as Gaussian noise, spike noise, and shot noise.

There are different techniques that can be used to remove the noise. Here, we are going to use a smooth operation, but depending on the type of noise, some are better than others. A median filter is normally used for removing salt-and-pepper noise; for example, consider the following image:

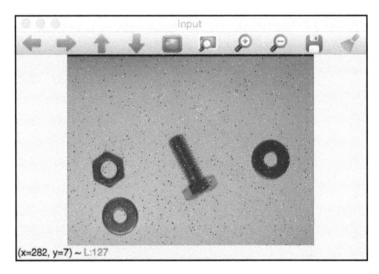

The preceding image is the original input with salt-and-pepper noise. If we apply a median blur, we get an awesome result in which we lose small details. For example, we lose the borders of the screw, but we maintain perfect edges. See the result in the following image:

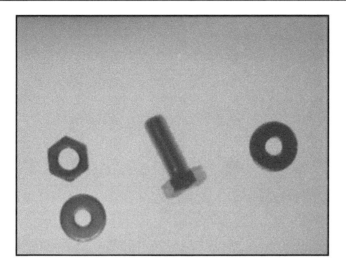

If we apply a box filter or Gaussian filter, the noise is not removed but made smooth, and the details of the objects are lost and smoothened too. See the following image for the result:

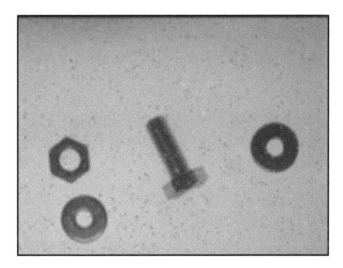

OpenCV brings us the `medianBlur` function, which requires three parameters:

- An input image with the 1, 3, or 4 channel's image. When the kernel size is bigger than 5, the image depth can only be CV_8U.
- An output image, which is the resulting image on applying median blur with the same type and depth as the input.

- Kernel size, which is an aperture size greater than 1 and odd, for example, 3, 5, 7, and so on.

The following code is used to remove noise:

```
Mat img_noise;
medianBlur(img, img_noise, 3);
```

Removing the background using the light pattern for segmentation

In this section, we are going to develop a basic algorithm that will enable us to remove the background using a light pattern. This preprocessing gives us better segmentation. The input image without noise is as follows:

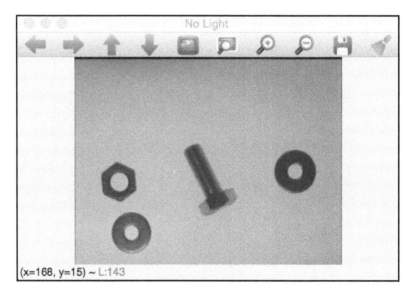

If we apply a basic threshold, we will obtain an image result like this:

We can see that the top image artifact has a lot of white noise. If we apply a light pattern and background removal technique, we can obtain an awesome result in which we can see that there are no artifacts in the top of image, like the previous threshold operation, and we will obtain better results when we have to segment. We can see the result of background removal and thresholding in the following image:

Now, how can we remove the light from our image? This is very simple: we only need a picture of our scenario without any objects, taken from exactly the same position and under the same lighting conditions that the other images were taken under; this is a very common technique in AOI because the external conditions are supervised and well-known. The image result for our case is similar to the following image:

Now, using a simple mathematical operation, we can remove this light pattern. There are two options for removing it:

- Difference
- Division

The difference option is the simplest approach. If we have the light pattern L and the image picture I, the resulting removal R is the difference between them:

```
R= L-I
```

This division is a bit more complex, but simple at the same time. If we have the light pattern matrix L and the image picture matrix I, the result removal R is as follows:

```
R= 255*(1-(I/L))
```

In this case, we divide the image by the light pattern, and we have the assumption that if our light pattern is white and the objects are darker than the background carrier tape, then the image pixel values are always the same or lower than the light pixel values. The result we obtain from I/L is between 0 and 1. Finally, we invert the result of this division to get the same color direction range and multiply it by 255 to get values within the range of 0-255.

In our code, we are going to create a new function called `removeLight` with the following parameters:

- An input image to remove the light/background
- A light pattern, `Mat`
- A method, with a `0` value for difference and `1` for division

The result is a new image matrix without light/background. The following code implements the removal of the background through the use of the light pattern:

```
Mat removeLight(Mat img, Mat pattern, int method)
{
  Mat aux;
  // if method is normalization
  if(method==1)
  {
    // Require change our image to 32 float for division
    Mat img32, pattern32;
    img.convertTo(img32, CV_32F);
    pattern.convertTo(pattern32, CV_32F);
    // Divide the image by the pattern
    aux= 1-(img32/pattern32);
    // Convert 8 bits format and scale
    aux.convertTo(aux, CV_8U, 255);
  }else{
    aux= pattern-img;
  }
  return aux;
}
```

Let's explore this. After creating the `aux` variable to save the result, we select the method chosen by the user and pass the parameter to the function. If the method that was selected is `1`, we apply the division method.

The division method requires a 32-bit float of images to allow us to divide the images and not truncate the numbers into integers. The first step is to convert the image and light pattern mat to floats of 32 bits. To convert images of this format, we can use the `convertTo` function of the `Mat` class. This function accepts four parameters; the output converted image and the format you wish to convert to the required parameters, but you can define alpha and beta parameters, which allow you to scale and shift the values following the next function, where O is the output image and I the input image:

$$O(x,y)=cast{<}Type{>}(\alpha * I(x,y)+\beta)$$

The following code changes the image to 32-bit float:

```
// Required to change our image to 32 float for division
Mat img32, pattern32;
img.convertTo(img32, CV_32F);
pattern.convertTo(pattern32, CV_32F);
```

Now, we can carry out the mathematical operations on our matrix as we described, by dividing the image by the pattern and inverting the result:

```
// Divide the image by the pattern
aux= 1-(img32/pattern32);
```

Now, we have the result but it is required to return it to an 8-bit depth image, and then use the convert function as we did previously to convert the image's mat and scale from 0 to 255 using the alpha parameter:

```
// Convert 8 bits format
aux.convertTo(aux, CV_8U, 255);
```

Now, we can return the aux variable with the result. For the difference method, the development is very easy because we don't have to convert our images; we only need to apply the difference between the pattern and image and return it. If we don't assume that the pattern is equal to or greater than an image, then we will require a few checks and truncate values that can be less than 0 or greater than 255:

```
aux= pattern-img;
```

The following images are the results of applying the image light pattern to our input image:

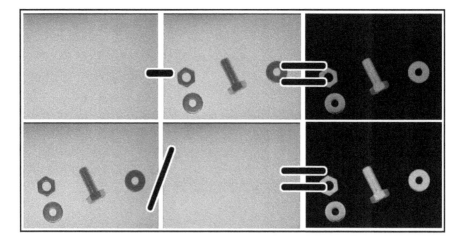

In the results that we obtain, we can check how the light gradient and the possible artifacts are removed. But what happens when we don't have a light/background pattern? There are a few different techniques to obtain this; we are going to present the most basic one here. Using a filter, we can create one that can be used, but there are better algorithms to learn about the background of images where the pieces appear in different areas. This technique sometimes requires a background estimation image initialization, where our basic approach can play very well. These advanced techniques will be explored in Chapter 8, *Video Surveillance, Background Modeling, and Morphological Operations*. To estimate the background image, we are going to use a blur with a large kernel size applied to our input image. This is a common technique used in **optical character recognition (OCR)**, where the letters are thin and small relative to the whole document, allowing us to do an approximation of the light patterns in the image. We can see the light/background pattern reconstruction in the left-hand image and the ground truth in the right-hand:

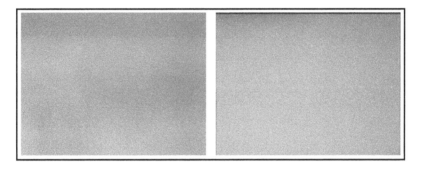

We can see that there are minor differences in the light patterns, but this result is enough to remove the background. We can also see the result in the following image when using different images. In the following image, the result of applying the image difference between the original input image and the estimated background image computed with the previous approach is depicted:

The `calculateLightPattern` function creates this light pattern or background approximation:

```
Mat calculateLightPattern(Mat img)
{
  Mat pattern;
  // Basic and effective way to calculate the light pattern from one image
  blur(img, pattern, Size(img.cols/3,img.cols/3));
  return pattern;
}
```

This basic function applies a blur to an input image by using a big kernel size relative to the image size. From the code, it is **one-third** of the original width and height.

Thresholding

After removing the background, we only have to binarize the image for future segmentation. We are going to do this with threshold. `Threshold` is a simple function that sets each pixel's values to a maximum value (255, for example). If the pixel's value is greater than the **threshold** value or if the pixel's value is lower than the **threshold** value, it will be set to a minimum (0):

$$I(x,y) = \begin{cases} 0, & \text{if } I(x,y) < \text{threshold} \\ 1, & \text{if } I(x,y) > \text{threshold} \end{cases}$$

Now, we are going to apply the `threshold` function using two different `threshold` values: we will use a 30 `threshold` value when we remove the light/background because all non-interesting regions are black. This is because we apply background removal. We will also a medium value `threshold` (140) when we do not use a light removal method, because we have a white background. This last option is used to allow us to check the results with and without background removal:

```
// Binarize image for segment
Mat img_thr;
if(method_light!=2){
  threshold(img_no_light, img_thr, 30, 255, THRESH_BINARY);
}else{
  threshold(img_no_light, img_thr, 140, 255, THRESH_BINARY_INV);
}
```

Now, we are going to continue with the most important part of our application: the segmentation. We are going to use two different approaches or algorithms here: connected components and find contours.

Segmenting our input image

Now, we are going to introduce two techniques to segment our threshold image:

- Connected components
- Find contours

With these two techniques, we are allowed to extract each **region of interest** (**ROI**) of our image where our targets objects appear. In our case, these are the nut, screw, and ring.

The connected components algorithm

The connected component algorithm is a very common algorithm that's used to segment and identify parts in binary images. The connected component is an iterative algorithm with the purpose of labeling an image using eight or four connectivity pixels. Two pixels are connected if they have the same value and are neighbors. In an image, each pixel has eight neighbor pixels:

Four-connectivity means that only the **2**, **4**, **5**, and **7** neighbors can be connected to the center if they have the same value as the center pixel. With eight-connectivity, the **1**, **2**, **3**, **4**, **5**, **6**, **7**, and **8** neighbors can be connected if they have the same value as the center pixel. We can see the differences in the following example from a four- and eight-connectivity algorithm. We are going to apply each algorithm to the next binarized image. We have used a small **9 x 9** image and zoomed in to show how connected components work and the differences between four- and eight-connectivity:

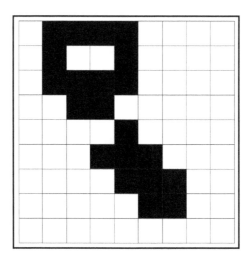

The four-connectivity algorithm detects two objects; we can see this in the left image. The eight-connectivity algorithm detects only one object (the right image) because two diagonal pixels are connected. Eight-connectivity takes care of diagonal connectivity, which is the main difference compared with four-connectivity, since this where only vertical and horizontal pixels are considered. We can see the result in the following image, where each object has a different gray color value:

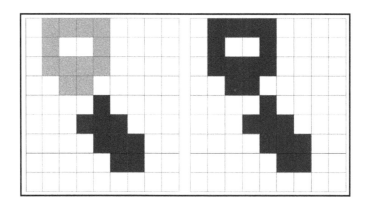

OpenCV brings us the connected components algorithm with two different functions:

- `connectedComponents` (image, labels, connectivity= 8, type= CV_32S)
- `connectedComponentsWithStats` (image, labels, stats, centroids, connectivity= 8, type= CV_32S)

Both functions return an integer with the number of detected labels, where label 0 represents the background. The difference between these two functions is basically the information that is returned. Let's check the parameters of each one. The `connectedComponents` function gives us the following parameters:

- **Image**: The input image to be labeled.
- **Labels**: An output mat that's the same size as the input image, where each pixel has the value of its label, where all OS represents the background, pixels with 1 value represent the first connected component object, and so on.
- **Connectivity**: Two possible values, 8 or 4, that represent the connectivity we want to use.
- **Type**: The type of label image we want to use. Only two types are allowed: CV32_S and CV16_U. By default, this is CV32_S.
- The `connectedComponentsWithStats` function has two more parameters defined. These are stats and centroids:
    - **Stats**: This is an output parameter that gives us the following statistical values for each label (background inclusive):
        - CC_STAT_LEFT: The leftmost x coordinate of the connected component object
        - CC_STAT_TOP: The topmost y coordinate of the connected component object
        - CC_STAT_WIDTH: The width of the connected component object defined by its bounding box
        - CC_STAT_HEIGHT: The height of the connected component object defined by its bounding box
        - CC_STAT_AREA: The number of pixels (area) of the connected component object
    - **Centroids**: The centroid points to the float type for each label, inclusive of the background that's considered for another connected component.

In our example application, we are going to create two functions so that we can apply these two OpenCV algorithms. We will then show the user the obtained result in a new image with colored objects in the basic connected component algorithm. If we select the connected component with the stats method, we are going to draw the respective calculated area that returns this function over each object.

Let's define the basic drawing for the connected component function:

```
void ConnectedComponents(Mat img)
{
  // Use connected components to divide our image in multiple connected
component objects
    Mat labels;
    auto num_objects= connectedComponents(img, labels);
  // Check the number of objects detected
    if(num_objects < 2 ){
       cout << "No objects detected" << endl;
       return;
     }else{
      cout << "Number of objects detected: " << num_objects - 1 << endl;
      }
  // Create output image coloring the objects
    Mat output= Mat::zeros(img.rows,img.cols, CV_8UC3);
    RNG rng(0xFFFFFFFF);
    for(auto i=1; i<num_objects; i++){
       Mat mask= labels==i;
       output.setTo(randomColor(rng), mask);
     }
    imshow("Result", output);
}
```

First of all, we call the OpenCV `connectedComponents` function, which returns the number of objects detected. If the number of objects is less than two, this means that only the background object is detected, and then we don't need to draw anything and we can finish. If the algorithm detects more than one object, we show the number of objects that have been detected on the console:

```
Mat labels;
auto num_objects= connectedComponents(img, labels);
// Check the number of objects detected
if(num_objects < 2){
  cout << "No objects detected" << endl;
  return;
}else{
  cout << "Number of objects detected: " << num_objects - 1 << endl;
```

Now, we are going to draw all detected objects in a new image with different colors. After this, we need to create a new black image with the same input size and three channels:

```
Mat output= Mat::zeros(img.rows,img.cols, CV_8UC3);
```

We will loop over each label, except for the 0 value, because this is the background:

```
for(int i=1; i<num_objects; i++){
```

To extract each object from the label image, we can create a mask for each i label using a comparison and save this in a new image:

```
Mat mask= labels==i;
```

Finally, we set a pseudo-random color to the output image using the mask:

```
output.setTo(randomColor(rng), mask);
}
```

After looping all of the images, we have all of the detected objects with different colors in our output and we only have to show the output image in a window:

```
imshow("Result", output);
```

This is the result in which each object is painted with different colors or a gray value:

Now, we are going to explain how to use the connected components with the stats OpenCV algorithm and show some more information in the resultant image. The following function implements this functionality:

```
void ConnectedComponentsStats(Mat img)
{
  // Use connected components with stats
  Mat labels, stats, centroids;
```

```
    auto num_objects= connectedComponentsWithStats(img, labels, stats,
centroids);
  // Check the number of objects detected
  if(num_objects < 2 ){
    cout << "No objects detected" << endl;
    return;
  }else{
    cout << "Number of objects detected: " << num_objects - 1 << endl;
  }
  // Create output image coloring the objects and show area
  Mat output= Mat::zeros(img.rows,img.cols, CV_8UC3);
  RNG rng( 0xFFFFFFFF );
  for(auto i=1; i<num_objects; i++){
    cout << "Object "<< i << " with pos: " << centroids.at<Point2d>(i) << "
with area " << stats.at<int>(i, CC_STAT_AREA) << endl;
    Mat mask= labels==i;
    output.setTo(randomColor(rng), mask);
    // draw text with area
    stringstream ss;
    ss << "area: " << stats.at<int>(i, CC_STAT_AREA);

    putText(output,
      ss.str(),
      centroids.at<Point2d>(i),
      FONT_HERSHEY_SIMPLEX,
      0.4,
      Scalar(255,255,255));
  }
  imshow("Result", output);
}
```

Let's understand this code. As we did in the non-stats function, we call the connected components algorithm, but here, we do this using the `stats` function, checking whether we detected more than one object:

```
  Mat labels, stats, centroids;
    auto num_objects= connectedComponentsWithStats(img, labels, stats,
centroids);
  // Check the number of objects detected
  if(num_objects < 2){
    cout << "No objects detected" << endl;
    return;
  }else{
    cout << "Number of objects detected: " << num_objects - 1 << endl;
  }
```

Now, we have two more output results: the stats and centroid variables. Then, for each detected label, we are going to show the centroid and area through the command line:

```
for(auto i=1; i<num_objects; i++){
    cout << "Object "<< i << " with pos: " << centroids.at<Point2d>(i) << "
with area " << stats.at<int>(i, CC_STAT_AREA) << endl;
```

You can check the call to the stats variable to extract the area using the column constant `stats.at<int>(I, CC_STAT_AREA)`. Now, like before, we paint the object labeled with `i` over the output image:

```
Mat mask= labels==i;
output.setTo(randomColor(rng), mask);
```

Finally, in the centroid position of each segmented object, we want to draw some information (such as the area) on the resultant image. To do this, we use the stats and centroid variables using the `putText` function. First, we have to create a `stringstream` so that we can add the stats area information:

```
// draw text with area
stringstream ss;
ss << "area: " << stats.at<int>(i, CC_STAT_AREA);
```

Then, we need to use `putText`, using the centroid as the text position:

```
putText(output,
    ss.str(),
    centroids.at<Point2d>(i),
    FONT_HERSHEY_SIMPLEX,
    0.4,
    Scalar(255,255,255));
```

The result for this function is as follows:

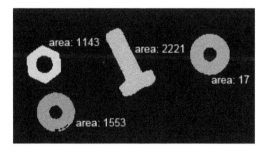

The findContours algorithm

The `findContours` algorithm is one of the most used OpenCV algorithms in regards to segment objects. This is because this algorithm was included in OpenCV from version 1.0 and gives developers more information and descriptors, including shapes, topological organizations, and so on:

```
void findContours(InputOutputArray image, OutputArrayOfArrays contours,
OutputArray hierarchy, int mode, int method, Point offset=Point())
```

Let's explain each parameter:

- **Image**: Input binary image.
- **Contours**: A contour's output where each detected contour is a vector of points.
- **Hierarchy**: This is the optional output vector where the hierarchy of contours is saved. This is the topology of the image where we can get the relations between each contour. The hierarchy is represented as a vector of four indices, which are (next contour, previous contour, first child, parent contour). Negative indices are given where the given contour has no relationship with other contours. A more detailed explanation can be found at https://docs.opencv.org/3.4/d9/d8b/tutorial_py_contours_hierarchy.html.
- **Mode**: This method is used to retrieve the contours:
    - `RETR_EXTERNAL` retrieves only the external contours.
    - `RETR_LIST` retrieves all contours without establishing the hierarchy.
    - `RETR_CCOMP` retrieves all contours with two levels of hierarchy, external and holes. If another object is inside one hole, this is put at the top of the hierarchy.
    - `RETR_TREE` retrieves all contours, creating a full hierarchy between contours.
- **Method**: This allows us to use the approximation method for retrieving the contour's shapes:
    - If `CV_CHAIN_APPROX_NONE` is set, then this does not apply any approximation to the contours and stores the contour's points.
    - `CV_CHAIN_APPROX_SIMPLE` compresses all horizontal, vertical, and diagonal segments, storing only the start and end points.
    - `CV_CHAIN_APPROX_TC89_L1` and `CV_CHAIN_APPROX_TC89_KCOS` apply the **Telchin chain approximation** algorithm.
- **Offset**: This is an optional point value to shift all contours. This is very useful when we are working in an ROI and need to retrieve global positions.

Note: The input image is modified by the `findContours` function. Create a copy of your image before sending it to this function if you need it.

Now that we know the parameters of the `findContours` function, let's apply this to our example:

```
void FindContoursBasic(Mat img)
{
  vector<vector<Point> > contours;
  findContours(img, contours, RETR_EXTERNAL, CHAIN_APPROX_SIMPLE);
  Mat output= Mat::zeros(img.rows,img.cols, CV_8UC3);
  // Check the number of objects detected
  if(contours.size() == 0 ){
    cout << "No objects detected" << endl;
    return;
  }else{
    cout << "Number of objects detected: " << contours.size() << endl;
  }
  RNG rng(0xFFFFFFFF);
  for(auto i=0; i<contours.size(); i++){
    drawContours(output, contours, i, randomColor(rng));
    imshow("Result", output);
  }
}
```

Let's explain our implementation, line by line.

In our case, we don't need any hierarchy, so we are only going to retrieve the external contours of all possible objects. To do this, we can use the RETR_EXTERNAL mode and basic contour encoding by using the CHAIN_APPROX_SIMPLE method:

```
vector<vector<Point> > contours;
vector<Vec4i> hierarchy;
findContours(img, contours, RETR_EXTERNAL, CHAIN_APPROX_SIMPLE);
```

Like the connected component examples we looked at before, first we check how many contours we have retrieved. If there are none, then we exit our function:

```
// Check the number of objects detected
  if(contours.size() == 0){
    cout << "No objects detected" << endl;
    return;
  }else{
    cout << "Number of objects detected: " << contours.size() << endl;
  }
```

Finally, we draw the contour for each detected object. We draw this in our output image with different colors. To do this, OpenCV gives us a function to draw the result of the find contours image:

```
for(auto i=0; i<contours.size(); i++)
    drawContours(output, contours, i, randomColor(rng));
  imshow("Result", output);
}
```

The `drawContours` function allows the following parameters:

- **Image**: The output image to draw the contours.
- **Contours**: The vector of contours.
- **Contour index**: A number indicating the contour to draw. If this is negative, all contours are drawn.
- **Color**: The color to draw the contour.
- **Thickness**: If it is negative, the contour is filled with the chosen color.
- **Line type**: This specifies whether we want to draw with anti-aliasing or another drawing method.
- **Hierarchy**: This is an optional parameter that is only needed if you want to draw some of the contours.
- **Max Level**: This is an optional parameter that is only taken into account when the hierarchy parameter is available. If it is set to 0, only the specified contour is drawn. If it is 1, the function draws the current contour and the nested contours too. If it is set to 2, then the algorithm draws all of the specified contour hierarchy.
- **Offset**: This is an optional parameter for shifting the contours.

The result of our example can be seen in the following image:

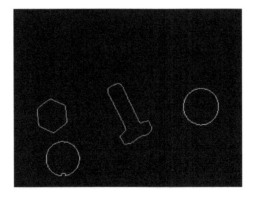

Summary

In this chapter, we explored the basics of object segmentation in a controlled situation where a camera takes pictures of different objects. Here, we learned how to remove background and light to allow us to binarize our image better, thus minimizing the noise. After binarizing the image, we learned about three different algorithms that we can use to divide and separate each object of one image, allowing us to isolate each object to manipulate or extract features.

We can see this whole process in the following image:

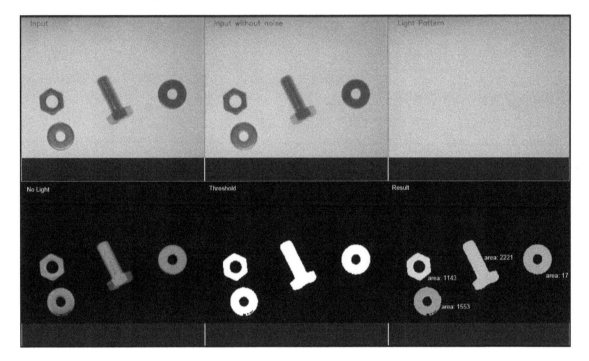

Finally, we extracted all of the objects on an image. You will need to do this to continue with the next chapter, where we are going to extract characteristics of each of these objects to train a machine learning system.

In the next chapter, we are going to predict the class of any objects in an image and then call a robot or any other system to pick any of them, or detect an object that is not in the correct carrier tape. We will then look at notifying a person to pick it up.

6
Learning Object Classification

In Chapter 5, *Automated Optical Inspection, Object Segmentation, and Detection*, we introduced the basic concepts of object segmentation and detection. This refers to isolating the objects that appear in an image for future processing and analysis. This chapter explains how to classify each of these isolated objects. To allow us to classify each object, we have to train our system to be capable of learning the required parameters so that it decide which specific label will be assigned to the detected object (depending on the different categories taken into account during the training phase).

This chapter introduces the basics concepts of machine learning to classify images with different labels. To do this, we are going to create a basic application based on the segmentation algorithm of Chapter 5, *Automated Optical Inspection, Object Segmentation, and Detection*. This segmentation algorithm extracts parts of images that contain unknown objects. For each detected object, we are going to extract different features that are going to be classified using a machine learning algorithm. Finally, we are going to show the obtained results using our user interface, together with the labels of each object detected in the input image.

This chapter involves different topics and algorithms, including the following:

- Introduction to machine learning concepts
- Common machine learning algorithms and processes
- Feature extraction
- support vector machines (SVM)
- Training and prediction

Technical requirements

This chapter requires familiarity with the basic C++ programming language. All of the code that's used in this chapter can be downloaded from the following GitHub link: `https://github.com/PacktPublishing/Learn-OpenCV-4-By-Building-Projects-Second-Edition/tree/master/Chapter_06`. This code can be executed on any operating system, though it is only tested on Ubuntu.

Check out the following video to see the Code in Action:
`http://bit.ly/2KGD4CO`

Introducing machine learning concepts

Machine learning is a concept that was defined by *Arthur Samuel* in 1959 as a field of study that gives computers the ability to learn without being explicitly programmed. *Tom M. Mitchel* provided a more formal definition for machine learning, in which he links the concept of samples with experience data, labels, and a performance measurement of algorithms.

The **machine learning** definition by *Arthur Samuel* is referenced in *Some Studies in Machine Learning Using the Game of Checkers* in *IBM Journal of Research and Development* (*Volume*: 3, *Issue*: 3), *p. 210*. It was also referenced in *The New Yorker* and *Office Management* in the same year.
The more formal definition from *Tom M. Mitchel* is referenced in *Machine Learning Book, McGray Hill*
1997: (`http://www.cs.cmu.edu/afs/cs.cmu.edu/user/mitchell/ftp/mlbook.html`).

Machine learning involves pattern recognition and learning theory in artificial intelligence, and is related with computational statistics. It is used in hundreds of applications, such as **optical character recognition** (OCR), spam filtering, search engines, and thousands of computer vision applications, such as the example that we will develop in this chapter, where a machine learning algorithm tries to classify objects that appear in the input image.

Depending on how machine learning algorithms learn from the input data, we can divide them into three categories:

- **Supervised learning**: The computer learns from a set of labeled data. The goal here is to learn the parameters of the model and rules that allow computers to map the relationship between data and output label results.

- **Unsupervised learning**: No labels are given and the computer tries to discover the input structure of the given data.
- **Reinforcement learning**: The computer interacts with a dynamic environment, reaching their goal and learning from their mistakes.

Depending on the results we wish to gain from our machine learning algorithm, we can categorize the results as follows:

- **Classification**: The space of the inputs can be divided into **N** classes, and the prediction results for a given sample are one of these training classes. This is one of the most used categories. A typical example can be email spam filtering, where there are only two classes: spam and non-spam. Alternatively, we can use OCR, where only N characters are available and each character is one class.
- **Regression**: The output is a continuous value instead of a discrete value like a classification result. One example of regression could be the prediction of a house price given the house's size, number of years since it was built, and location.
- **Clustering**: The input is to be divided into N groups, which is typically done using unsupervised training.
- **Density estimation**: Finds the (probability) distribution of inputs.

In our example, we are going to use a supervised learning and classification algorithm where a training dataset with labels is used to train the model and the result of the model's prediction is one of the possible labels. In machine learning, there are several approaches and methods for this. Some of the more popular ones include the following: **support vector machines** (**SVM**), **artificial neural networks** (**ANN**), clustering, k-nearest neighbors, decision trees, and deep learning. Almost all of these methods and approaches are supported, implemented, and well documented in OpenCV. In this chapter, we are going to explain support vector machines.

OpenCV machine learning algorithms

OpenCV implements eight of these machine learning algorithms. All of them are inherited from the `StatModel` class:

- Artificial neural networks
- Random trees
- Expectation maximization
- k-nearest neighbors
- Logistic regression
- Normal Bayes classifiers

- support vector machine
- Stochastic gradient descent SVMs

Version 3 supports deep learning at a basic level, but version 4 is stable and more supported. We will delve into deep learning in detail in further chapters.

 To get more information about each algorithm, read the OpenCV document page for machine learning at http://docs.opencv.org/trunk/dc/dd6/ml_intro.html.

The following diagram shows the machine learning class hierarchy:

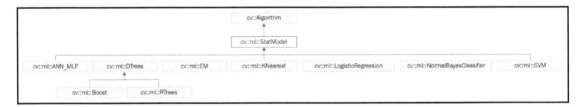

The `StatModel` class is the base class for all machine learning algorithms. This provides the prediction and all the read and write functions that are very important for saving and reading our machine learning parameters and training data.

In machine learning, the most time-consuming and computing resource-consuming part is the training method. Training can take from seconds to weeks or months for large datasets and complex machine learning structures. For example, in deep learning, big neural network structures with more than 100,000 image datasets can take a long time to train. With deep learning algorithms, it is common to use parallel hardware processing such as GPUs with CUDA technology to decrease the computing time during training, or most new chip devices such as Intel Movidius. This means that we cannot train our algorithm each time we run our application, and therefore it's recommended to save our trained model with all of the parameters that have been learned. In future executions, we only have to load/read from our saved model without training, except if we need to update our model with more sample data.

`StatModel` is the base class of all machine learning classes, such as SVM or ANN, except deep learning methods. `StatModel` is basically a virtual class that defines the two most important functions—`train` and `predict`. The `train` method is the main method that's responsible for learning model parameters using a training dataset. This has the following three possible calls:

```
bool train(const Ptr<TrainData>& trainData, int flags=0 );
bool train(InputArray samples, int layout, InputArray responses);
Ptr<_Tp> train(const Ptr<TrainData>& data, int flags=0 );
```

The train function has the following parameters:

- `TrainData`: Training data that can be loaded or created from the `TrainData` class. This class is new in OpenCV 3 and helps developers create training data and abstract from the machine learning algorithm. This is done because different algorithms require different types of structures of arrays for training and prediction, such as the ANN algorithm.
- `samples`: An array of training array samples such as training data in the format required by the machine learning algorithm.
- `layout`: `ROW_SAMPLE` (training samples are the matrix rows) or `COL_SAMPLE` (training samples are the matrix columns).
- `responses`: Vector of responses associated with the sample data.
- `flags`: Optional flags defined by each method.

The last train method creates and trains a model of the `_TP` class type. The only classes accepted are the classes that implement a static create method with no parameters or with all default parameter values.

The `predict` method is much simpler and has only one possible call:

```
float StatModel::predict(InputArray samples, OutputArray results=noArray(),
int flags=0)
```

The predict function has the following parameters:

- `samples`: The input samples to predict results from the model can consist of any amount of data, whether single or multiple.
- `results`: The results of each input row sample (computed by the algorithm from the previously trained model).
- `flags`: These optional flags are model-dependent. Some models, such as Boost, are recognized by the SVM `StatModel::RAW_OUTPUT` flag, which makes the method return the raw results (the sum), and not the class label.

The `StatModel` class provides an interface for other very useful methods:

- `isTrained()` returns true if the model is trained
- `isClassifier()` returns true if the model is a classifier, or false in the case of regression
- `getVarCount()` returns the number of variables in training samples
- `save(const string& filename)` saves the model in the filename
- `Ptr<_Tp> load(const string& filename)` loads the `<indexentry content="StatModel class:Ptr load(const string& filename)">` model from a filename, for example—`Ptr<SVM> svm = StatModel::load<SVM>("my_svm_model.xml")`
- `calcError(const Ptr<TrainData>& data, bool test, OutputArray resp)` calculates the error from test data, where the data is the training data. If the test parameter is true, the method calculates the error from a test subset of data; if its false, the method calculates the error from all training data. `resp` is the optional output result.

Now, we are going to introduce how a basic application that uses machine learning in a computer vision application is constructed.

Computer vision and the machine learning workflow

Computer vision applications with machine learning have a common basic structure. This structure is divided into different steps:

1. **Pre-process**
2. **Segmentation**
3. **Feature extraction**
4. **Classification result**
5. **Post-process**

These are common in almost all computer vision applications, while others are omitted. In the following diagram, you can see the different steps that are involved:

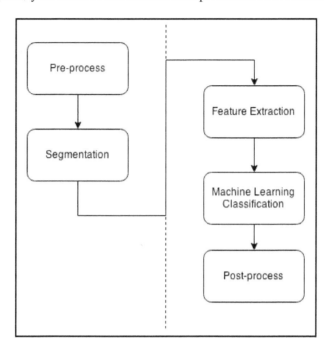

Almost all computer vision applications start with a **Pre-process** applied to the input image, which consists of the removal of light and noise, filtering, blurring, and so on. After applying all pre-processing required to the input image, the second step is **Segmentation**. In this step, we have to extract the regions of interest in the image and isolate each one as a unique object of interest. For example, in a face detection system, we have to separate the faces from the rest of the parts in the scene. After detecting the objects inside the image, we continue to the next step. Here, we have to extract the features of each one; the features are normally a vector of characteristics of objects. A characteristic describes our objects and can be the area of an object, contour, texture pattern, pixels, and so on.

Now, we have the descriptor, also known as a feature vector or feature set, of our object. Descriptors are the features that describe an object, and we use these to train or predict a model. To do this, we have to create a large dataset of features where thousands of images are pre-processed. We then use the extracted features (image/object characteristics) such as area, size, and aspect ration, in the **Train** model function we choose. In the following diagram, we can see how a dataset is fed into a **Machine Learning Algorithm** to train and **generate** a **Model**:

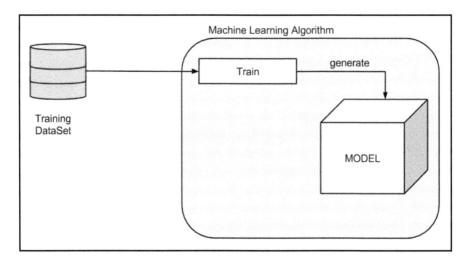

When we **Train** with a dataset, the **Model** learns all the parameters required to be able to predict when a new vector of features with an unknown label is given as input to our algorithm. In the following diagram, we can see how an unknown vector of features is used to **Predict** using the generated **Model**, thus returning the **Classification result** or regression:

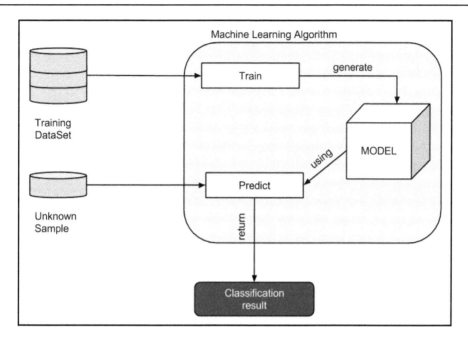

After predicting the result, the post-processing of output data is sometimes required, for example, merging multiple classifications to decrease the prediction error or merging multiple labels. A sample case in Optical Character recognition is where the **Classification result** is according to each predicted character, and by combining the results of character recognition, we construct a word. This means that we can create a post-processing method to correct errors in detected words. With this small introduction to machine learning for computer vision, we are going to implement our own application that uses machine learning to classify objects in a slide tape. We are going to use support vector machines as our classification method and explain how to use them. The other machine learning algorithms are used in a very similar way. The OpenCV documentation has detailed information about all of the machine learning algorithms at the following link: `https://docs.opencv.org/master/dd/ded/group__ml.html`.

Automatic object inspection classification example

In Chapter 5, *Automated Optical Inspection, Object Segmentation, and Detection*, we looked at an example of automatic object inspection segmentation where a carrier tape contained three different types of object: nuts, screws, and rings. With computer vision, we will be able to recognize each one of these so that we can send notifications to a robot or put each one in a different box. The following is a basic diagram of the carrier tape:

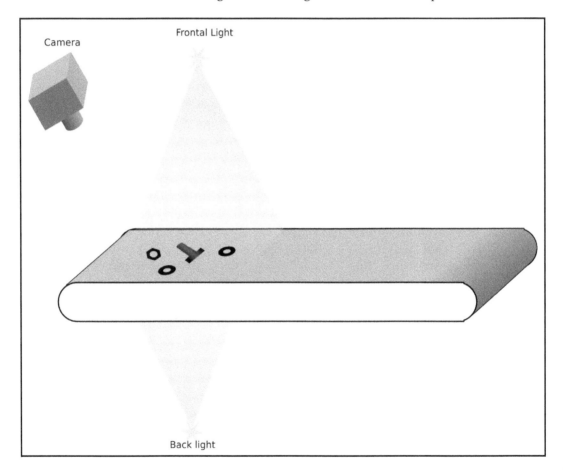

In `Chapter 5`, *Automated Optical Inspection, Object Segmentation, and Detection*, we pre-processed the input images and extracted the regions of interest, isolating each object using different techniques. Now, we are going to apply all the concepts we explained in the previous sections in this example to extract features and classify each object, allowing the robot to put each one in a different box. In our application, we are only going to show the labels of each image, but we could send the positions in the image and the label to other devices, such as a robot. At this point, our goal is to give an input image with different objects, allowing the computer to detect the objects and show the objects' names over each image, as demonstrated in the following images. However, to learn the steps of the whole process, we are going to train our system by creating a plot to show the feature distribution that we are going to use, and visualize it with different colors. We will also show the pre-processed input image, and the output classification result obtained. The final result looks as follows:

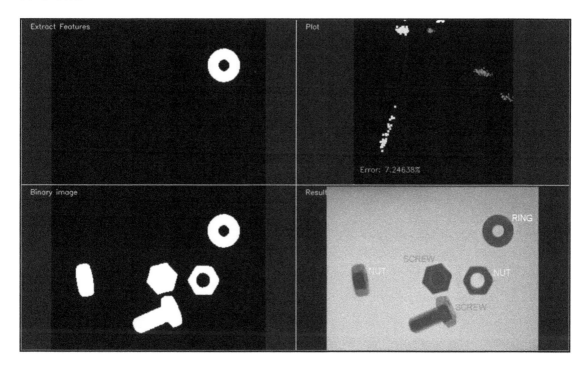

We are going to follow these steps for our example application:

1. For each input image:

    - Preprocess the image
    - Segment the image

2. For each object in an image:
   - Extract the features
   - Add the features to the training feature vector with a corresponding label (nut, screw, ring)
3. Create an SVM model.
4. Train our SVM model with the training feature vector.
5. Preprocess the input image to classify each segmented object.
6. Segment the input image.
7. For each object detected:
   - Extract the features
   - Predict it with the SVM
   - model
   - Paint the result in the output image

For pre-processing and segmentation, we are going to use the code found in `Chapter 5`, *Automated Optical Inspection, Object Segmentation, and Detection.* We are then going to explain how to extract the features and create the vectors required to **train** and **predict** our model.

Feature extraction

The next thing we need to do is extract the features for each object. To understand the feature vector concept, we are going to extract very simple features in our example, as this is enough to get good results. In other solutions, we can get more complex features such as texture descriptors, contour descriptors, and so on. In our example, we only have nuts, rings, and screws in different positions and orientations in the image. The same object can be in any position of image and orientation, for example, the screw or the nut. We can see different orientations in the following image:

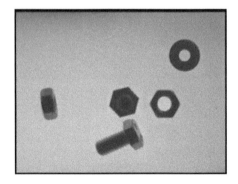

We are going to explore some features or characteristics that could improve the accuracy of our machine learning algorithm. These possible characteristics of our different objects (nuts, screws, and rings) are as follows:

- The area of the object
- The aspect ratio, that is, the width divided by the height of the bounding rectangle
- The number of holes
- The number of contour sides

These characteristics can describe our objects very well, and if we use all of them, the classification error will be very small. However, in our implemented example, we are only going to use the first two characteristics, area and aspect ratio, for learning purposes, because we can plot these characteristics in a 2D graphic and show that these values correctly describe our objects. We can also show that we can visually differentiate between one kind of object and another in the graphic plot. To extract these features, we are going to use the black/white ROI image as input, where only one object appears in white with a black background. This input is the segmentation result of Chapter 5, *Automated Optical Inspection, Object Segmentation, and Detection*. We are going to use the findCountours algorithm for segmenting objects and create the ExtractFeatures function for this purpose, as we can see in the following code:

```
vector< vector<float> > ExtractFeatures(Mat img, vector<int>* left=NULL,
vector<int>* top=NULL)
{
  vector< vector<float> > output;
  vector<vector<Point> > contours;
  Mat input= img.clone();
  vector<Vec4i> hierarchy;
  findContours(input, contours, hierarchy, RETR_CCOMP,
CHAIN_APPROX_SIMPLE);
  // Check the number of objects detected
  if(contours.size() == 0){
    return output;
  }
  RNG rng(0xFFFFFFFF);
  for(auto i=0; i<contours.size(); i++){
    Mat mask= Mat::zeros(img.rows, img.cols, CV_8UC1);
    drawContours(mask, contours, i, Scalar(1), FILLED, LINE_8, hierarchy,
1);
    Scalar area_s= sum(mask);
    float area= area_s[0];

    if(area>500){ //if the area is greater than min.
      RotatedRect r= minAreaRect(contours[i]);
```

```
        float width= r.size.width;
        float height= r.size.height;
        float ar=(width<height)?height/width:width/height;

        vector<float> row;
        row.push_back(area);
        row.push_back(ar);
        output.push_back(row);
        if(left!=NULL){
            left->push_back((int)r.center.x);
        }
        if(top!=NULL){
            top->push_back((int)r.center.y);
        }
        // Add image to the multiple image window class, See the class on
    full github code
        miw->addImage("Extract Features", mask*255);
        miw->render();
        waitKey(10);
    }
  }
  return output;
}
```

Let's explain the code that we use to extract features. We are going to create a function that has one image as input and return two vectors of the left and top position for each object detected in the image as a parameter. This data will be used for drawing the corresponding label over each object. The output of a function is a vector of vectors of floats. In other words, it is a matrix where each row contains the features of each object that's detected.

First, we have to create the output vector variable and the contours variable that are going to be used in our find contours algorithm segmentation. We also have to create a copy of our input image, because the `findCoutours` OpenCV functions modify the input image:

```
    vector< vector<float> > output;
    vector<vector<Point> > contours;
    Mat input= img.clone();
    vector<Vec4i> hierarchy;
    findContours(input, contours, hierarchy, RETR_CCOMP,
CHAIN_APPROX_SIMPLE);
```

Now, we can use the `findContours` function to retrieve each object in an image. If we don't detect any contour, we return an empty output matrix, as we can see in the following snippet:

```
if(contours.size() == 0){
    return output;
}
```

If objects are detected, for each contour we are going to draw the object in white on a black image (zero values). This will be done using 1 values, like a mask image. The following piece of code generates the mask image:

```
for(auto i=0; i<contours.size(); i++){
    Mat mask= Mat::zeros(img.rows, img.cols, CV_8UC1);
    drawContours(mask, contours, i, Scalar(1), FILLED, LINE_8, hierarchy,
1);
```

It's important to use the value of 1 to draw inside the shape because we can calculate the area by summing all of the values inside the contour, as shown in the following code:

```
Scalar area_s= sum(mask);
float area= area_s[0];
```

This area is our first feature. We are going to use this value as a filter to remove all possible small objects that we have to avoid. All objects with an area less than the minimum threshold area that we considered will be discarded. After passing the filter, we create the second feature and the aspect ratio of the object. This refers to the maximum of the width or height, divided by the minimum of the width or height. This feature can tell the difference between the screw and other objects easily. The following code describes how to calculate the aspect ratio:

```
if(area>MIN_AREA){ //if the area is greater than min.
    RotatedRect r= minAreaRect(contours[i]);
    float width= r.size.width;
    float height= r.size.height;
    float ar=(width<height)?height/width:width/height;
```

Now we have the features, we only have to add them to the output vector. To do this, we will create a row vector of floats and add the values, followed by adding this row to the output vector, as shown in the following code:

```
vector<float> row;
row.push_back(area);
row.push_back(ar);
output.push_back(row);
```

If the left and top parameters are passed, then add the top-left values to output the parameters:

```
if(left!=NULL){
    left->push_back((int)r.center.x);
}
if(top!=NULL){
    top->push_back((int)r.center.y);
}
```

Finally, we are going to show the detected objects in a window for user feedback. When we finish processing all of the objects in the image, we are going to return the output feature vector, as described in the following code snippet:

```
miw->addImage("Extract Features", mask*255);
miw->render();
waitKey(10);
    }
}
return output;
```

Now that we have extracted the features of each input image, we can continue with the next step.

Training an SVM model

We are now going to use supervised learning and then obtain a set of images for each object and its corresponding label. There is no minimum number of images in the dataset; if we provide more images for the training process, we will get a better classification model (in most cases). However, for simple classifiers, it could be enough to train simple models. To do this, we created three folders (screw, nut, and ring), where all of the images of each type are placed together. For each image in the folder, we have to extract the features, add them to the train feature matrix and, at the same time, create a new vector with the labels for each row corresponding to each training matrix. To evaluate our system, we will split each folder into a number of images according to testing and training. We will leave around 20 images for testing and the others for training. We are then going to create two vectors of labels and two matrices for training and testing.

Let's go inside of our code. First, we have to create our model. We are going to declare the model out of all functions to be able to gain access to it as a global variable. OpenCV uses the Ptr template class for pointer management:

```
Ptr<SVM> svm;
```

After declaring the pointer to the new SVM model, we are going to create it and train it. We created the `trainAndTest` function for this purpose. The complete function code is as follows:

```
void trainAndTest()
{
  vector< float > trainingData;
  vector< int > responsesData;
  vector< float > testData;
  vector< float > testResponsesData;

  int num_for_test= 20;

  // Get the nut images
  readFolderAndExtractFeatures("../data/nut/nut_%04d.pgm", 0, num_for_test,
trainingData, responsesData, testData, testResponsesData);
  // Get and process the ring images
  readFolderAndExtractFeatures("../data/ring/ring_%04d.pgm", 1,
num_for_test, trainingData, responsesData, testData, testResponsesData);
  // get and process the screw images
  readFolderAndExtractFeatures("../data/screw/screw_%04d.pgm", 2,
num_for_test, trainingData, responsesData, testData, testResponsesData);
  cout << "Num of train samples: " << responsesData.size() << endl;

  cout << "Num of test samples: " << testResponsesData.size() << endl;
  // Merge all data
  Mat trainingDataMat(trainingData.size()/2, 2, CV_32FC1,
&trainingData[0]);
  Mat responses(responsesData.size(), 1, CV_32SC1, &responsesData[0]);

  Mat testDataMat(testData.size()/2, 2, CV_32FC1, &testData[0]);
  Mat testResponses(testResponsesData.size(), 1, CV_32FC1,
&testResponsesData[0]);
  Ptr<TrainData> tdata= TrainData::create(trainingDataMat, ROW_SAMPLE,
responses);

  svm = cv::ml::SVM::create();
  svm->setType(cv::ml::SVM::C_SVC);
  svm->setNu(0.05);
  svm->setKernel(cv::ml::SVM::CHI2);
  svm->setDegree(1.0);
  svm->setGamma(2.0);
  svm->setTermCriteria(TermCriteria(TermCriteria::MAX_ITER, 100, 1e-6));
  svm->train(tdata);

  if(testResponsesData.size()>0){
    cout << "Evaluation" << endl;
    cout << "==========" << endl;
```

```
    // Test the ML Model
    Mat testPredict;
    svm->predict(testDataMat, testPredict);
    cout << "Prediction Done" << endl;
    // Error calculation
    Mat errorMat= testPredict!=testResponses;
    float error= 100.0f * countNonZero(errorMat) /
testResponsesData.size();
    cout << "Error: " << error << "%" << endl;
    // Plot training data with error label
    plotTrainData(trainingDataMat, responses, &error);

  }else{
    plotTrainData(trainingDataMat, responses);
  }
}
```

Now, let's explain the code. First of all, we have to create the required variables to store the training and testing data:

```
    vector< float > trainingData;
    vector< int > responsesData;
    vector< float > testData;
    vector< float > testResponsesData;
```

As we mentioned previously, we have to read all of the images from each folder, extract the features, and save them in our training and testing data. To do this, we are going to use the `readFolderAndExtractFeatures` function, as follows:

```
    int num_for_test= 20;
    // Get the nut images
    readFolderAndExtractFeatures("../data/nut/tuerca_%04d.pgm", 0,
num_for_test, trainingData, responsesData, testData, testResponsesData);
    // Get and process the ring images
    readFolderAndExtractFeatures("../data/ring/arandela_%04d.pgm", 1,
num_for_test, trainingData, responsesData, testData, testResponsesData);
    // get and process the screw images
    readFolderAndExtractFeatures("../data/screw/tornillo_%04d.pgm", 2,
num_for_test, trainingData, responsesData, testData, testResponsesData);
```

The `readFolderAndExtractFeatures` function uses the `VideoCapture` OpenCV function to read all of the images in a folder, including videos and camera frames. For each image that's read, we extract the features and add them to the corresponding output vector:

```
    bool readFolderAndExtractFeatures(string folder, int label, int
    num_for_test,
      vector<float> &trainingData, vector<int> &responsesData,
      vector<float> &testData, vector<float> &testResponsesData)
```

```
{
  VideoCapture images;
  if(images.open(folder)==false){
    cout << "Can not open the folder images" << endl;
    return false;
  }
  Mat frame;
  int img_index=0;
  while(images.read(frame)){
    //// Preprocess image
    Mat pre= preprocessImage(frame);
    // Extract features
    vector< vector<float> > features= ExtractFeatures(pre);
    for(int i=0; i< features.size(); i++){
      if(img_index >= num_for_test){
        trainingData.push_back(features[i][0]);
        trainingData.push_back(features[i][1]);
        responsesData.push_back(label);
      }else{
        testData.push_back(features[i][0]);
        testData.push_back(features[i][1]);
        testResponsesData.push_back((float)label);
      }
    }
    img_index++;
  }
  return true;
}
```

After filling all of the vectors with features and labels, we have to convert from vectors to an OpenCV `Mat` format so that we can send it to the training function:

```
// Merge all data
Mat trainingDataMat(trainingData.size()/2, 2, CV_32FC1, &trainingData[0]);
Mat responses(responsesData.size(), 1, CV_32SC1, &responsesData[0]);
Mat testDataMat(testData.size()/2, 2, CV_32FC1, &testData[0]);
Mat testResponses(testResponsesData.size(), 1, CV_32FC1,
&testResponsesData[0]);
```

Now, we are ready to create and train our machine learning model. As we stated previously, we are going to use the support vector machine for this. First, we are going to set up the basic model parameters, as follows:

```
// Set up SVM's parameters
svm = cv::ml::SVM::create();
svm->setType(cv::ml::SVM::C_SVC);
svm->setNu(0.05);
svm->setKernel(cv::ml::SVM::CHI2);
```

```
svm->setDegree(1.0);
svm->setGamma(2.0);
svm->setTermCriteria(TermCriteria(TermCriteria::MAX_ITER, 100, 1e-6));
```

We are now going to define the SVM type and kernel to use, as well as the criteria to stop the learning process. In our case, we are going to use a number of maximum iterations, stopping at 100 iterations. For more information about each parameter and what it does, check the OpenCV documentation at the following link: `https://docs.opencv.org/master/d1/d2d/classcv_1_1ml_1_1SVM.html`. After creating the setup parameters, we are going to create the model by calling the `train` method and using `trainingDataMat` and response matrices as a `TrainData` object:

```
// Train the SVM
svm->train(tdata);
```

We use the test vector (setting the `num_for_test` variable to greater than 0) to obtain an approximation error of our model. To get the error estimation, we are going to predict all test vector features to obtain the SVM prediction results and compare these results to the original labels:

```
if(testResponsesData.size()>0){
    cout << "Evaluation" << endl;
    cout << "==========" << endl;
    // Test the ML Model
    Mat testPredict;
    svm->predict(testDataMat, testPredict);
    cout << "Prediction Done" << endl;
    // Error calculation
    Mat errorMat= testPredict!=testResponses;
    float error= 100.0f * countNonZero(errorMat) /
testResponsesData.size();
    cout << "Error: " << error << "%" << endl;
    // Plot training data with error label
    plotTrainData(trainingDataMat, responses, &error);

}else{
    plotTrainData(trainingDataMat, responses);
}
```

We use the `predict` function by using the `testDataMat` features and a new `Mat` for prediction results. The `predict` function makes it possible to make multiple predictions at the same time, giving a matrix as the result instead of only one row or vector. After prediction, we only have to compute the differences of `testPredict` with our `testResponses` (the original labels). If there are differences, we only have to count how many there are and divide this by the total number of tests in order to calculate the error.

We can use the new `TrainData` class to generate the feature vectors, samples, and split our train data between test and train vectors.

Finally, we are going to show the training data in a 2D plot, where the *y*-axis is the aspect ratio feature and the *x*-axis is the area of objects. Each point has different colors and shapes (cross, square, and circle) that show each different kind of object, and we can clearly see the groups of objects in the following image:

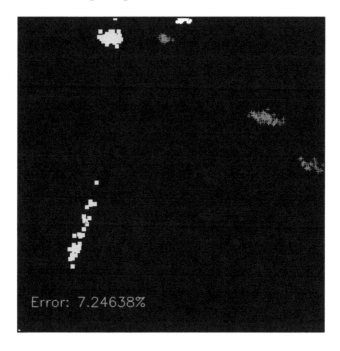

We are now very close to finishing our application sample. At this point, we have trained the SVM model; we can now use it for classification to detect the type of a new incoming and unknown feature vector. The next step is to predict an input image with unknown objects.

Input image prediction

We are now ready to explain the main function, which loads the input image and predicts the objects that appear inside it. We are going to use something like the following picture as the input image. Here, multiple different objects appear in the image. We did not have the labels or names of these, but the computer must be able to identify them:

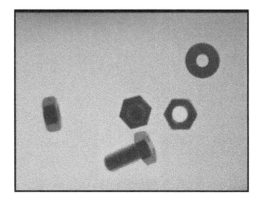

As with all training images, we have to load and pre-process the input image, as follows:

1. First, we load and convert the image into gray color values.
2. Then, we apply the pre-processing tasks (as we learned in Chapter 5, *Automated Optical Inspection, Object Segmentation, and Detection*) using the preprocessImage function:

```
Mat pre= preprocessImage(img);
```

3. Now, we are going to extract the feature of vectors for all objects that appear in the image and the top-left positions of each one by using the ExtractFeatures that we previously described:

```
// Extract features
vector<int> pos_top, pos_left;
vector< vector<float> >
features=ExtractFeatures(pre, &pos_left,      &pos_top);
```

4. We store each object we detect as a feature row and then convert each row as a Mat of one row and two features:

```
for(int i=0; i< features.size(); i++){
    Mat trainingDataMat(1, 2, CV_32FC1, &features[i][0]);
```

5. After this, we can predict the single object using the `predict` function of our `StatModel` SVM. The float result of the prediction is the label of the object detected. Then, to finish the application, we have to draw the label of each object that's detected and classified over the output image:

```
float result= svm->predict(trainingDataMat);
```

6. We are going to use a `stringstream` to store the text and a `Scalar` to store the color for each different label:

```
stringstream ss;
Scalar color;
if(result==0){
  color= green; // NUT
  ss << "NUT";
}else if(result==1){
  color= blue; // RING
  ss << "RING" ;
}else if(result==2){
  color= red; // SCREW
  ss << "SCREW";
}
```

7. We are also going to draw the label text over each object using its detected position in the `ExtractFeatures` function:

```
putText(img_output,
        ss.str(),
        Point2d(pos_left[i], pos_top[i]),
        FONT_HERSHEY_SIMPLEX,
        0.4,
        color);
```

8. Finally, we are going to draw our results in the output window:

```
miw->addImage("Binary image", pre);
miw->addImage("Result", img_output);
miw->render();
waitKey(0);
```

The final result of our application shows a window tiled with four screens. Here, the top-left image is the input training image, the top-right is the plot training image, the bottom left is the input image to analyze pre-processed images, and the bottom-right is the final result of the prediction:

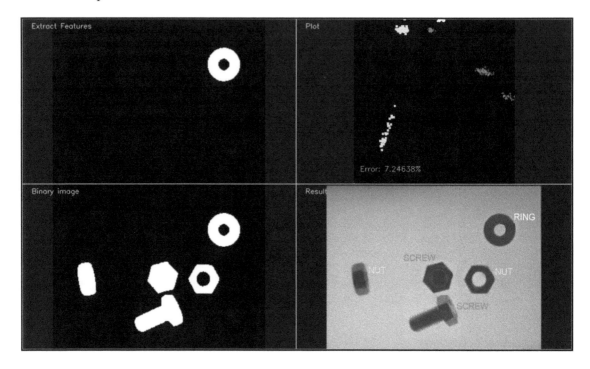

Summary

In this chapter, we learned about the basics of machine learning and applied them to a small sample application. This allowed us to understand the basic techniques that we can use to create our own machine learning application. Machine learning is complex and involves different techniques for each use case (supervised learning, unsupervised, clustering, and so on). We also learned how to create the most typical machine learning application, the supervised learning application, with SVM. The most important concepts in supervised machine learning are as follows: you must have an appropriate number of samples or a dataset, you must accurately choose the features that describe our objects (for more information on image features, go to Chapter 8, *Video Surveillance, Background Modeling, and Morphological Operations*), and you must choose a model that gives the best predictions.

If we don't get the correct predictions, we have to check each one of these concepts to find the issue.

In the next chapter, we are going to introduce background subtraction methods, which are very useful for video surveillance applications where the background doesn't give us any interesting information and must be discarded so that we can segment the image to detect and analyze the image objects.

7
Detecting Face Parts and Overlaying Masks

In Chapter 6, *Learning Object Classification*, we learned about object classification and how machine learning can be used to achieve it. In this chapter, we are going to learn how to detect and track different face parts. We will start the discussion by understanding the face detection pipeline and how it's built. We will then use this framework to detect face parts, such as the eyes, ears, mouth, and nose. Finally, we will learn how to overlay funny masks on these face parts in a live video.

By the end of this chapter, we should be familiar with the following topics:

- Understanding Haar cascades
- Integral images and why we need them
- Building a generic face detection pipeline
- Detecting and tracking faces, eyes, ears, noses, and mouths in a live video stream from the webcam
- Automatically overlaying a face mask, sunglasses, and a funny nose on a person's face in a video

Technical requirements

This chapter requires basic familiarity with the C++ programming language. All the code used in this chapter can be downloaded from the following GitHub link: `https://github.com/PacktPublishing/Learn-OpenCV-4-By-Building-Projects-Second-Edition/tree/master/Chapter_07`. The code can be executed on any operating system, though it is only tested on Ubuntu.

Check out the following video to see the Code in Action:
`http://bit.ly/2SlpTK6`

Understanding Haar cascades

Haar cascades are cascade classifiers that are based on Haar features. What is a cascade classifier? It is simply a concatenation of a set of weak classifiers that can be used to create a strong classifier. What do we mean by **weak** and **strong** classifiers? Weak classifiers are classifiers whose performance is limited. They don't have the ability to classify everything correctly. If you keep the problem really simple, they might perform at an acceptable level. Strong classifiers, on the other hand, are really good at classifying our data correctly. We will see how it all comes together in the next couple of paragraphs. Another important part of Haar cascades is **Haar features**. These features are simple summations of rectangles and differences of those areas across the image. Let's consider the following diagram:

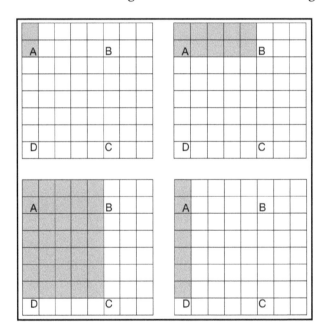

If we want to compute the Haar features for region ABCD, we just need to compute the difference between the white pixels and the blue pixels in that region. As we can see from the four diagrams, we use different patterns to build Haar features. There are a lot of other patterns that are used as well. We do this at multiple scales to make the system scale-invariant. When we say multiple scales, we just scale the image down to compute the same features again. This way, we can make it robust against size variations of a given object.

As it turns out, this concatenation system is a very good method for detecting objects in an image. In 2001, Paul Viola and Michael Jones published a seminal paper where they described a fast and effective method for object detection. If you are interested in learning more about it, you can check out their paper at `http://www.cs.ubc.ca/~lowe/425/slides/13-ViolaJones.pdf`.

Let's dive deeper into it to understand what they actually did. They basically described an algorithm that uses a boosted cascade of simple classifiers. This system is used to build a strong classifier that can perform really well. Why did they use these simple classifiers instead of complex classifiers, which can be more accurate? Well, using this technique they were able to avoid the problem of having to build a single classifier that can perform with high precision. These single-step classifiers tend to be complex and computationally intensive. The reason their technique works so well is because the simple classifiers can be weak learners, which means they don't need to be complex. Consider the problem of building a table detector. We want to build a system that will automatically learn what a table looks like. Based on that knowledge, it should be able to identify whether there is a table in any given image. To build this system, the first step is to collect images that can be used to train our system. There are a lot of techniques available in the machine learning world that can be used to train a system such as this. Bear in mind that we need to collect a lot of table and non-table images if we want our system to perform well. In machine learning lingo, table images are called **positive** samples and the non-table images are called **negative** samples. Our system will ingest this data and then learn to differentiate between these two classes. In order to build a real-time system, we need to keep our classifier nice and simple. The only concern is that simple classifiers are not very accurate. If we try to make them more accurate, then the process will end up being computationally intensive, and hence slow. This trade-off between accuracy and speed is very common in machine learning. So, we overcome this problem by concatenating a bunch of weak classifiers to create a strong and unified classifier. We don't need the weak classifiers to be very accurate. To ensure the quality of the overall classifier, Viola and Jones have described a nifty technique in the cascading step. You can go through the paper to understand the full system.

Now that we understand the general pipeline, let's see how to build a system that can detect faces in a live video. The first step is to extract features from all the images. In this case, the algorithms need these features to learn and understand what faces look like. They used Haar features in their paper to build the feature vectors. Once we extract these features, we pass them through a cascade of classifiers. We just check all the different rectangular sub-regions and keep discarding the ones that don't have faces in them. This way, we arrive at the final answer quickly to see whether a given rectangle contains a face or not.

What are integral images?

In order to extract these Haar features, we will have to calculate the sum of the pixel values enclosed in many rectangular regions of the image. To make it scale-invariant, we are required to compute these areas at multiple scales (for various rectangle sizes). Implemented naively, this would be a very computationally-intensive process; we would have to iterate over all the pixels of each rectangle, including reading the same pixels multiple times if they are contained in different overlapping rectangles. If you want to build a system that can run in real-time, you cannot spend so much time in computation. We need to find a way to avoid this huge redundancy during the area computation because we iterate over the same pixels multiple times. To avoid it, we can use something called integral images. These images can be initialized at a linear time (by iterating only twice over the image) and then provide the sum of the pixels inside any rectangle of any size by reading only four values. To understand it better, let's look at the following diagram:

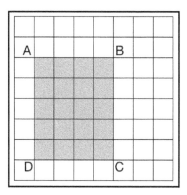

If we want to calculate the area of any rectangle in our diagram, we don't have to iterate through all the pixels in that region. Let's consider a rectangle formed by the top-left point in the image and any point, P, as the opposite corner. Let A_P denote the area of this rectangle. For example, in the previous image, A_B denotes the area of the 5 x 2 rectangle formed by taking the top-left point and **B** as opposite corners. Let's look at the following diagram for clarity:

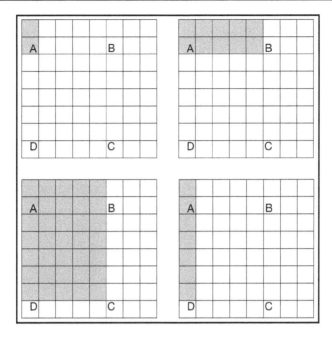

Let's consider the top-left square in the previous image. The blue pixels indicate the the the area between the top-left pixel and point **A**. This is denoted by A_A. The remaining diagrams are denoted by their respective names: A_B, A_C, and A_D. Now, if we want to calculate the area of the ABCD rectangle, as shown in the preceding diagram, we would use the following formula:

Area of the rectangle: $ABCD = A_C - (A_B + A_D - A_A)$

What's so special about this particular formula? As we know, extracting Haar features from the image includes computing these summations and we would have to do it for a lot of rectangles at multiple scales in the image. A lot of those calculations are repetitive because we would be iterating over the same pixels over and over again. It is so slow that building a real-time system wouldn't be feasible. Hence, we need this formula. As you can see, we don't have to iterate over the same pixels multiple times. If we want to compute the area of any rectangle, all the values on the right-hand side of the preceding equation are readily available in our integral image. We just pick up the right values, substitute them in the preceding equation, and extract the features.

Overlaying a face mask in a live video

OpenCV provides a nice face detection framework. We just need to load the cascade file and use it to detect the faces in an image. When we capture a video stream from the webcam, we can overlay funny masks on our faces. It will look something like this:

Let's look at the main parts of the code to see how to overlay this mask on the face in the input video stream. The full code is available in the downloadable code bundle provided along with this book:

```
#include "opencv2/core/utility.hpp"
#include "opencv2/objdetect/objdetect.hpp"
#include "opencv2/imgproc.hpp"
#include "opencv2/highgui.hpp"

using namespace cv;
using namespace std;

...

int main(int argc, char* argv[])
{
```

```
    string faceCascadeName = argv[1];
    // Variable declaration and initialization
    ...
    // Iterate until the user presses the Esc key
    while(true)
    {
        // Capture the current frame
        cap >> frame;
        // Resize the frame
        resize(frame, frame, Size(), scalingFactor, scalingFactor,
INTER_AREA);
        // Convert to grayscale
        cvtColor(frame, frameGray, COLOR_BGR2GRAY);
        // Equalize the histogram
        equalizeHist(frameGray, frameGray);
        // Detect faces
        faceCascade.detectMultiScale(frameGray, faces, 1.1, 2,
0|HAAR_SCALE_IMAGE, Size(30, 30) );
```

Let's take a quick stop to see what happened here. We start reading input frames from the webcam and resize it to our size of choice. The captured frame is a color image and face detection works on grayscale images. So, we convert it to grayscale and equalize the histogram. Why do we need to equalize the histogram? We need to do this to compensate for any issues, such as lighting or saturation. If the image is too bright or too dark, the detection will be poor. So, we need to equalize the histogram to ensure that our image has a healthy range of pixel values:

```
        // Draw green rectangle around the face
        for(auto& face:faces)
        {
            Rect faceRect(face.x, face.y, face.width, face.height);
            // Custom parameters to make the mask fit your face. You may
    have to play around with them to make sure it works.
            int x = face.x - int(0.1*face.width);
            int y = face.y - int(0.0*face.height);
            int w = int(1.1 * face.width);
            int h = int(1.3 * face.height);
            // Extract region of interest (ROI) covering your face
            frameROI = frame(Rect(x,y,w,h));
```

At this point, we know where the face is. So we extract the region of interest to overlay the mask in the right position:

```
                // Resize the face mask image based on the dimensions of the
    above ROI
                resize(faceMask, faceMaskSmall, Size(w,h));
                // Convert the previous image to grayscale
                cvtColor(faceMaskSmall, grayMaskSmall, COLOR_BGR2GRAY);
                // Threshold the previous image to isolate the pixels
    associated only with the face mask
                threshold(grayMaskSmall, grayMaskSmallThresh, 230, 255,
    THRESH_BINARY_INV);
```

We isolate the pixels associated with the face mask. We want to overlay the mask in such a way that it doesn't look like a rectangle. We want the exact boundaries of the overlaid object so that it looks natural. Let's go ahead and overlay the mask now:

```
                // Create mask by inverting the previous image (because we
    don't want the background to affect the overlay)
                bitwise_not(grayMaskSmallThresh, grayMaskSmallThreshInv);
                // Use bitwise "AND" operator to extract precise boundary of
    face mask
                bitwise_and(faceMaskSmall, faceMaskSmall, maskedFace,
    grayMaskSmallThresh);
                // Use bitwise "AND" operator to overlay face mask
                bitwise_and(frameROI, frameROI, maskedFrame,
    grayMaskSmallThreshInv);
                // Add the previously masked images and place it in the
    original frame ROI to create the final image
                add(maskedFace, maskedFrame, frame(Rect(x,y,w,h)));
            }
        // code dealing with memory release and GUI

        return 1;
    }
```

What happened in the code?

The first thing to note is that this code takes two input arguments—the **face cascade XML** file and the **mask image**. You can use the `haarcascade_frontalface_alt.xml` and `facemask.jpg` files that are provided under the `resources` folder. We need a classifier model that can be used to detect faces in an image and OpenCV provides a prebuilt XML file that can be used for this purpose. We use the `faceCascade.load()` function to load the XML file and also check whether the file is loaded correctly. We initiate the video-capture object to capture the input frames from the webcam. We then convert it to grayscale to run the detector. The `detectMultiScale` function is used to extract the boundaries of all the faces in the input image. We may have to scale down the image according to our needs, so the second argument in this function takes care of this. This scaling factor is the jump we take at each scale; since we need to look for faces at multiple scales, the next size will be 1.1 times bigger than the current size. The last parameter is a threshold that specifies the number of adjacent rectangles needed to keep the current rectangle. It can be used to increase the robustness of the face detector. We start the `while` loop and keep detecting the face in every frame until the user presses the *Esc* key. Once we detect a face, we need to overlay a mask on it. We may have to modify the dimensions slightly to ensure that the mask fits nicely. This customization is slightly subjective and it depends on the mask that's being used. Now that we have extracted the region of interest, we need to place our mask on top of this region. If we overlay the mask with its white background, it will look weird. We have to extract the exact curvy boundaries of the mask and then overlay it. We want the skull mask pixels to be visible and the remaining area should be transparent.

As we can see, the input mask has a white background. So, we create a mask by applying a threshold to the mask image. Using trial and error, we can see that a threshold of 240 works well. In the image, all the pixels with an intensity value greater than 240 will become 0, and all others will become 255. As far as the region of interest is concerned, we have to black out all the pixels in this region. To do that, we simply use the inverse of the mask that was just created. In the last step, we just add the masked versions to produce the final output image.

Get your sunglasses on

Now that we understand how to detect faces, we can generalize that concept to detect different parts of the face. We will be using an eye detector to overlay sunglasses in a live video. It's important to understand that the Viola-Jones framework can be applied to any object. The accuracy and robustness will depend on the uniqueness of the object. For example, the human face has very unique characteristics, so it's easy to train our system to be robust. On the other hand, an object such as a towel is too generic, and it has no distinguishing characteristics as such, so it's more difficult to build a robust towel detector. Once you build the eye detector and overlay the glasses, it will look something like this:

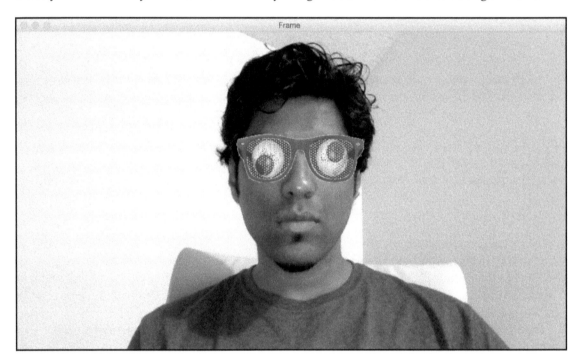

Let's look at the main parts of the code:

```
...
int main(int argc, char* argv[])
{
    string faceCascadeName = argv[1];
    string eyeCascadeName = argv[2];

    // Variable declaration and initialization
    ....
    // Face detection code
```

```
    . . . .
    vector<Point> centers;
    . . . .
    // Draw green circles around the eyes
    for( auto& face:faces )
    {
        Mat faceROI = frameGray(face[i]);
        vector<Rect> eyes;
        // In each face, detect eyes eyeCascade.detectMultiScale(faceROI,
    eyes, 1.1, 2, 0 |CV_HAAR_SCALE_IMAGE, Size(30, 30));
```

As we can see here, we run the eye detector only in the face region. We don't need to search the entire image for eyes because we know eyes will always be on a face:

```
        // For each eye detected, compute the center
        for(auto& eyes:eyes)
        {
            Point center( face.x + eye.x + int(eye.width*0.5), face.y +
    eye.y + int(eye.height*0.5) );
            centers.push_back(center);
        }
    }
    // Overlay sunglasses only if both eyes are detected
    if(centers.size() == 2)
    {
        Point leftPoint, rightPoint;
        // Identify the left and right eyes
        if(centers[0].x < centers[1].x)
        {
            leftPoint = centers[0];
            rightPoint = centers[1];
        }
        else
        {
            leftPoint = centers[1];
            rightPoint = centers[0];
        }
```

We detect the eyes and store them only when we find both of them. We then use their coordinates to determine which one is the left eye and which one is the right eye:

```
        // Custom parameters to make the sunglasses fit your face. You
    may have to play around with them to make sure it works.
        int w = 2.3 * (rightPoint.x - leftPoint.x);
        int h = int(0.4 * w);
        int x = leftPoint.x - 0.25*w;
        int y = leftPoint.y - 0.5*h;
        // Extract region of interest (ROI) covering both the eyes
```

```
              frameROI = frame(Rect(x,y,w,h));
              // Resize the sunglasses image based on the dimensions of the
  above ROI
              resize(eyeMask, eyeMaskSmall, Size(w,h));
```

In the preceding code, we adjusted the size of the sunglasses to fit the scale of our faces in the webcam. Let's check the remaining code:

```
              // Convert the previous image to grayscale
              cvtColor(eyeMaskSmall, grayMaskSmall, COLOR_BGR2GRAY);
              // Threshold the previous image to isolate the foreground
  object
              threshold(grayMaskSmall, grayMaskSmallThresh, 245, 255,
  THRESH_BINARY_INV);
              // Create mask by inverting the previous image (because we
  don't want the background to affect the overlay)
              bitwise_not(grayMaskSmallThresh, grayMaskSmallThreshInv);
              // Use bitwise "AND" operator to extract precise boundary of
  sunglasses
              bitwise_and(eyeMaskSmall, eyeMaskSmall, maskedEye,
  grayMaskSmallThresh);
              // Use bitwise "AND" operator to overlay sunglasses
              bitwise_and(frameROI, frameROI, maskedFrame,
  grayMaskSmallThreshInv);
              // Add the previously masked images and place it in the
  original frame ROI to create the final image
              add(maskedEye, maskedFrame, frame(Rect(x,y,w,h)));
          }

      // code for memory release and GUI

      return 1;
  }
```

Looking inside the code

You may have noticed that the flow of the code looks similar to the face detection code that we discussed in the *Overlaying a face mask in a live video* section. We load a face detection cascade classifier as well as the eye detection cascade classifier. Now, why do we need to load the face cascade classifier when we are detecting eyes? Well, we don't really need to use the face detector, but it helps us in limiting our search for the eyes' location. We know that the eyes are always located on somebody's face, so we can limit eye detection to the face region. The first step would be to detect the face and then run our eye detector code on this region. Since we would be operating on a smaller region, it would be faster and way more efficient.

For each frame, we start by detecting the face. We then go ahead and detect the location of the eyes by operating on this region. After this step, we need to overlay the sunglasses. To do that, we need to resize the sunglasses image to make sure it fits our face. To get the proper scale, we can consider the distance between the two eyes that are being detected. We overlay the sunglasses only when we detect both eyes. That's why we run the eye detector first, collect all the centers, and then overlay the sunglasses. Once we have this, we just need to overlay the sunglasses mask. The principle used for masking is very similar to the principle we used to overlay the face mask. You may have to customize the sizing and position of the sunglasses, depending on what you want. You can play around with different types of sunglasses to see what they look like.

Tracking the nose, mouth, and ears

Now that you know how to track different things using the framework, you can try tracking your nose, mouth, and ears too. Let's use a nose detector to overlay a funny nose:

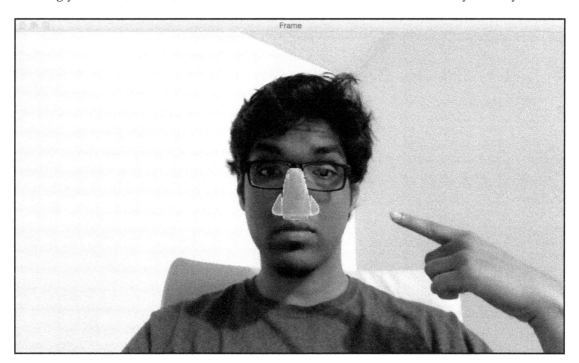

You can refer to the code files for a full implementation of this detector. The `haarcascade_mcs_nose.xml`, `haarcascade_mcs_mouth.xml`, `haarcascade_mcs_leftear.xml`, and `haarcascade_mcs_rightear.xml` cascade files can be used to track the different face parts. Play around with them and try to overlay a mustache or Dracula ears on yourself.

Summary

In this chapter, we discussed Haar cascades and integral images. We looked at how the face detection pipeline is built. We learned how to detect and track faces in a live video stream. We discussed using the face detection framework to detect various face parts, such as eyes, ears, nose, and mouth. Finally, we learned how to overlay masks on the input image using the results of face part detection.

In the next chapter, we are going to learn about video surveillance, background removal, and morphological image processing.

8
Video Surveillance, Background Modeling, and Morphological Operations

In this chapter, we are going to learn how to detect a moving object in a video taken from a static camera. This is used extensively in video surveillance systems. We will discuss the different characteristics that can be used to build this system. We will learn about background modeling and see how we can use it to build a model of the background in a live video. Once we do this, we will combine all the blocks to detect the object of interest in the video.

By the end of this chapter, you should be able to answer the following questions:

- What is naive background subtraction?
- What is frame differencing?
- How do we build a background model?
- How do we identify a new object in a static video?
- What is morphological image processing and how is it related to background modeling?
- How do we achieve different effects using morphological operators?

Technical requirements

This chapter requires familiarity with the basics of the C++ programming language. All the code used in this chapter can be downloaded from the following GitHub link: `https://github.com/PacktPublishing/Learn-OpenCV-4-By-Building-Projects-Second-Edition/tree/master/Chapter_08`. The code can be executed on any operating system, though it is only tested on Ubuntu.

Check out the following video to see the Code in Action:

`http://bit.ly/2SfqzRo`

Understanding background subtraction

Background subtraction is very useful in video surveillance. Basically, the background subtraction technique performs really well in cases where we have to detect moving objects in a static scene. How is this useful for video surveillance? The process of video surveillance involves dealing with constant data flow. The data stream keeps coming in and we need to analyze it to recognize any suspicious activity. Let's consider the example of a hotel lobby. All the walls and furniture have a fixed location. If we build a background model, we can use it to identify suspicious activity in the lobby. We are taking advantage of the fact that the background scene remains static (which happens to be true in this case). This helps us avoid any unnecessary computational overhead. As the name indicates, this algorithm works by detecting and assigning each pixel of an image to two classes, either the background (assumed static and stable) or the foreground, and subtracting it from the current frame to obtain the foreground image part, which includes moving objects such as persons, cars, and so on. With the static assumption, the foreground objects will naturally correspond to objects or people moving in front of the background.

In order to detect moving objects, we need to build a model of the background. This is not the same as direct frame differencing, because we are actually modeling the background and using this model to detect moving objects. When we say that we are modeling the background, we are basically building a mathematical formula that can be used to represent the background. This is much better than the simple frame-differencing technique. This technique tries to detect static parts of the scene and then include small updates in the build statistic formula of the background model. This background model is then used to detect background pixels. So, it's an adaptive technique that can adjust according to the scene.

Naive background subtraction

Let's start the discussion from the beginning. What does a background subtraction process look like? Consider the following image:

The previous image represents the background scene. Now, let's introduce a new object into this scene:

As we can see, there is a new object in the scene. So, if we compute the difference between this image and our background model, you should be able to identify the location of the TV remote:

The overall process looks like this:

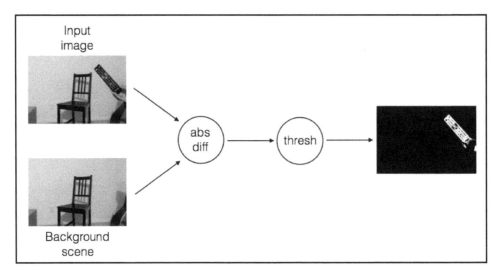

Does it work well?

There's a reason we call it the **naive** approach! It works under ideal conditions and, as we know, nothing is ideal in the real world. It does a reasonably good job of computing the shape of the given object, but it does so under some constraints. One of the main requirements of this approach is that the color and intensity of the object should be sufficiently different from that of the background. Some of the factors that affect this kind of algorithm are image noise, lighting conditions, and autofocus in cameras.

Once a new object enters our scene and stays there, it will be difficult to detect new objects that are in front of it. This is because we are not updating our background model, and the new object is now a part of our background. Consider the following image:

Now, let's say a new object enters our scene:

We detect this to be a new object, which is fine! Let's say another object comes into the scene:

It will be difficult to identify the location of these two different objects because their locations are overlapping. Here's what we get after subtracting the background and applying the threshold:

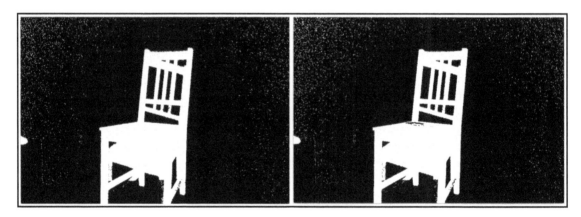

In this approach, we assume that the background is static. If some parts of our background start moving, those parts will start getting detected as new objects. So, even movements that are minor, say a waving flag, will cause problems in our detection algorithm. This approach is also sensitive to changes in illumination and it cannot handle any camera movement. Needless to say, it's a delicate approach! We need something that can handle all these things in the real world.

Frame differencing

We know that we cannot keep a static background image pattern that can be used to detect objects. One of the ways to fix this would be by using frame differencing. It is one of the simplest techniques we can use to see what parts of the video are moving. When we consider a live video stream, the difference between successive frames gives a lot of information. The concept is fairly straightforward! We just take the difference between successive frames and display the differences between them.

If I move my laptop rapidly, we can see something like this:

Instead of the laptop, let's move the object and see what happens. If I rapidly shake my head, it will look something like this:

As you can see from the previous images, only the moving parts of the video get highlighted. This gives us a good starting point to see what areas are moving in the video. Let's look at the function to compute the frame differences:

```
Mat frameDiff(Mat prevFrame, Mat curFrame, Mat nextFrame)
{
    Mat diffFrames1, diffFrames2, output;
    // Compute absolute difference between current frame and the next
    absdiff(nextFrame, curFrame, diffFrames1);
    // Compute absolute difference between current frame and the previous
    absdiff(curFrame, prevFrame, diffFrames2);
    // Bitwise "AND" operation between the previous two diff images
    bitwise_and(diffFrames1, diffFrames2, output);
    return output;
}
```

Frame differencing is fairly straightforward! You compute the absolute differences between the current frame and the previous frame, and between the current frame and the next frame. We then take these frame differences and apply a bitwise **AND** operator. This will highlight the moving parts in the image. If you just compute the difference between the current frame and the previous frame, it tends to be noisy. Hence, we need to use the bitwise AND operator between successive frame differences to get some stability when we see the moving objects.

Let's look at the function that can extract and return a frame from the webcam:

```
Mat getFrame(VideoCapture cap, float scalingFactor)
{
    Mat frame, output;

    // Capture the current frame
    cap >> frame;

    // Resize the frame
    resize(frame, frame, Size(), scalingFactor, scalingFactor, INTER_AREA);

    // Convert to grayscale
    cvtColor(frame, output, COLOR_BGR2GRAY);

    return output;
}
```

As we can see, it's pretty straightforward. We just need to resize the frame and convert it to grayscale. Now that we have the helper functions ready, let's look at the main function and see how it all comes together:

```cpp
int main(int argc, char* argv[])
{
    Mat frame, prevFrame, curFrame, nextFrame;
    char ch;

    // Create the capture object
    // 0 -> input arg that specifies it should take the input from the
webcam
    VideoCapture cap(0);

    // If you cannot open the webcam, stop the execution!
    if(!cap.isOpened())
        return -1;

    //create GUI windows
    namedWindow("Frame");


    // Scaling factor to resize the input frames from the webcam
    float scalingFactor = 0.75;

    prevFrame = getFrame(cap, scalingFactor);
    curFrame = getFrame(cap, scalingFactor);
    nextFrame = getFrame(cap, scalingFactor);

    // Iterate until the user presses the Esc key
    while(true)
    {
        // Show the object movement
        imshow("Object Movement", frameDiff(prevFrame, curFrame,
nextFrame));

        // Update the variables and grab the next frame
        prevFrame = curFrame;
        curFrame = nextFrame;
        nextFrame = getFrame(cap, scalingFactor);

        // Get the keyboard input and check if it's 'Esc'
        // 27 -> ASCII value of 'Esc' key
        ch = waitKey( 30 );
        if (ch == 27) {
            break;
        }
    }
```

```
// Release the video capture object
cap.release();

// Close all windows
destroyAllWindows();

return 1;
}
```

How well does it work?

As we can see, frame differencing addresses a couple of important problems we faced earlier. It can quickly adapt to lighting changes or camera movement. If an object comes in to the frame and stays there, it will not be detected in future frames. One of the main concerns of this approach is about detecting uniformly colored objects. It can only detect the edges of a uniformly colored object. The reason is that a large portion of this object will result in very low pixel differences:

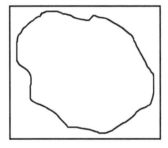

Let's say this object moved slightly. If we compare this with the previous frame, it will look like this:

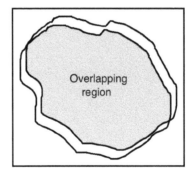

Hence, we have very few pixels that are labeled on that object. Another concern is that it is difficult to detect whether an object moving toward the camera or away from it.

The Mixture of Gaussians approach

Before we talk about **Mixture of Gaussians** (**MOG**), let's see what a **mixture model** is. A mixture model is just a statistical model that can be used to represent the presence of subpopulations within our data. We don't really care about what category each data point belongs to. All we need to do is identify that the data has multiple groups inside it. If we represent each subpopulation using the Gaussian function, then it's called Mixture of Gaussians. Let's consider the following photograph:

Now, as we gather more frames in this scene, every part of the image will gradually become a part of the background model. This is what we discussed earlier in the *Frame differencing* section as well. If a scene is static, the model adapts itself to make sure the background model is updated. The foreground mask, which is supposed to represent the foreground object, looks like a black image at this point because every pixel is part of the background model.

OpenCV has multiple algorithms implemented for the Mixture of Gaussians approach. One of them is called **MOG** and the other is called **MOG2**: refer to this link for a detailed explanation: http://docs.opencv.org/master/db/d5c/tutorial_py_bg_subtraction. html#gsc.tab=0. You will also be able check out the original research papers that were used to implement these algorithms.

Let's wait for some time and then introduce a new object into the scene. Let's look at what the new foreground mask looks like, using the MOG2 approach:

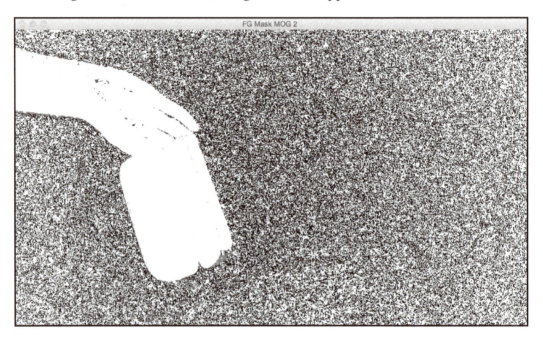

As you can see, the new objects are being identified correctly. Let's look at the interesting part of the code (you can get the full code in the .cpp files):

```
int main(int argc, char* argv[])
{

    // Variable declaration and initialization
    ....
    // Iterate until the user presses the Esc key
    while(true)
    {
        // Capture the current frame
        cap >> frame;

        // Resize the frame
        resize(frame, frame, Size(), scalingFactor, scalingFactor,
INTER_AREA);

        // Update the MOG2 background model based on the current frame
        pMOG2->apply(frame, fgMaskMOG2);

        // Show the MOG2 foreground mask
```

```
            imshow("FG Mask MOG 2", fgMaskMOG2);

            // Get the keyboard input and check if it's 'Esc'
            // 27 -> ASCII value of 'Esc' key
            ch = waitKey( 30 );
            if (ch == 27) {
                break;
            }
        }

        // Release the video capture object
        cap.release();

        // Close all windows
        destroyAllWindows();

        return 1;
    }
```

What happened in the code?

Let's quickly go through the code and see what's happening there. We use the Mixture of Gaussians model to create a background subtractor object. This object represents the model that will be updated as and when we encounter new frames from the webcam. We initialized two background subtraction models—BackgroundSubtractorMOG and BackgroundSubtractorMOG2. They represent two different algorithms that are used for background subtraction. The first one refers to the paper by *P. KadewTraKuPong* and *R. Bowden*, titled *An Improved Adaptive Background Mixture Model for Real-time Tracking with Shadow Detection*. You can check it out at http://personal.ee.surrey.ac.uk/Personal/R.Bowden/publications/avbs01/avbs01.pdf. The second one refers to the paper by *Z. Zivkovic*, titled *Improved Adaptive Gaussian Mixture Model for Background Subtraction*. You can check it out here: http://www.zoranz.net/Publications/zivkovic2004ICPR.pdf.
We start an infinite while loop and continuously read the input frames from the webcam. With each frame, we update the background model, as indicated in the following lines:

```
    pMOG2->apply(frame, fgMaskMOG2);
```

The background model gets updated in these steps. Now, if a new object enters the scene and stays there, it will become part of the background model. This helps us overcome one of the biggest shortcomings of the **naive** background subtraction model.

Morphological image processing

As we discussed earlier, background subtraction methods are affected by many factors. Their accuracy depends on how we capture the data and how it's processed. One of the biggest factors that affects these algorithms is the noise level. When we say **noise**, we are talking about things such as graininess in an image and isolated black/white pixels. These issues tend to affect the quality of our algorithms. This is where morphological image processing comes into play. Morphological image processing is used extensively in a lot of real-time systems to ensure the quality of the output. Morphological image processing refers to processing the shapes of features in the image; for example, you can make a shape thicker or thinner. Morphological operators rely not on how the pixels are ordered in an image, but on their values. This is why they are really well suited to manipulating shapes in binary images. Morphological image processing can be applied to grayscale images as well, but the pixel values will not matter much.

What's the underlying principle?

Morphological operators use a structuring element to modify an image. What is a structuring element? A structuring element is basically a small shape that can be used to inspect a small region in the image. It is positioned at all the pixel locations in the image so that it can inspect that neighborhood. We basically take a small window and overlay it on a pixel. Depending on the response, we take appropriate action at that pixel location.

Let's consider the following input image:

We are going to apply a bunch of morphological operations to this image to see how the shape changes.

Slimming the shapes

We achieve this effect using an operation called **erosion**. This is the operation that makes a shape thinner by peeling the boundary layers of all the shapes in the image:

Output image after erosion

Let's look at the function that performs morphological erosion:

```cpp
Mat performErosion(Mat inputImage, int erosionElement, int erosionSize)
{

    Mat outputImage;
    int erosionType;

    if(erosionElement == 0)
        erosionType = MORPH_RECT;
    else if(erosionElement == 1)
        erosionType = MORPH_CROSS;
    else if(erosionElement == 2)
        erosionType = MORPH_ELLIPSE;

    // Create the structuring element for erosion
    Mat element = getStructuringElement(erosionType, Size(2*erosionSize +
1, 2*erosionSize + 1), Point(erosionSize, erosionSize));

    // Erode the image using the structuring element
    erode(inputImage, outputImage, element);

    // Return the output image
    return outputImage;
}
```

You can check out the full code in the .cpp files to understand how to use this function. We basically build a structuring element using a built-in OpenCV function. This object is used as a probe to modify each pixel based on certain conditions. These conditions refer to what's happening around that particular pixel in the image. For example, is it surrounded by white pixels? Or is it surround by black pixels? Once we have an answer, we take the appropriate action.

Thickening the shapes

We use an operation called **dilation** to achieve thickening. This is the operation that makes a shape thicker by adding boundary layers to all the shapes in the image:

Here is the code to do it:

```
Mat performDilation(Mat inputImage, int dilationElement, int dilationSize)
{
    Mat outputImage;
    int dilationType;

    if(dilationElement == 0)
        dilationType = MORPH_RECT;
    else if(dilationElement == 1)
        dilationType = MORPH_CROSS;
    else if(dilationElement == 2)
        dilationType = MORPH_ELLIPSE;

    // Create the structuring element for dilation
    Mat element = getStructuringElement(dilationType, Size(2*dilationSize +
1, 2*dilationSize + 1), Point(dilationSize, dilationSize));

    // Dilate the image using the structuring element
    dilate(inputImage, outputImage, element);

    // Return the output image
    return outputImage;
}
```

Other morphological operators

Here are some other interesting morphological operators. Let's look at the output image first. We can look at the code at the end of this section.

Morphological opening

This is the operation that **opens** a shape. This operator is frequently used for noise removal in images. It's basically erosion followed by dilation. Morphological opening removes small objects from the foreground in the image by placing them in the background:

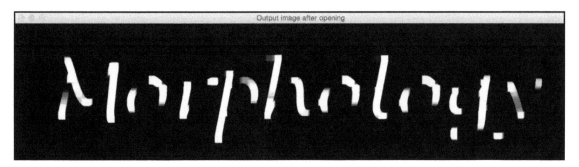

Here is the function to perform morphological opening:

```
Mat performOpening(Mat inputImage, int morphologyElement, int
morphologySize)
{

    Mat outputImage, tempImage;
    int morphologyType;

    if(morphologyElement == 0)
        morphologyType = MORPH_RECT;
    else if(morphologyElement == 1)
        morphologyType = MORPH_CROSS;
    else if(morphologyElement == 2)
        morphologyType = MORPH_ELLIPSE;

    // Create the structuring element for erosion
    Mat element = getStructuringElement(morphologyType,
Size(2*morphologySize + 1, 2*morphologySize + 1), Point(morphologySize,
morphologySize));

    // Apply morphological opening to the image using the structuring
```

```
element
    erode(inputImage, tempImage, element);
    dilate(tempImage, outputImage, element);

    // Return the output image
    return outputImage;
}
```

As we can see here, we apply **erosion** and **dilation** on the image to perform morphological opening.

Morphological closing

This is the operation that **closes** a shape by filling the gaps, as shown in the following screenshot. This operation is also used for noise removal. It's basically dilation followed by erosion. This operation removes tiny holes in the foreground by changing small objects in the background into the foreground:

Let's quickly look at the function to perform morphological closing:

```
Mat performClosing(Mat inputImage, int morphologyElement, int
morphologySize)
{

    Mat outputImage, tempImage;
    int morphologyType;

    if(morphologyElement == 0)
        morphologyType = MORPH_RECT;
    else if(morphologyElement == 1)
        morphologyType = MORPH_CROSS;
    else if(morphologyElement == 2)
        morphologyType = MORPH_ELLIPSE;
```

```
    // Create the structuring element for erosion
    Mat element = getStructuringElement(morphologyType,
Size(2*morphologySize + 1, 2*morphologySize + 1), Point(morphologySize,
morphologySize));

    // Apply morphological opening to the image using the structuring
element
    dilate(inputImage, tempImage, element);
    erode(tempImage, outputImage, element);
    // Return the output image
    return outputImage;
}
```

Drawing the boundary

We achieve this using a morphological gradient. This is the operation that draws the boundary around a shape by taking the difference between the dilation and erosion of an image:

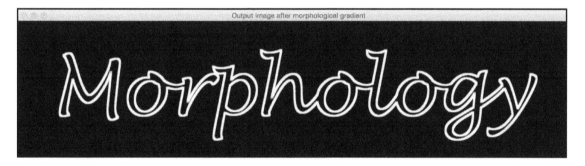

Let's look at the function to perform morphological gradient:

```
Mat performMorphologicalGradient(Mat inputImage, int morphologyElement, int
morphologySize)
{
    Mat outputImage, tempImage1, tempImage2;
    int morphologyType;

    if(morphologyElement == 0)
        morphologyType = MORPH_RECT;
    else if(morphologyElement == 1)
        morphologyType = MORPH_CROSS;
    else if(morphologyElement == 2)
        morphologyType = MORPH_ELLIPSE;
```

```
    // Create the structuring element for erosion
    Mat element = getStructuringElement(morphologyType,
Size(2*morphologySize + 1, 2*morphologySize + 1), Point(morphologySize,
morphologySize));
    // Apply morphological gradient to the image using the structuring
element
    dilate(inputImage, tempImage1, element);
    erode(inputImage, tempImage2, element);

    // Return the output image
    return tempImage1 - tempImage2;
}
```

Top Hat transform

This transform extracts finer details from the images. This is the difference between the input image and its morphological opening. This gives us the objects in the image that are smaller than the structuring element and brighter than the surroundings. Depending on the size of the structuring element, we can extract various objects in the given image:

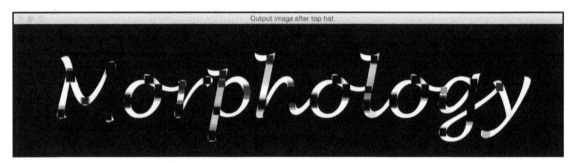

If you look at the output image carefully, you can see those black rectangles. It means that the structuring element was able to fit in there, and so those regions are blackened out. Here is the function:

```
Mat performTopHat(Mat inputImage, int morphologyElement, int
morphologySize)
{

    Mat outputImage;
    int morphologyType;

    if(morphologyElement == 0)
        morphologyType = MORPH_RECT;
    else if(morphologyElement == 1)
```

```
        morphologyType = MORPH_CROSS;
    else if(morphologyElement == 2)
        morphologyType = MORPH_ELLIPSE;

    // Create the structuring element for erosion
    Mat element = getStructuringElement(morphologyType,
Size(2*morphologySize + 1, 2*morphologySize + 1), Point(morphologySize,
morphologySize));

    // Apply top hat operation to the image using the structuring element
    outputImage = inputImage - performOpening(inputImage,
morphologyElement, morphologySize);

    // Return the output image
    return outputImage;
}
```

Black Hat transform

This transform extract finer details from the image as well. This is the difference between the morphological closing of an image and the image itself. This gives us the objects in the image that are smaller than the structuring element and darker than its surroundings:

Let's look at the function to perform a Black Hat transform:

```
Mat performBlackHat(Mat inputImage, int morphologyElement, int
morphologySize)
{
    Mat outputImage;
    int morphologyType;

    if(morphologyElement == 0)
        morphologyType = MORPH_RECT;
    else if(morphologyElement == 1)
        morphologyType = MORPH_CROSS;
```

```
    else if(morphologyElement == 2)
        morphologyType = MORPH_ELLIPSE;

    // Create the structuring element for erosion
    Mat element = getStructuringElement(morphologyType,
Size(2*morphologySize + 1, 2*morphologySize + 1), Point(morphologySize,
morphologySize));

    // Apply black hat operation to the image using the structuring element
    outputImage = performClosing(inputImage, morphologyElement,
morphologySize) - inputImage;

    // Return the output image
    return outputImage;
}
```

Summary

In this chapter, we learned about the algorithms that are used for background modeling and morphological image processing. We discussed naive background subtraction and its limitations. We looked at how to get motion information using frame differencing and how it can be limiting when we want to track different types of objects. This led to our discussion about the Mixture of Gaussians. We discussed the formula and how we can implement it. We then discussed morphological image processing, which can be used for various purposes, and different operations were covered to show the use cases.

In the next chapter, we are going to discuss object tracking and the various techniques that can be used to do it.

Learning Object Tracking

9

In the previous chapter, we learned about video surveillance, background modeling, and morphological image processing. We discussed how we can use different morphological operators to apply cool visual effects to input images. In this chapter, we are going to learn how to track an object in a live video. We will discuss the different characteristics of an object that can be used to track it. We will also learn about different methods and techniques for object tracking. Object tracking is used extensively in robotics, self-driving cars, vehicle tracking, player tracking in sports, and video compression.

By the end of this chapter, you will know the following:

- How to track objects of a specific color
- How to build an interactive object tracker
- What a corner detector is
- How to detect good features to track
- How to build an optical flow-based feature tracker

Technical requirements

This chapter requires familiarity with the basics of the C++ programming language. All the code used in this chapter can be downloaded from the following GitHub link: `https://github.com/PacktPublishing/Learn-OpenCV-4-By-Building-Projects-Second-Edition/tree/master/Chapter_09`. The code can be executed on any operating system, though it is only tested on Ubuntu.

Check out the following video to see the Code in Action:
`http://bit.ly/2SidbMc`

Tracking objects of a specific color

In order to build a good object tracker, we need to understand what characteristics can be used to make our tracking robust and accurate. So, let's take a baby step in that direction and see whether we can use colorspace information to come up with a good visual tracker. One thing to keep in mind is that color information is sensitive to lighting conditions. In real-world applications, you will have to do some preprocessing to take care of that. But for now, let's assume that somebody else is doing that and we are getting clean color images.

There are many different colorspaces, and picking a good one will depend on the different applications that a user is using. While RGB is the native representation on a computer screen, it's not necessarily ideal for humans. When it comes to humans, we give names to colors more naturally based on their hue, which is why **hue saturation value** (**HSV**) is probably one of the most informative colorspaces. It closely aligns with how we perceive colors. Hue refers to the color spectrum, saturation refers to the intensity of a particular color, and value refers to the brightness of that pixel. This is actually represented in a cylindrical format. You can find a simple explanation at `http://infohost.nmt.edu/tcc/help/pubs/colortheory/web/hsv.html`. We can take the pixels of an image to the HSV colorspace and then use this colorspace to measure distances in this colorspace and threshold in this space thresholding to track a given object.

Consider the following frame in the video:

If you run it through the colorspace filter and track the object, you will see something like this:

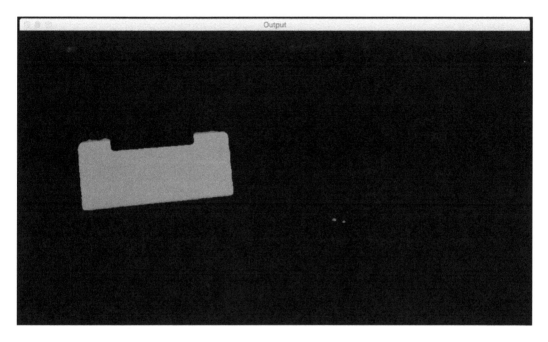

As we can see here, our tracker recognizes a particular object in the video based on the color characteristics. In order to use this tracker, we need to know the color distribution of our target object. Here is the code to track a colored object, which selects only pixels that have a certain given hue. The code is well-commented, so read the explanation about each term to see what's happening:

```
int main(int argc, char* argv[])
{
    // Variable declarations and initializations
    // Iterate until the user presses the Esc key
    while(true)
    {
        // Initialize the output image before each iteration
        outputImage = Scalar(0,0,0);
        // Capture the current frame
        cap >> frame;
        // Check if 'frame' is empty
        if(frame.empty())
            break;
        // Resize the frame
        resize(frame, frame, Size(), scalingFactor, scalingFactor,
```

```
INTER_AREA);
        // Convert to HSV colorspace
        cvtColor(frame, hsvImage, COLOR_BGR2HSV);
        // Define the range of "blue" color in HSV colorspace
        Scalar lowerLimit = Scalar(60,100,100);
        Scalar upperLimit = Scalar(180,255,255);
        // Threshold the HSV image to get only blue color
        inRange(hsvImage, lowerLimit, upperLimit, mask);
        // Compute bitwise-AND of input image and mask
        bitwise_and(frame, frame, outputImage, mask=mask);
        // Run median filter on the output to smoothen it
        medianBlur(outputImage, outputImage, 5);
        // Display the input and output image
        imshow("Input", frame);
        imshow("Output", outputImage);
        // Get the keyboard input and check if it's 'Esc'
        // 30 -> wait for 30 ms
        // 27 -> ASCII value of 'ESC' key
        ch = waitKey(30);
        if (ch == 27) {
            break;
        }
    }
    return 1;
}
```

Building an interactive object tracker

A colorspace-based tracker gives us the freedom to track a colored object, but we are also constrained to a predefined color. What if we just want to pick an object at random? How do we build an object tracker that can learn the characteristics of the selected object and just track it automatically? This is where the **continuously-adaptive meanshift** (**CAMShift**) algorithm comes into picture. It's basically an improved version of the meanshift algorithm.

The concept of meanshift is actually nice and simple. Let's say we select a region of interest and we want our object tracker to track that object. In this region, we select a bunch of points based on the color histogram and we compute the centroid of spatial points. If the centroid lies at the center of this region, we know that the object hasn't moved. But if the centroid is not at the center of this region, then we know that the object is moving in some direction. The movement of the centroid controls the direction in which the object is moving. So, we move the bounding box of the object to a new location so that the new centroid becomes the center of this bounding box. Hence, this algorithm is called meanshift, because the mean (the centroid) is shifting. This way, we keep ourselves updated with the current location of the object.

But the problem with meanshift is that the size of the bounding box is not allowed to change. When you move the object away from the camera, the object will appear smaller to the human eye, but meanshift will not take that into account. The size of the bounding box will remain the same throughout the tracking session. Hence, we need to use CAMShift. The advantage of CAMShift is that it can adapt the size of the bounding box to the size of the object. Along with that, it can also keep track of the orientation of the object.

Let's consider the following frame, in which the object is highlighted:

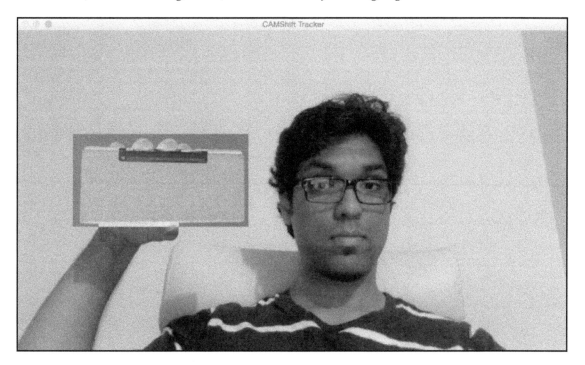

Now that we have selected the object, the algorithm computes the histogram backprojection and extracts all the information. What is histogram backprojection? It's just a way of identifying how well the image fits into our histogram model. We compute the histogram model of a particular thing and then use this model to find that thing in an image. Let's move the object and see how it's getting tracked:

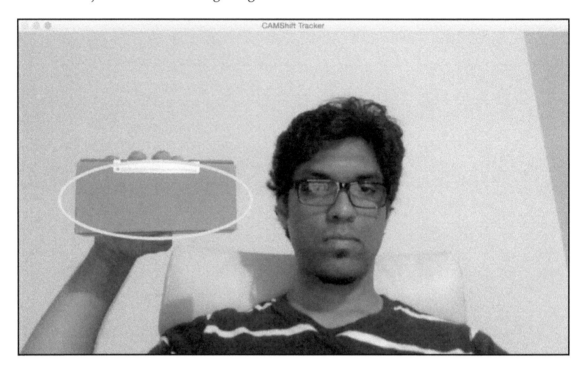

It looks like the object is getting tracked fairly well. Let's change the orientation and see whether the tracking is maintained:

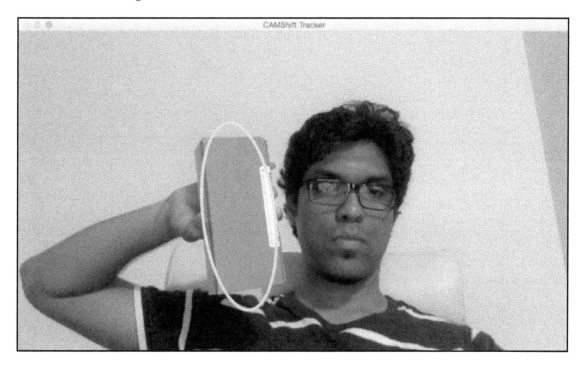

As we can see, the bounding ellipse has changed its location as well as orientation. Let's change the perspective of the object and see whether it's still able to track it:

We're still good! The bounding ellipse has changed the aspect ratio to reflect the fact that the object looks skewed now (because of the perspective transformation). Let's look at the user interface functionality in the code:

```
Mat image;
Point originPoint;
Rect selectedRect;
bool selectRegion = false;
int trackingFlag = 0;

// Function to track the mouse events
void onMouse(int event, int x, int y, int, void*)
{
    if(selectRegion)
    {
        selectedRect.x = MIN(x, originPoint.x);
        selectedRect.y = MIN(y, originPoint.y);
        selectedRect.width = std::abs(x - originPoint.x);
        selectedRect.height = std::abs(y - originPoint.y);
```

```
            selectedRect &= Rect(0, 0, image.cols, image.rows);
        }
    switch(event)
    {
        case EVENT_LBUTTONDOWN:
            originPoint = Point(x,y);
            selectedRect = Rect(x,y,0,0);
            selectRegion = true;
            break;
        case EVENT_LBUTTONUP:
            selectRegion = false;
            if( selectedRect.width > 0 && selectedRect.height > 0 )
            {
                trackingFlag = -1;
            }
            break;
    }
}
```

This function basically captures the coordinates of the rectangle that was selected in the window. The user just needs to click and drag with the mouse. There are a set of built-in functions in OpenCV that help us to detect these different mouse events.

Here is the code for performing object tracking based on CAMShift:

```
int main(int argc, char* argv[])
{
    // Variable declaration and initialization
    ....
    // Iterate until the user presses the Esc key
    while(true)
    {
        // Capture the current frame
        cap >> frame;
        // Check if 'frame' is empty
        if(frame.empty())
            break;
        // Resize the frame
        resize(frame, frame, Size(), scalingFactor, scalingFactor,
INTER_AREA);
        // Clone the input frame
        frame.copyTo(image);
        // Convert to HSV colorspace
        cvtColor(image, hsvImage, COLOR_BGR2HSV);
```

We now have the HSV image waiting to be processed. Let's go ahead and see how we can use our thresholds to process this image:

```
        if(trackingFlag)
        {
            // Check for all the values in 'hsvimage' that are within the
specified range
            // and put the result in 'mask'
            inRange(hsvImage, Scalar(0, minSaturation, minValue),
Scalar(180, 256, maxValue), mask);
            // Mix the specified channels
            int channels[] = {0, 0};
            hueImage.create(hsvImage.size(), hsvImage.depth());
            mixChannels(&hsvImage, 1, &hueImage, 1, channels, 1);
            if(trackingFlag < 0)
            {
                // Create images based on selected regions of interest
                Mat roi(hueImage, selectedRect), maskroi(mask,
selectedRect);
                // Compute the histogram and normalize it
                calcHist(&roi, 1, 0, maskroi, hist, 1, &histSize,
&histRanges);

                normalize(hist, hist, 0, 255, NORM_MINMAX);
                trackingRect = selectedRect;
                trackingFlag = 1;

            }
```

As we can see here, we use the HSV image to compute the histogram of the region. We use our thresholds to locate the required color in the HSV spectrum and then filter out the image based on that. Let's go ahead and see how we can compute the histogram backprojection:

```
            // Compute the histogram backprojection
            calcBackProject(&hueImage, 1, 0, hist, backproj, &histRanges);
            backproj &= mask;
            RotatedRect rotatedTrackingRect = CamShift(backproj,
trackingRect, TermCriteria(TermCriteria::EPS | TermCriteria::COUNT, 10,
1));
            // Check if the area of trackingRect is too small
            if(trackingRect.area() <= 1)
            {
                // Use an offset value to make sure the trackingRect has a
minimum size
                int cols = backproj.cols, rows = backproj.rows;
                int offset = MIN(rows, cols) + 1;
                trackingRect = Rect(trackingRect.x - offset, trackingRect.y
- offset, trackingRect.x + offset, trackingRect.y + offset) & Rect(0, 0,
cols, rows);
```

```
        }
```

We are now ready to display the results. Using the rotated rectangle, let's draw an ellipse around our region of interest:

```
        // Draw the ellipse on top of the image
        ellipse(image, rotatedTrackingRect, Scalar(0,255,0), 3,
LINE_AA);
        }
        // Apply the 'negative' effect on the selected region of interest
        if(selectRegion && selectedRect.width > 0 && selectedRect.height >
0)
        {
            Mat roi(image, selectedRect);
            bitwise_not(roi, roi);
        }
        // Display the output image
        imshow(windowName, image);
        // Get the keyboard input and check if it's 'Esc'
        // 27 -> ASCII value of 'Esc' key
        ch = waitKey(30);
        if (ch == 27) {
            break;
        }
    }
    return 1;
}
```

Detecting points using the Harris corner detector

Corner detection is a technique used to detect points of interest in an image. These interest points are also called feature points, or simply features, in computer vision terminology. A corner is basically an intersection of two edges. An interest point is basically something that can be uniquely detected in an image. A corner is a particular case of an interest point. These interest points help us characterize an image. These points are used extensively in applications such as object tracking, image classification, and visual search. Since we know that the corners are interesting, let's see how can detect them.

In computer vision, there is a popular corner detection technique called the Harris corner detector. We basically construct a 2 x 2 matrix based on partial derivatives of the grayscale image, and then analyze the eigenvalues. What does that even mean? Well, let's dissect it so that we can understand it better. Let's consider a small patch in the image. Our goal is to identify whether this patch has a corner in it. So, we consider all the neighboring patches and compute the intensity difference between our patch and all those neighboring patches. If the difference is high in all directions, then we know that our patch has a corner in it. This is an oversimplification of the actual algorithm, but it covers the gist. If you want to understand the underlying mathematical details, you can check out the original paper by *Harris* and *Stephens* at `http://www.bmva.org/bmvc/1988/avc-88-023.pdf`. A corner is a point with strong intensity differences along two directions.

If we run the Harris corner detector, it will look like this:

As we can see, the green circles on the TV remote are the detected corners. This will change based on the parameters you choose for the detector. If you modify the parameters, you can see that more points might get detected. If you make it strict, you might not be able to detect soft corners. Let's look at the code to detect Harris corners:

```
int main(int argc, char* argv[])
{
// Variable declaration and initialization

// Iterate until the user presses the Esc key
while(true)
{
    // Capture the current frame
    cap >> frame;

    // Resize the frame
    resize(frame, frame, Size(), scalingFactor, scalingFactor, INTER_AREA);

    dst = Mat::zeros(frame.size(), CV_32FC1);

    // Convert to grayscale
    cvtColor(frame, frameGray, COLOR_BGR2GRAY );

    // Detecting corners
    cornerHarris(frameGray, dst, blockSize, apertureSize, k,
BORDER_DEFAULT);

    // Normalizing
    normalize(dst, dst_norm, 0, 255, NORM_MINMAX, CV_32FC1, Mat());
    convertScaleAbs(dst_norm, dst_norm_scaled);
```

We converted the image to grayscale and detected corners using our parameters. You can find the full code in the .cpp files. These parameters play an important role in the number of points that will be detected. You can check out the OpenCV documentation of cornerHarris() at https://docs.opencv.org/master/dd/d1a/group__imgproc__feature.html#gac1fc3598018010880e370e2f709b4345.

We now have all the information we need. Let's go ahead and draw circles around our corners to display the results:

```
    // Drawing a circle around each corner
    for(int j = 0; j < dst_norm.rows ; j++)
    {
        for(int i = 0; i < dst_norm.cols; i++)
        {
            if((int)dst_norm.at<float>(j,i) > thresh)
            {
```

```
                        circle(frame, Point(i, j), 8, Scalar(0,255,0), 2, 8,
    0);
                    }
                }
            }

            // Showing the result
            imshow(windowName, frame);

            // Get the keyboard input and check if it's 'Esc'
            // 27 -> ASCII value of 'Esc' key
            ch = waitKey(10);
            if (ch == 27) {
                break;
            }
        }

        // Release the video capture object
        cap.release();

        // Close all windows
        destroyAllWindows();

        return 1;
    }
```

As we can see, this code takes an input argument: `blockSize`. Depending on the size you choose, the performance will vary. Start with a value of four and play around with it to see what happens.

Good features to track

Harris corner detector performs well in many cases, but it can still be improved. Around six years after the original paper by *Harris* and *Stephens*, *Shi* and *Tomasi* came up with something better and they called it *Good Features to Track*. You can read the original paper here: `http://www.ai.mit.edu/courses/6.891/handouts/shi94good.pdf`. They used a different scoring function to improve the overall quality. Using this method, we can find the N strongest corners in the given image. This is very useful when we don't want to use every single corner to extract information from the image. As we discussed, a good interest point detector is very useful in applications such as object tracking, object recognition, and image search.

If you apply the Shi-Tomasi corner detector to an image, you will see something like this:

As we can see here, all the important points in the frame are captured. Let's look at the code to track these features:

```
int main(int argc, char* argv[])
{
    // Variable declaration and initialization
    // Iterate until the user presses the Esc key
    while(true)
    {
        // Capture the current frame
        cap >> frame;
        // Resize the frame
        resize(frame, frame, Size(), scalingFactor, scalingFactor,
INTER_AREA);
        // Convert to grayscale
        cvtColor(frame, frameGray, COLOR_BGR2GRAY );
        // Initialize the parameters for Shi-Tomasi algorithm
        vector<Point2f> corners;
        double qualityThreshold = 0.02;
        double minDist = 15;
        int blockSize = 5;
```

```
bool useHarrisDetector = false;
double k = 0.07;
// Clone the input frame
Mat frameCopy;
frameCopy = frame.clone();
// Apply corner detection
goodFeaturesToTrack(frameGray, corners, numCorners,
qualityThreshold, minDist, Mat(), blockSize, useHarrisDetector, k);
```

As we can see, we extracted the frame and used goodFeaturesToTrack to detect the corners. It's important to understand that the number of corners detected will depend on our choice of parameters. You can find a detailed explanation at http://docs.opencv.org/2.4/modules/imgproc/doc/feature_detection.html?highlight=goodfeaturestotrack#goodfeaturestotrack. Let's go ahead and draw circles on these points to display the output image:

```
// Parameters for the circles to display the corners
int radius = 8;       // radius of the circles
int thickness = 2;    // thickness of the circles
int lineType = 8;
// Draw the detected corners using circles
for(size_t i = 0; i < corners.size(); i++)
{
    Scalar color = Scalar(rng.uniform(0,255), rng.uniform(0,255),
rng.uniform(0,255));
        circle(frameCopy, corners[i], radius, color, thickness,
lineType, 0);
}
/// Show what you got
imshow(windowName, frameCopy);
// Get the keyboard input and check if it's 'Esc'
// 27 -> ASCII value of 'Esc' key
ch = waitKey(30);
if (ch == 27) {
    break;
}
}
// Release the video capture object
cap.release();
// Close all windows
destroyAllWindows();
return 1;
}
```

This program takes an input argument: `numCorners`. This value indicates the maximum number of corners you want to track. Start with a value of `100` and play around with it to see what happens. If you increase this value, you will see more feature points getting detected.

Feature-based tracking

Feature-based tracking refers to tracking individual feature points across successive frames in the video. The advantage here is that we don't have to detect feature points in every single frame. We can just detect them once and keep tracking them after that. This is more efficient than running the detector on every frame. We use a technique called optical flow to track these features. Optical flow is one of the most popular techniques in computer vision. We choose a bunch of feature points and track them through the video stream. When we detect the feature points, we compute the displacement vectors and show the motion of those keypoints between consecutive frames. These vectors are called motion vectors. A motion vector for a particular point is basically just a directional line indicating where that point has moved, as compared to the previous frame. Different methods are used to detect these motion vectors. The two most popular algorithms are the **Lucas-Kanade** method and the **Farneback** algorithm.

Lucas-Kanade method

The Lucas-Kanade method is used for sparse optical flow tracking. By sparse, we mean that the number of feature points is relatively low. You can refer to their original paper here: `http://cseweb.ucsd.edu/classes/sp02/cse252/lucaskanade81.pdf`. We start the process by extracting the feature points. For each feature point, we create 3 x 3 patches with the feature point at the center. The assumption here is that all the points within each patch will have a similar motion. We can adjust the size of this window depending on the problem at hand.

For each feature point in the current frame, we take the surrounding 3 x 3 patch as our reference point. For this patch, we look in its neighborhood in the previous frame to get the best match. This neighborhood is usually bigger than 3 x 3 because we want to get the patch that's closest to the patch under consideration. Now, the path from the center pixel of the matched patch in the previous frame to the center pixel of the patch under consideration in the current frame will become the motion vector. We do that for all the feature points and extract all the motion vectors.

Let's consider the following frame:

We need to add some points that we want to track. Just go ahead and click on a bunch of points on this window with your mouse:

If I move into a different position, you will see that the points are still being tracked correctly within a small margin of error:

Let's add a lot of points and see what happens:

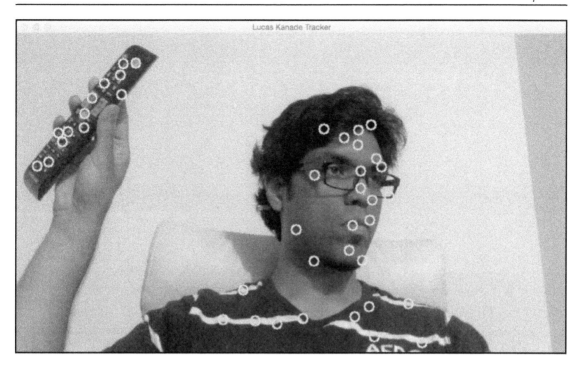

As we can see, it will keep tracking those points. But, you will notice that some of the points will be dropped because of factors such as prominence or speed of movement. If you want to play around with it, you can just keep adding more points to it. You can also let the user select a region of interest in the input video. You can then extract feature points from this region of interest and track the object by drawing a bounding box. It will be a fun exercise!

Here is the code to do Lucas-Kanade-based tracking:

```
int main(int argc, char* argv[])
{
    // Variable declaration and initialization
    // Iterate until the user hits the Esc key
    while(true)
    {
        // Capture the current frame
        cap >> frame;
        // Check if the frame is empty
        if(frame.empty())
            break;
        // Resize the frame
        resize(frame, frame, Size(), scalingFactor, scalingFactor,
INTER_AREA);
        // Copy the input frame
```

```
        frame.copyTo(image);
        // Convert the image to grayscale
        cvtColor(image, curGrayImage, COLOR_BGR2GRAY);
        // Check if there are points to track
        if(!trackingPoints[0].empty())
        {
            // Status vector to indicate whether the flow for the
corresponding features has been found
            vector<uchar> statusVector;
            // Error vector to indicate the error for the corresponding
feature
            vector<float> errorVector;
            // Check if previous image is empty
            if(prevGrayImage.empty())
            {
                curGrayImage.copyTo(prevGrayImage);
            }
            // Calculate the optical flow using Lucas-Kanade algorithm
            calcOpticalFlowPyrLK(prevGrayImage, curGrayImage,
trackingPoints[0], trackingPoints[1], statusVector, errorVector,
windowSize, 3, terminationCriteria, 0, 0.001);
```

We use the current image and the previous image to compute the optical flow information. Needless to say, the quality of the output will depend on the parameters chosen. You can find more details about the parameters at http://docs.opencv.org/2.4/modules/video/doc/motion_analysis_and_object_tracking.html#calcopticalflowpyrlk. To increase quality and robustness, we need to filter out the points that are very close to each other because they're not adding new information. Let's go ahead and do that:

```
        int count = 0;
        // Minimum distance between any two tracking points
        int minDist = 7;
        for(int i=0; i < trackingPoints[1].size(); i++)
        {
            if(pointTrackingFlag)
            {
                // If the new point is within 'minDist' distance from
an existing point, it will not be tracked
                if(norm(currentPoint - trackingPoints[1][i]) <=
minDist)
                {
                    pointTrackingFlag = false;
                    continue;
                }
            }
            // Check if the status vector is good
```

```
        if(!statusVector[i])
            continue;
        trackingPoints[1][count++] = trackingPoints[1][i];

        // Draw a filled circle for each of the tracking points
        int radius = 8;
        int thickness = 2;
        int lineType = 8;
        circle(image, trackingPoints[1][i], radius,
Scalar(0,255,0), thickness, lineType);
        }
        trackingPoints[1].resize(count);
    }
```

We now have the tracking points. The next step is to refine the location of those points. What exactly does **refine** mean in this context? To increase the speed of computation, there is some level of quantization involved. In layman's terms, you can think of it as rounding off. Now that we have the approximate region, we can refine the location of the point within that region to get a more accurate outcome. Let's go ahead and do that:

```
        // Refining the location of the feature points
        if(pointTrackingFlag && trackingPoints[1].size() < maxNumPoints)
        {
            vector<Point2f> tempPoints;
            tempPoints.push_back(currentPoint);
            // Function to refine the location of the corners to subpixel
accuracy.
            // Here, 'pixel' refers to the image patch of size 'windowSize'
and not the actual image pixel
            cornerSubPix(curGrayImage, tempPoints, windowSize, Size(-1,-1),
terminationCriteria);
            trackingPoints[1].push_back(tempPoints[0]);
            pointTrackingFlag = false;
        }
        // Display the image with the tracking points
        imshow(windowName, image);
        // Check if the user pressed the Esc key
        char ch = waitKey(10);
        if(ch == 27)
            break;
        // Swap the 'points' vectors to update 'previous' to 'current'
        std::swap(trackingPoints[1], trackingPoints[0]);
        // Swap the images to update previous image to current image
        cv::swap(prevGrayImage, curGrayImage);
    }
    return 1;
}
```

Farneback algorithm

Gunnar Farneback proposed this optical flow algorithm and it's used for dense tracking. Dense tracking is used extensively in robotics, augmented reality, and 3D mapping. You can check out the original paper here: `http://www.diva-portal.org/smash/get/diva2:273847/FULLTEXT01.pdf`. The Lucas-Kanade method is a sparse technique, which means that we only need to process some pixels in the entire image. The Farneback algorithm, on the other hand, is a dense technique that requires us to process all the pixels in the given image. So, obviously, there is a trade-off here. Dense techniques are more accurate, but they are slower. Sparse techniques are less accurate, but they are faster. For real-time applications, people tend to prefer sparse techniques. For applications where time and complexity are not a factor, people tend to prefer dense techniques to extract finer details.

In his paper, Farneback describes a method for dense optical-flow estimation based on polynomial expansion for two frames. Our goal is to estimate the motion between these two frames, which is basically a three-step process. In the first step, each neighborhood in both frames is approximated by polynomials. In this case, we are only interested in quadratic polynomials. The next step is to construct a new signal by global displacement. Now that each neighborhood is approximated by a polynomial, we need to see what happens if this polynomial undergoes an ideal translation. The last step is to compute the global displacement by equating the coefficients in the yields of these quadratic polynomials.

Now, how this is feasible? If you think about it, we are assuming that an entire signal is a single polynomial and there is a global translation relating the two signals. This is not a realistic scenario! So, what are we looking for? Well, our goal is to find out whether these errors are small enough so that we can build a useful algorithm that can track the features.

Let's look at a static image:

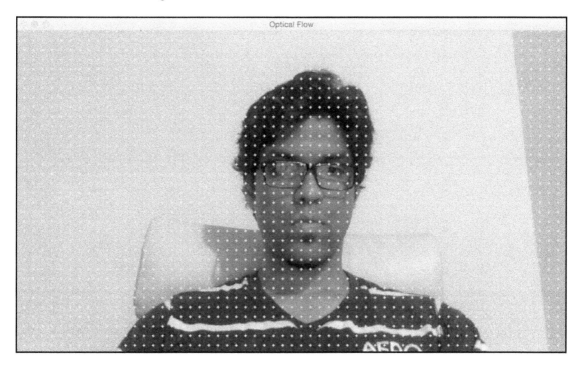

If I move sideways, we can see that the motion vectors are pointing in a horizontal direction. It is simply tracking the movement of my head:

If I move away from the webcam, you can see that the motion vectors are pointing in a direction perpendicular to the image plane:

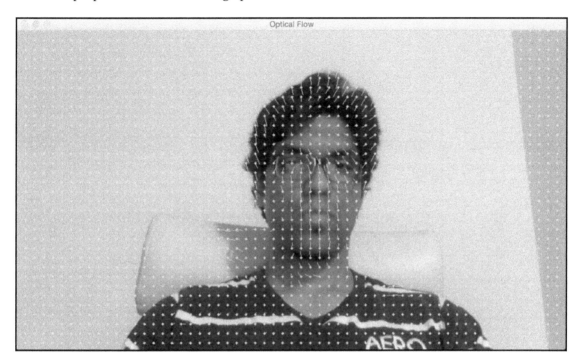

Here is the code to do optical-flow-based tracking using the Farneback algorithm:

```
int main(int, char** argv)
{
    // Variable declaration and initialization
    // Iterate until the user presses the Esc key
    while(true)
    {
        // Capture the current frame
        cap >> frame;
        if(frame.empty())
            break;
        // Resize the frame
        resize(frame, frame, Size(), scalingFactor, scalingFactor,
INTER_AREA);
        // Convert to grayscale
        cvtColor(frame, curGray, COLOR_BGR2GRAY);
        // Check if the image is valid
        if(prevGray.data)
        {
```

```
                    // Initialize parameters for the optical flow algorithm
                    float pyrScale = 0.5;
                    int numLevels = 3;
                    int windowSize = 15;
                    int numIterations = 3;
                    int neighborhoodSize = 5;
                    float stdDeviation = 1.2;
                    // Calculate optical flow map using Farneback algorithm
                    calcOpticalFlowFarneback(prevGray, curGray, flowImage,
        pyrScale, numLevels, windowSize, numIterations, neighborhoodSize,
        stdDeviation, OPTFLOW_USE_INITIAL_FLOW);
```

As we can see, we use the Farneback algorithm to compute the optical flow vectors. The input parameters to `calcOpticalFlowFarneback` are important when it comes to the quality of tracking. You can find details about those parameters at `http://docs.opencv.org/3.0-beta/modules/video/doc/motion_analysis_and_object _tracking.html`. Let's go ahead and draw those vectors on the output image:

```
                    // Convert to 3-channel RGB
                    cvtColor(prevGray, flowImageGray, COLOR_GRAY2BGR);
                    // Draw the optical flow map
                    drawOpticalFlow(flowImage, flowImageGray);
                    // Display the output image
                    imshow(windowName, flowImageGray);
                }
                // Break out of the loop if the user presses the Esc key
                ch = waitKey(10);
                if(ch == 27)
                    break;
                // Swap previous image with the current image
                std::swap(prevGray, curGray);
            }
            return 1;
        }
```

We used a function called `drawOpticalFlow` to draw those optical flow vectors. These vectors indicate the direction of motion. Let's look at the function to see how we draw those vectors:

```
    // Function to compute the optical flow map
    void drawOpticalFlow(const Mat& flowImage, Mat& flowImageGray)
    {
        int stepSize = 16;
        Scalar color = Scalar(0, 255, 0);
        // Draw the uniform grid of points on the input image along with the
    motion vectors
        for(int y = 0; y < flowImageGray.rows; y += stepSize)
```

```
    {
        for(int x = 0; x < flowImageGray.cols; x += stepSize)
        {
            // Circles to indicate the uniform grid of points
            int radius = 2;
            int thickness = -1;
            circle(flowImageGray, Point(x,y), radius, color, thickness);
            // Lines to indicate the motion vectors
            Point2f pt = flowImage.at<Point2f>(y, x);
            line(flowImageGray, Point(x,y), Point(cvRound(x+pt.x),
cvRound(y+pt.y)), color);
        }
    }
}
```

Summary

In this chapter, we learned about object tracking. We learned how to use HSV colorspace to track objects of a specific color. We discussed clustering techniques for object tracking and how we can build an interactive object tracker using the CAMShift algorithm. We looked at corner detectors and how we can track corners in a live video. We discussed how to track features in a video using optical flow. Finally, we understood the concepts behind the Lucas-Kanade and Farneback algorithms and then implemented them.

In the next chapter, we are going to discuss segmentation algorithms and how we can use them for text recognition.

10
Developing Segmentation Algorithms for Text Recognition

In the previous chapters, we learned about a wide range of image processing techniques such as thresholding, contours descriptors, and mathematical morphology. In this chapter, we will discuss common problems that you may face while dealing with scanned documents, such as identifying where the text is or adjusting its rotation. We will also learn how to combine techniques presented in the previous chapters to solve those problems. By the end of this chapter, we will have segmented regions of text that can be sent to an **optical character recognition** (**OCR**) library.

By the end of this chapter, you should be able to answer the following questions:

- What kind of OCR applications exists?
- What are the common problems while writing an OCR application?
- How do I identify regions of documents?
- How do I deal with problems like skewing and other elements in the middle of the text?
- How do I use Tesseract OCR to identify my text?

Technical requirements

This chapter requires familiarity with the basic C++ programming language. All of the code that's used in this chapter can be downloaded from the following GitHub link:`https://github.com/PacktPublishing/Learn-OpenCV-4-By-Building-Projects-Second-Edition/tree/master/Chapter_10`. The code can be executed on any operating system, though it has only been tested on Ubuntu.

Check out the following video to see the Code in Action:
`http://bit.ly/2KIoJFX`

Introducing optical character recognition

Identifying text in an image is a very popular application for computer vision. This process is commonly called **optical character recognition**, and is divided as follows:

- **Text preprocessing and segmentation**: During this step, the computer must deal with image noise, and rotation (skewing), and identify what areas are candidate text.
- **Text identification**: This is the process of identifying each letter in text. Although this is also a computer vision topic, we will not show how you to do this in this book purely using OpenCV. Instead, we will show you how to use the Tesseract library to do this step, since it was integrated in OpenCV 3.0. If you are interested in learning how to do what Tesseract does by yourself, take a look at Packt's *Mastering OpenCV* book, which presents a chapter on car plate recognition.

The preprocessing and segmentation phase can vary greatly depending on the source of the text. Let's take a look at common situations where preprocessing is done:

- **Production OCR applications with a scanner**: This is a very reliable source of text. In this scenario, the background of the image is usually white and the document is almost aligned with the scanner margins. The content that's being scanned contains basically text, with almost no noise. This kind of application relies on simple preprocessing techniques that can adjust text quickly and maintain a fast scanning pace. When writing production OCR software, it is common to delegate the identification of important text regions to the user, and create a quality pipeline for text verification and indexing.

- **Scanning text in a casually taken picture or in a video**: This is a much more complex scenario, since there's no indication of where the text can be. This scenario is called **scene text recognition**, and OpenCV 4.0 contains a contrib library to deal with it. We will cover this in `Chapter 11`, *Text Recognition with Tesseract*. Usually, the preprocessor will use texture analysis techniques to identify the text patterns.

- **Creating a production quality OCR for historical texts**: Historical texts are also scanned, but they have several additional problems, such as noise that's created by the old paper color and the use of ink. Other common problems are decorated letters and specific text fonts, and low contrast content that's created by ink that is erased over time. It's not uncommon to write specific OCR software for the documents at hand.

- **Scanning maps, diagrams, and charts**: Maps, diagrams, and charts pose an especially difficult scenario since the text is usually in any orientation and in the middle of image content. For example, city names are often clustered, and ocean names often follow country shore contour lines. Some charts are heavily colored, with text appearing in both clear and dark tones.

OCR application strategies also vary according to the objective of the identification. Will it be used for a full text search? Or should the text be separated into logical fields to index a database with information for a structured search?

In this chapter, we will focus on preprocessing scanned text, or text that's been photographed by a camera. We'll consider that the text is the main purpose of the image, such as in a photographed piece of paper or card, for example, in this parking ticket:

We'll try to remove common noise, deal with text rotation (if any), and crop the possible text regions. While most OCR APIs already do these things automatically – and probably with state-of-the-art algorithms—it is still worth knowing how things happen under the hood. This will allow you to better understand most OCR APIs parameters and will give you better knowledge about the potential OCR problems you may face.

Preprocessing stage

Software that identifies letters does so by comparing text with previously recorded data. Classification results can be improved greatly if the input text is clear, if the letters are in a vertical position, and if there's no other elements, such as images sent to the classification software. In this section, we'll learn how to adjust text by using **preprocessing**.

Thresholding the image

We usually start preprocessing by thresholding the image. This eliminates all color information. Most OpenCV functions consider information to be written in white, and the background to be black. So, let's start by creating a threshold function to match this criteria:

```
#include opencv2/opencv.hpp;
#include vector;

using namespace std;
using namespace cv;

Mat binarize(Mat input)
{
    //Uses otsu to threshold the input image
    Mat binaryImage;
    cvtColor(input, input, COLOR_BGR2GRAY);
    threshold(input, binaryImage, 0, 255, THRESH_OTSU);

    //Count the number of black and white pixels
    int white = countNonZero(binaryImage);
    int black = binaryImage.size().area() - white;

    //If the image is mostly white (white background), invert it
    return white black ? binaryImage : ~binaryImage;
}
```

The `binarize` function applies a threshold, similar to what we did in `Chapter 4`, *Delving into Histogram and Filters*. But here, we will use the Otsu method by passing `THRESH_OTSU` in the fourth parameter of the function. The Otsu method maximizes inter-class variance. Since a threshold creates only two classes (the black and white pixels), this is the same as minimizing the intraclass variance. This method works using the image histogram. Then, it iterates through all the possible threshold values and calculates the spread for the pixel values for each side of the threshold, that is, the pixels that are either in the background or in the foreground of the image. The purpose of this process is to find the threshold value where the sum of both spreads are at their minimum.

After the thresholding is done, the function counts how many white pixels are in the image. The black pixels are simply the total number of pixels in the image, given by the image area, minus the white pixel count. Since text is usually written over a plain background, we will verify whether there are more white pixels than there are black pixels. In this case, we are dealing with black text over a white background, so we will invert the image for further processing.

The result of the thresholding process with the parking ticket image is as follows:

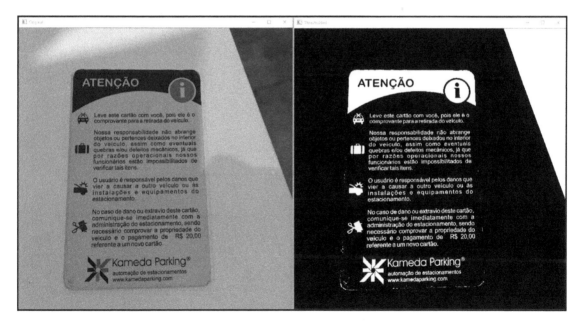

Text segmentation

The next step is to find where the text is located and extract it. There are two common strategies for this:

- **Using connected component analysis**: Searching groups of connected pixels in the image. This will be the technique that will be used in this chapter.
- **Use classifiers to search for a previously trained letter texture pattern**: with texture features such as **Haralick** features, wavelet transforms are often used. Anther option is to identify **maximally stable extremal regions** (**MSER**s) in this task. This approach is more robust for text in a complex background and will be studied in Chapter 11, *Text Recognition with Tesseract*. You can read about Haralick features at his own website, which can be found at http://haralick.org/journals/TexturalFeatures.pdf.

Creating connected areas

If you take a closer look at the image, you'll notice that the letters are always together in blocks, formed by text paragraphs. That leaves us with the question, how do we detect and remove these blocks?

The first step is to make these blocks even more evident. We can do this by using the dilation morphological operator. Recall from Chapter 8, *Video Surveillance, Background Modeling, and Morphological Operations*, that dilation makes the image elements thicker. Let's look at a small code snippet that does the trick:

```
auto kernel = getStructuringElement(MORPH_CROSS, Size(3,3));
Mat dilated;
dilate(input, dilated, kernel, cv::Point(-1, -1), 5);
imshow("Dilated", dilated);
```

In the preceding code, we start by creating a 3 x 3 cross kernel that will be used in the morphological operation. Then, we apply dilation five times, centered on this kernel. The exact kernel size and number of times vary according to the situation. Just make sure that the values glue all of the letters in the same line together.

The result of this operation is presented in the following screenshot:

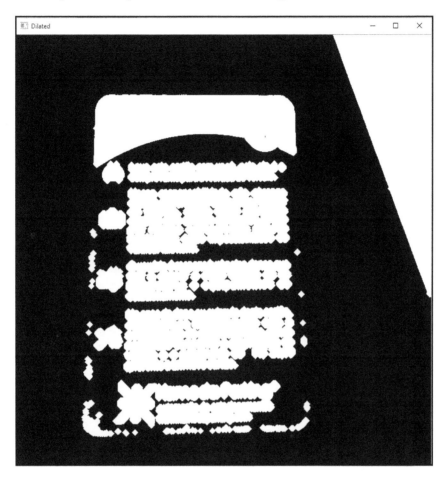

Notice that we now have huge white blocks. They match exactly with each paragraph of text, and also match with other non-textual elements, like images or the border noise.

> The ticket image that comes with the code is a low resolution image. OCR engines usually work with high resolution images (200 or 300 DPI), so it may be necessary to apply dilation more than five times.

Identifying paragraph blocks

The next step is to perform connect component analysis to find blocks that correspond with paragraphs. OpenCV has a function for this, which we previously used in Chapter 5, *Automated Optical Inspection, Object Segmentation, and Detection*. This is the findContours function:

```
vector;vector;Point;contours;
findContours(dilated, contours, RETR_EXTERNAL, CHAIN_APPROX_SIMPLE);
```

In the first parameter, we pass our dilated image. The second parameter is the vector of detected contours. Then, we use the option to retrieve only external contours and to use simple approximation. The image contours are presented as follows. Each tone of gray represents a different contour:

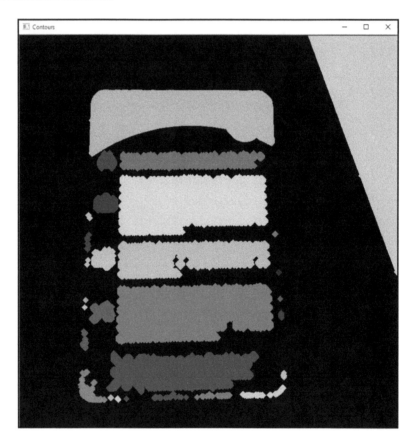

The last step is to identify the minimum rotated bounding rectangle of each contour. OpenCV provides a handy function for this operation called `minAreaRect`. This function receives a vector of arbitrary points and returns a `RoundedRect` containing the bounding box. This is also a good opportunity to discard unwanted rectangles, that is, rectangles that are obviously not text. Since we are making software for OCR, we'll assume that the text contains a group of letters. With this assumption, we'll discard text in the following situations:

- The rectangle width or size is too small, that is, smaller than 20 pixels. This will help discard border noises and other small artifacts.
- The rectangle of the image has a width/height proportion smaller than two. That is, rectangles that resemble a square, such as the image icons, or are much taller, will also be discarded.

There's a little caveat in the second condition. Since we are dealing with rotated bounding boxes, we must test whether the bounding box angle is smaller than -45 degrees. If it is, the text is vertically rotated, so the proportion that we must take into account is height/width.

Let's check this out by looking at the following code:

```
//For each contour

vector;RotatedRect; areas;
for (const auto& contour : contours)
{
    //Find it's rotated rect
    auto box = minAreaRect(contour);

    //Discard very small boxes
    if (box.size.width 20 || box.size.height 20)
        continue;

    //Discard squares shaped boxes and boxes
    //higher than larger
    double proportion = box.angle -45.0 ?
        box.size.height / box.size.width :
        box.size.width / box.size.height;

    if (proportion 2)
        continue;

    //Add the box
    areas.push_back(box);
}
```

Let's see which boxes this algorithm selected:

That's certainly a good result!

We should notice that the algorithm described in step 2, in the preceding code, will also discard single letters. This is not a big issue since we are creating an OCR preprocessor, and single symbols are usually meaningless with context information; one example of such a case is the page numbers. The page numbers will be discarded with this process since they usually appear alone at the bottom of the page, and the size and proportion of the text will also be disturbed. But this will not be a problem, since after the text passes through the OCR, you will end up with a huge amount of text files with no page division at all.

We'll place all of this code in a function with the following signature:

```
vector RotatedRect; findTextAreas(Mat input)
```

Text extraction and skewing adjustment

Now, all we must do is extract the text and adjust the text skew. This is done by the deskewAndCrop function, as follows:

```
Mat deskewAndCrop(Mat input, const RotatedRect& box)
{
    double angle = box.angle;
    auto size = box.size;

    //Adjust the box angle
    if (angle -45.0)
    {
        angle += 90.0;
         std::swap(size.width, size.height);
    }
    //Rotate the text according to the angle
    auto transform = getRotationMatrix2D(box.center, angle, 1.0);
    Mat rotated;
    warpAffine(input, rotated, transform, input.size(), INTER_CUBIC);

    //Crop the result
    Mat cropped;
    getRectSubPix(rotated, size, box.center, cropped);
    copyMakeBorder(cropped,cropped,10,10,10,10,BORDER_CONSTANT,Scalar(0));
    return cropped;
}
```

First, we start by reading the desired region angle and size. As we saw earlier, the angle may be less than -45 degrees. This means that the text is vertically aligned, so we must add 90 degrees to the rotation angle and switch the width and height properties. Next, we need to rotate the text. First, we start by creating a 2D affine transformation matrix that describes the rotation. We do so by using the `getRotationMatrix2D` OpenCV function. This function takes three parameters:

- **CENTER**: The central position of the rotation. The rotation will pivot around this center. In our case, we use the box center.
- **ANGLE**: The rotation angle. If the angle is negative, the rotation will occur in a clockwise direction.
- **SCALE**: The isotropic scale factor. We will use `1.0` since we want to keep the box's original scale untouched.

The rotation itself is made by using the `warpAffine` function. This function takes four mandatory arguments:

- **SRC**: The input `mat` array to be transformed.
- **DST**: The destination `mat` array.
- **M**: A transformation matrix. This matrix is a 2 x 3 affine transformation matrix. This may be a translation, scale, or rotation matrix. In our case, we will just use the matrix we recently created.
- **SIZE**: The size of the output image. We will generate an image that's the same size as our input image.

The following are another three optional arguments:

- **FLAGS**: These indicate how the image should be interpolated. We use `BICUBIC_INTERPOLATION` for better quality. The default is `LINEAR_INTERPOLATION`.
- **BORDER**: Border mode. We use the default, `BORDER_CONSTANT`.
- **BORDER VALUE**: The color of the border. We use the default, which is black. Then, we use the `getRectSubPix` function. After we rotate our image, we need to crop the rectangle area of our bounding box. This function takes four mandatory arguments and one optional argument, and returns the cropped image:
  - **IMAGE**: The image to crop.
  - **SIZE**: A `cv::Size` object describing the width and height of the box to be cropped.

- **CENTER**: The central pixel of the area to be cropped. Notice that since we rotated around the center, this point is conveniently the same.
- **PATCH**: The destination image.
- **PATCH_TYPE**: The depth of the destination image. We use the default value, representing the same depth of the source image.

The final step is done by the `copyMakeBorder` function. This function adds a border around the image. This is important, since the classification stage usually expects a margin around the text. The function parameters are very simple: the input and output images, the border thickness at the top, bottom, left, and right, the border type, and the color of the new border.

For the card image, the following images will be generated:

Now, it's time to put every function together. Let's present the main method that does the following:

- Loads the ticket image
- Calls our binarization function
- Find all text regions
- Shows each region in a window

We will present the main method as follows:

```
int main(int argc, char* argv[])
{
    //Loads the ticket image and binarize it
    auto ticket = binarize(imread("ticket.png"));
    auto regions = findTextAreas(ticket);
    //For each region
    for (const auto& region : regions) {
        //Crop
        auto cropped = deskewAndCrop(ticket, region);

        //Show
        imshow("Cropped text", cropped);
        waitKey(0);
        destroyWindow("Border Skew");
    }
}
```

For the complete source code, take a look at the segment.cpp file that comes with this book.

Installing Tesseract OCR on your operating system

Tesseract is an open source OCR engine that was originally developed by Hewlett-Packard Laboratories Bristol and Hewlett-Packard Co. All of its code is licensed under the Apache License and hosted on GitHub at `https://github.com/tesseract-ocr`. It is considered one of the most accurate OCR engines available: it can read a wide variety of image formats and can convert text written in more than 60 languages. In this session, we will teach you how to install Tesseract on Windows or Mac. Since there's lots of Linux distributions, we will not teach you how to install it on this operating system. Normally, Tesseract offers installation packages in your package repository, so, before compiling Tesseract yourself, just search for it there.

Installing Tesseract on Windows

Tesseract uses the **C++ Archive Network** (**CPPAN**) as its dependency manager. To install Tesseract, follow these steps.

Building the latest library

1. Download the latest CPPAN client from `https://cppan.org/client/`.
2. In the command line, run
   `cppan --build pvt.cppan.demo.google.tesseract.tesseract-master`.

Setting up Tesseract in Visual Studio

1. Set up `vcpkg`, the Visual C++ Package Manager, at `https://github.com/Microsoft/vcpkg`.
2. For a 64-bit compilation, use `vcpkg install tesseract:x64-windows`. You may also add `--head` for the master branch.

Static linking

It's also possible to static link (`https://github.com/tesseract-ocr/tesseract/wiki/Compiling#static-linking`) Tesseract in your project. This will avoid `dlls` to be packaged with your executable files. To do this, use `vcpkg`, like we did previously, with the following command for a 32-bit installation:

```
vcpkg install tesseract:x86-windows-static
```

Alternatively, you can use the following command for a 64-bit installation:

```
vckpg install tesseract:x64-windows-static
```

Installing Tesseract on Mac

The easiest way to install Tesseract OCR on Mac is using **Homebrew**. If you don't have Homebrew installed, just go to Homebrew's site (`http://brew.sh/`), open your console, and run the **Ruby script** that is on the front page. You may be required to type in your administrator password.

After Homebrew is installed, just type in the following:

```
brew install tesseract
```

The English language is already included in this installation. If you want to install other language packs, just run the following command:

```
brew install tesseract --all-languages
```

This will install all of the language packs. Then, just go to the Tesseract installation directory and delete any unwanted languages. Homebrew usually installs stuff in the `/usr/local/` directory.

Using the Tesseract OCR library

While Tesseract OCR is already integrated with OpenCV 3.0, it's still worth studying its API since it allows for finer grained control over Tesseract parameters. This integration will be studied in `Chapter 11`, *Text Recognition with Tesseract*.

Creating an OCR function

We'll change the previous example to work with Tesseract. Start by adding
`tesseract/baseapi.h` and `fstream` to the `include` list:

```
#include opencv2/opencv.hpp;
#include tesseract/baseapi.h;

#include vector;
#include fstream;
```

Then, we'll create a global `TessBaseAPI` object that represents our Tesseract OCR engine:

```
tesseract::TessBaseAPI ocr;
```

The `ocr` engine is completely self-contained. If you want to create a multi-threaded piece of OCR software, just add a different `TessBaseAPI` object in each thread, and the execution will be fairly thread-safe. You just need to guarantee that file writing is not done over the same file, otherwise you'll need to guarantee safety for this operation.

Next, we will create a function called **identify text** (`identifyText`) that will run the `ocr`:

```
const char* identifyText(Mat input, const char* language = "eng")
{
    ocr.Init(NULL, language, tesseract::OEM_TESSERACT_ONLY);
    ocr.SetPageSegMode(tesseract::PSM_SINGLE_BLOCK);
    ocr.SetImage(input.data, input.cols, input.rows, 1, input.step);
    const char* text = ocr.GetUTF8Text();
    cout  "Text:"  endl;
    cout  text  endl;
    cout  "Confidence: "  ocr.MeanTextConf() endl;
     // Get the text
    return text;
}
```

Let's explain this function line-by-line. In the first line, we start by initializing `tesseract`. This is done by calling the `Init` function. This function has the following signature:

```
int Init(const char* datapath, const char* language,
  OcrEngineMode oem)
```

Let's explain each parameter:

- `datapath`: This is the path to the root directory of `tessdata` files. The path must end with a backslash / character. The `tessdata` directory contains the language files that you installed. Passing `NULL` to this parameter will make `tesseract` search its installation directory, which is the location that this folder is normally present in. It's common to change this value to `args[0]` when deploying an application, and include the `tessdata` folder in your application path.

- `language`: This is a three letter word for the language code (for example, eng for English, por for Portuguese, or hin for Hindi). Tesseract supports loading multiple language codes by using the + sign. Therefore, passing `eng+por` will load both the English and Portuguese languages. Of course, you can only use languages you have previously installed, otherwise the loading process will fail. A language config file may specify that two or more languages must be loaded together. To prevent that, you may use a tilde ~. For example, you can use `hin+~eng` to guarantee that English is not loaded with Hindi, even if it is configured to do so.

- `OcrEngineMode`: These are the OCR algorithms that will be used. It can have one of the following values:
    - `OEM_TESSERACT_ONLY`: Uses just `tesseract`. It's the fastest method, but it also has less precision.
    - `OEM_CUBE_ONLY`: Uses the Cube engine. It's slower, but more precise. This will only work if your language was trained to support this engine mode. To check if that's the case, look for `.cube` files for your language in the `tessdata` folder. The support for English language is guaranteed.
    - `OEM_TESSERACT_CUBE_COMBINED`: This combines both Tesseract and Cube to achieve the best possible OCR classification. This engine has the best accuracy and the slowest execution time.
    - `OEM_DEFAULT`: This infers the strategy based on the language config file, command-line config file or, in the absence of both, uses `OEM_TESSERACT_ONLY`.

It's important to emphasize that the `Init` function can be executed many times. If a different language or engine mode is provided, Tesseract will clear the previous configuration and start again. If the same parameters are provided, Tesseract is smart enough to simply ignore the command. The `init` function returns 0 in case of success and −1 in case of failure.

Our program will then proceed by setting the page segmentation mode:

```
ocr.SetPageSegMode(tesseract::PSM_SINGLE_BLOCK);
```

There are several segmentation modes available:

- PSM_OSD_ONLY: Using this mode, Tesseract will just run its preprocessing algorithms to detect orientation and script detection.
- PSM_AUTO_OSD: This tells Tesseract to do automatic page segmentation with orientation and script detection.
- PSM_AUTO_ONLY: This does page segmentation, but avoids doing orientation, script detection, or OCR.
- PSM_AUTO: This does page segmentation and OCR, but avoids doing orientation or script detection.
- PSM_SINGLE_COLUMN: This assumes that the text of variable sizes is displayed in a single column.
- PSM_SINGLE_BLOCK_VERT_TEXT: This treats the image as a single uniform block of vertically aligned text.
- PSM_SINGLE_BLOCK: This assumes a single block of text, and is the default configuration. We will use this flag since our preprocessing phase guarantees this condition.
- PSM_SINGLE_LINE: Indicates that the image contains only one line of text.
- PSM_SINGLE_WORD: Indicates that the image contains just one word.
- PSM_SINGLE_WORD_CIRCLE: Informs us that the image is a just one word disposed in a circle.
- PSM_SINGLE_CHAR: Indicates that the image contains a single character.

Notice that Tesseract already has **deskewing** and text segmentation algorithms implemented, just like most OCR libraries do. But it's interesting to know of such algorithms since you may provide your own preprocessing phase for specific needs. This allows you to improve text detection in many cases. For example, if you are creating an OCR application for old documents, the default threshold used by Tesseract may create a dark background. Tesseract may also be confused by borders or severe text skewing.

Next, we call the SetImage method with the following signature:

```
void SetImage(const unsigned char* imagedata, int width,
  int height, int bytes_per_pixel, int bytes_per_line);
```

The parameters are almost self-explanatory, and most of them can be read directly from our `Mat` object:

- `data`: A raw byte array containing image data. OpenCV contains a function called `data()` in the `Mat` class that provides a direct pointer to the data.
- `width`: Image width.
- `height`: Image height.
- `bytes_per_pixel`: Number of bytes per pixel. We are using 1, since we are dealing with a binary image. If you want the code to be more generic, you could also use the `Mat::elemSize()` function, which provides the same information.
- `bytes_per_line`: Number of bytes in a single line. We are using the `Mat::step` property since some images add trailing bytes.

Then, we call `GetUTF8Text` to run the recognition itself. The recognized text is returned, encoded with UTF8 and without BOM. Before returning it, we also print some debug information.

`MeanTextConf` returns a confidence index, which may by a number from 0 to 100:

```
auto text = ocr.GetUTF8Text();
cout   "Text:"   endl;
cout   text   endl;
cout   "Confidence: "   ocr.MeanTextConf()   endl;
```

Sending the output to a file

Let's change our main method to send the recognized output to a file. We do this by using a standard `ofstream`:

```
int main(int argc, char* argv[])
{
   //Loads the ticket image and binarize it
   Mat ticket = binarize(imread("ticket.png"));
   auto regions = findTextAreas(ticket);

   std::ofstream file;
   file.open("ticket.txt", std::ios::out | std::ios::binary);

   //For each region
   for (const auto& region : regions) {
       //Crop
       auto cropped = deskewAndCrop(ticket, region);
       auto text = identifyText(cropped, "por");
```

```
        file.write(text, strlen(text));
        file endl;
    }
    file.close();
}
```

The following line opens the file in binary mode:

```
file.open("ticket.txt", std::ios::out | std::ios::binary);
```

This is important since Tesseract returns text encoded in UTF-8, taking into account special characters that are available in Unicode. We also write the output directly using the following command:

```
file.write(text, strlen(text));
```

In this sample, we called the `identify` function using Portuguese as an input language (this is the language the ticket was written in). You may use another photo, if you like.

The complete source file is provided in the `segmentOcr.cpp` file, which comes with this book.

`ticket.png` is a low resolution image, since we imagined you would want to display a window with the image while studying this code. For this image, the Tesseract results are rather poor. If you want to test with a higher resolution image, the code for this book provides you with a `ticketHigh.png` image. To test with this image, change the dilation repetitions to `12` and the minimum box size from `20` to `60`. You'll get a much higher confidence rate (about 87%), and the resulting text will be almost fully readable. The `segmentOcrHigh.cpp` file contains these modifications.

Summary

In this chapter, we presented a brief introduction to OCR applications. We saw that the preprocessing phase of such systems must be adjusted according to the type of document we are planning to identify. We have learned about common operations while preprocessing text files, such as thresholding, cropping, skewing, and text region segmentation. Finally, we learned how to install and use Tesseract OCR to convert our image into text.

In the next chapter, we'll use a more sophisticated OCR technique to identify text in a casually taken picture or video –a situation known as scene text recognition. This is a much more complex scenario, since the text can be anywhere, in any font, and with different illuminations and orientations. There can even be no text at all! We'll also learn how to use the OpenCV 3.0 text contribution module, which is fully integrated with Tesseract.

11
Text Recognition with Tesseract

In `Chapter 10`, *Developing Segmentation Algorithms for Text Recognition*, we covered the very basic OCR processing functions. Although they are quite useful for scanned or photographed documents, they are almost useless when dealing with text that casually appears in a picture.

In this chapter, we'll explore the OpenCV 4.0 text module, which deals specifically with scene text detection. Using this API, it is possible to detect the text that appears in a webcam video, or to analyze photographed images (like the ones in Street View or taken by a surveillance camera) to extract text information in real time. This allows for a wide range of applications to be created, from accessibility, to marketing, and even robotics fields.

By the end of this chapter, you will be able to do the following:

- Understand what scene text recognition is
- Understand how the text API works
- Use the OpenCV 4.0 text API to detect text
- Extract the detected text into an image
- Use the text API and Tesseract integration to identify letters

Technical requirements

This chapter requires familiarity with the basic C++ programming language. All of the code used in this chapter can be downloaded from the following GitHub link: `https://github.com/PacktPublishing/Learn-OpenCV-4-By-Building-Projects-Second-Edition/tree/master/Chapter_11`. The code can be executed on any operating system, though it is only tested on Ubuntu.

Check out the following video to see the Code in Action:
`http://bit.ly/2Slht5A`

How the text API works

The text API implements the algorithm that was proposed by *Lukás Neumann* and *Jiri Matas* in the article *Real-Time Scene Text Localization and Recognition* during the **computer vision and pattern recognition** (**CVPR**) conference in 2012. This algorithm represented a significant increase in scene text detection, performing state-of-the art detection both in the CVPR database, as well as in the Google Street View database. Before using the API, let's take a look at how this algorithm works under to hood, and how it addresses the scene text detection problem.

 Remember: The OpenCV 4.0 text API does not come with the standard OpenCV modules. It's an additional module that's present in the OpenCV `contrib` package. If you installed OpenCV using the Windows Installer, you should take a look back at `Chapter 1`, *Getting Started with OpenCV*; this will guide you on how to install these modules.

The scene detection problem

Detecting text that randomly appears in a scene is a problem that's harder than it looks. There are several new variables that you need to take into account when you're comparing to identified scanned text, such as the following:

- **Tridimensionality**: The text may be in any scale, orientation, or perspective. Also, the text may be partially occluded or interrupted. There are literally thousands of possible regions where it may appear in the image.
- **Variety**: Text can be in several different fonts and colors. The font may have outline borders. The background can be dark, light, or a complex image.
- **Illumination and shadows**: The sunlight's position and apparent color changes over time. Different weather conditions like fog or rain can generate noise. Illumination may be a problem even in closed spaces, since light reflects over colored objects and hits the text.

- **Blurring**: Text may appear in a region that's not prioritized by lens auto-focus. Blurring is also common in moving cameras, in perspective text, or in the presence of fog.

The following picture, taken from Google Street View, illustrates these problems. Note how several of these situations occur simultaneously in just a single image:

Performing text detection to deal with such situations may prove computationally expensive, since there are 2^n subsets of pixels, n being the number of pixels in the image.

To reduce complexity, two strategies are commonly applied:

- **Use a sliding window to search just a subset of image rectangles**: This strategy just reduces the number of subsets to a smaller amount. The amount of regions varies according to the complexity of text being considered. Algorithms that deal just with text rotation may use small values, compared to the ones that also deal with rotation, skewing, perspective, and so on. The advantage of this approach is its simplicity, but they are usually limited to a narrow range of fonts and often to a lexicon of specific words.

- **Use of connected component analysis**: This approach assumes that pixels can be grouped into regions, where pixels have similar properties. These regions are supposed to have higher chances to be identified as characters. The advantage of this approach is that it does not depend on several text properties (orientation, scale, fonts, and so on), and they also provide a segmentation region that can be used to crop text to the OCR. This was the approach that we used in Chapter 10, *Developing Segmentation Algorithms for Text Recognition*. Lighting could also affect the result, for example, if a shadow is cast over the letters, creating two distinct regions. However, since scene detection is commonly used in moving vehicles (for example, drones or cars) and with videos, the text will end up being detected eventually, since these lighting conditions will differ from frame to frame.

The OpenCV 4.0 algorithm uses the second strategy by performing connected component analysis and searching for extremal regions.

Extremal regions

Extremal regions are connected areas that are characterized by almost uniform intensity, which is surrounded by a contrasted background. The stability of a region can be measured by calculating how resistant to thresholding variance the region is. This variance can be measured with a simple algorithm:

1. Apply the threshold, generating an image, A. Detect its connected pixels regions (extremal regions).
2. Increase the threshold by a delta amount, generating an image, B. Detect its connected pixels regions (extremal regions).
3. Compare image B with A. If a region in image A is similar to the same region in image B, add it to the same branch in the tree. The criteria of similarity may vary from implementation to implementation, but it's usually related to the image area or general shape. If a region in image A appears to be split in image B, create two new branches in the tree for the new regions and associate it with the previous branch.
4. Set $A = B$ and go back to step 2, until the maximum threshold is applied.

This will assemble a tree of regions, as follows:

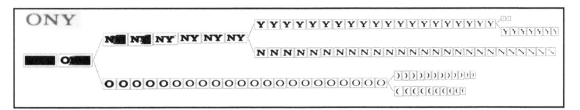

The resistance to variance is determined by counting how many nodes are in the same level. By analyzing this tree, it's also possible to determine the **maximally stable extremal regions** (**MSER**s), that is, the regions where the area remains stable in a wide variety of thresholds. In the previous diagram, it is clear that these areas would contain the letters *O*, *N*, and *Y*. The main disadvantage of maximally extremal regions is that they are weak in the presence of blur. OpenCV provides a MSER feature detector in the **feature2d** module. Extremal regions are interesting because they are strongly invariant to illumination, scale, and orientation. They are good candidates for text as well, since they are also invariant, with regards to the type of font used, even when the font is styled. Each region can also be analyzed to determine its boundary ellipsis, and can have properties like affine transformation and area numerically determined. Finally, it's worth mentioning that this entire process is fast, which makes it a very good candidate for real-time applications.

Extremal region filtering

Although MSERs are a common approach to define which extremal regions are worth working with, the *Neumann* and *Matas* algorithm uses a different approach, by submitting all extremal regions to a sequential classifier that's been trained for character detection. This classifier works in two different stages:

1. The first stage incrementally computes descriptors (bounding box, perimeter, area, and Euler number) for each region. These descriptors are submitted to a classifier that estimates how probable the region is to be a character in the alphabet. Then, only the regions of high probability are selected for stage 2.
2. In this stage, the features of the whole area ratio, convex hull ratio, and the number of outer boundary inflexion points are calculated. This provides more detailed information that allows the classifier to discard non-text characters, but they are also much slower to calculate.

Under OpenCV, this process is implemented in a class called `ERFilter`. It is also possible to use different image single channel projections, such as *R*, *G*, *B*, Luminance, or gray scale conversion to increase the character recognition rates. Finally, all of the characters must be grouped into text blocks (such as words or paragraphs). OpenCV 3.0 provides two algorithms for this purpose:

- **Prune exhaustive search**: Also proposed by *Mattas* in 2011, this algorithm does not need any previous training or classification, but is limited to horizontally aligned text
- **Hierarchical method for oriented text**: This deals with text in any orientation, but needs a trained classifier

Note that since these operations require classifiers, it is also necessary to provide a trained set as input. OpenCV 4.0 provides some of these trained sets in the following sample package: `https://github.com/opencv/opencv_contrib/tree/master/modules/text/samples`. This also means that this algorithm is sensitive to the fonts used in classifier training.

A demonstration of this algorithm can be seen in the following video, which is provided by Neumann himself: `https://www.youtube.com/watch?v=ejd5gGea2Fofeature=youtu.be`. Once the text is segmented, it just needs to be sent to an OCR like Tesseract, similarly to what we did in `Chapter 10`, *Developing Segmentation Algorithms for Text Recognition*. The only difference is that now we will use OpenCV text module classes to interface with Tesseract, since they provide a way to encapsulate the specific OCR engine we are using.

Using the text API

Enough theory. It's time to see how the text module works in practice. Let's study how we can use it to perform text detection, extraction, and identification.

Text detection

Let's start by creating a simple program so that we can perform text segmentation using **ERFilters**. In this program, we will use the trained classifiers from text API samples. You may download this from the OpenCV repository, but they are also available in this book's companion code.

First, we start by including all of the necessary `libs` and `usings`:

```
#include   "opencv2/highgui.hpp"
#include   "opencv2/imgproc.hpp"
#include   "opencv2/text.hpp"

#include   <vector>
#include   <iostream>

using namespace std;
using namespace cv;
using namespace cv::text;
```

Recall from the *Extremal region filtering* section that the `ERFilter` works separately in each image channel. Therefore, we must provide a way to separate each desired channel in a different single channel, `cv::Mat`. This is done by the `separateChannels` function:

```
vector<Mat> separateChannels(const Mat& src)
{
    vector<Mat> channels;
    //Grayscale images
    if (src.type() == CV_8U || src.type() == CV_8UC1) {
        channels.push_back(src);
        channels.push_back(255-src);
        return channels;
    }

    //Colored images
    if (src.type() == CV_8UC3) {
        computeNMChannels(src, channels);
        int size = static_cast<int>(channels.size())-1;
        for (int c = 0; c < size; c++)
            channels.push_back(255-channels[c]);
        return channels;
    }

    //Other types
    cout << "Invalid image format!" << endl;
    exit(-1);
}
```

First, we verify whether the image is already a single channel image (grayscale image). If that's the case, we just add this image – it does not need to be processed. Otherwise, we check if it's an **RGB** image. For colored images, we call the `computeNMChannels` function to split the image into several channels. This function is defined as follows:

```
void computeNMChannels(InputArray src, OutputArrayOfArrays channels, int
mode = ERFILTER_NM_RGBLGrad);
```

The following are its parameters:

- `src`: The source input array. It must be a colored image of type 8UC3.
- `channels`: A vector of `Mat`s that will be filled with the resulting channels.
- `mode`: Defines which channels will be computed. Two possible values can be used:
  - `ERFILTER_NM_RGBLGrad`: Indicates whether the algorithm will use RGB color, lightness, and gradient magnitude as channels (default)
  - `ERFILTER_NM_IHSGrad`: Indicates whether the image will be split by its intensity, hue, saturation, and gradient magnitude

We also append the negative of all color components in the vector. Since the image will have three distinct channels (*R*, *G*, and *B*), this is usually enough. It's also possible to add the non-flipped channels, just like we did with the de-grayscaled image, but we'll end up with six channels, and this could be computer-intensive. Of course, you're free to test with your images if this leads to a better result. Finally, if another kind of image is provided, the function will terminate the program with an error message.

Negatives are appended, so the algorithms will cover both bright text in a dark background and dark text in a bright background. There is no sense in adding a negative for the gradient magnitude.

Let's proceed to the main method. We'll use this program to segment the `easel.png` image, which is provided with the source code:

This picture was taken by a mobile phone camera while I was walking on the street. Let's code this so that you may also use a different image easily by providing its name in the first program argument:

```
int main(int argc, const char * argv[])
{
    const char* image = argc < 2 ? "easel.png" : argv[1];
    auto input = imread(image);
```

Next, we'll convert the image to grayscale and separate its channels by calling the `separateChannels` function:

```
    Mat processed;
    cvtColor(input, processed, COLOR_RGB2GRAY);

    auto channels = separateChannels(processed);
```

If you want to work with all of the channels in a colored image, just replace the two first lines of this code extract to the following:

```
    Mat processed = input;
```

We will need to analyze six channels (RGB and inverted) instead of two (gray and inverted). Actually, the processing times will increase much more than the improvements that we can get. With the channels in hand, we need to create `ERFilters` for both stages of the algorithm. Luckily, the OpenCV text contribution module provides functions for this:

```
// Create ERFilter objects with the 1st and 2nd stage classifiers
auto filter1 = createERFilterNM1(
    loadClassifierNM1("trained_classifierNM1.xml"),  15, 0.00015f,
    0.13f, 0.2f,true,0.1f);

auto filter2 = createERFilterNM2(
    loadClassifierNM2("trained_classifierNM2.xml"),0.5);
```

For the first stage, we call the `loadClassifierNM1` function to load a previously trained classification model. The .xml containing the training data is its only argument. Then, we call `createERFilterNM1` to create an instance of the `ERFilter` class that will perform the classification. The function has the following signature:

```
Ptr<ERFilter> createERFilterNM1(const Ptr<ERFilter::Callback>& cb, int
thresholdDelta = 1, float minArea = 0.00025, float maxArea = 0.13, float
minProbability = 0.4, bool nonMaxSuppression = true, float
minProbabilityDiff = 0.1);
```

The parameters for this function are as follows:

- `cb`: The classification model. This is the same model we loaded with the `loadCassifierNM1` function.
- `thresholdDelta`: The amount to be summed to the threshold in each algorithm iteration. The default value is 1, but we'll use 15 in our example.
- `minArea`: The minimum area of the **extremal region** (**ER**), where text may be found. This is measured by the percentage of the image's size. ERs with areas smaller than this are immediately discarded.
- `maxArea`: The maximum area of the ER where text may be found. This is also measured by the percentage of the image's size. ERs with areas greater than this are immediately discarded.
- `minProbability`: The minimum probability that a region must have to be a character in order to remain for the next stage.
- `nonMaxSupression`: This is used to indicate if non-maximum suppression will be done in each branch probability.
- `minProbabilityDiff`: The minimum probability difference between the minimum and maximum extreme region.

The process for the second stage is similar. We call `loadClassifierNM2` to load the classifier model for the second stage and `createERFilterNM2` to create the second stage classifier. This function only takes the input parameters of the loaded classification model and a minimum probability that a region must achieve to be considered as a character. So, let's call these algorithms in each channel to identify all possible text regions:

```
//Extract text regions using Newmann & Matas algorithm
cout << "Processing " << channels.size() << " channels...";
cout << endl;
vector<vector<ERStat> > regions(channels.size());
for (int c=0; c < channels.size(); c++)
{
    cout << "    Channel " << (c+1) << endl;
    filter1->run(channels[c], regions[c]);
    filter2->run(channels[c], regions[c]);
}
filter1.release();
filter2.release();
```

In the previous code, we used the `run` function of the `ERFilter` class. This function takes two arguments:

- **The input channel**: This includes the image to be processed.
- **The regions**: In the first stage algorithm, this argument will be filled with the detected regions. In the second stage (performed by `filter2`), this argument must contain the regions selected in stage 1. These will be processed and filtered by stage 2.

Finally, we release both filters, since they will not be needed in the program anymore. The final segmentation step is grouping all ERRegions into possible words and defining their bounding boxes. This is done by calling the `erGrouping` function:

```
//Separate character groups from regions
vector< vector<Vec2i> > groups;
vector<Rect> groupRects;
erGrouping(input, channels, regions, groups, groupRects,
ERGROUPING_ORIENTATION_HORIZ);
```

This function has the following signature:

```
void erGrouping(InputArray img, InputArrayOfArrays channels,
std::vector<std::vector<ERStat> > &regions, std::vector<std::vector<Vec2i>
> &groups, std::vector<Rect> &groups_rects, int method =
ERGROUPING_ORIENTATION_HORIZ, const std::string& filename = std::string(),
float minProbablity = 0.5);
```

Let's take a look at the meaning of each parameter:

- `img`: Input image, also called the original image.
- `regions`: Vector of single channel images where regions were extracted.
- `groups`: An output vector of indexes of grouped regions. Each group region contains all extremal regions of a single word.
- `groupRects`: A list of rectangles with the detected text regions.
- `method`: This is the method of grouping. It can be any of the following:
    - `ERGROUPING_ORIENTATION_HORIZ`: The default value. This only generates groups with horizontally oriented text by doing an exhaustive search, as proposed originally by *Neumann* and *Matas*.
    - `ERGROUPING_ORIENTATION_ANY`: This generates groups with text in any orientation, using single linkage clustering and classifiers. If you use this method, the filename of the classifier model must be provided in the next parameter.
    - `Filename`: The name of the classifier model. This is only needed if `ERGROUPING_ORIENTATION_ANY` is selected.
    - `minProbability`: The minimum detected probability of accepting a group. This is also only needed if `ERGROUPING_ORIENTATION_ANY` is selected.

The code also provides a call to the second method, but it's commented out. You may switch between the two to test this out. Just comment the previous call and uncomment this one:

```
erGrouping(input, channels, regions,
    groups, groupRects, ERGROUPING_ORIENTATION_ANY,
    "trained_classifier_erGrouping.xml", 0.5);
```

For this call, we also used the default trained classifier that's provided in the text module sample package. Finally, we draw the region boxes and show the results:

```
// draw groups boxes
for (const auto& rect : groupRects)
    rectangle(input, rect, Scalar(0, 255, 0), 3);

imshow("grouping",input);
waitKey(0);
```

This program outputs the following result:

You may check the entire source code in the detection.cpp file.

While most OpenCV text module functions are written to support both grayscale and colored images as its input parameter, at the time of writing this book, there were bugs preventing us from using grayscale images in functions such as erGrouping. For more information, take a look at the following GitHub link: https://github.com/Itseez/opencv_contrib/issues/309.
Always remember that the OpenCV contrib modules package is not as stable as the default OpenCV packages.

Text extraction

Now that we have detected the regions, we must crop the text before submitting it to the OCR. We could simply use a function like `getRectSubpix` or `Mat::copy`, using each region rectangle as a **region of interest** (**ROI**) but, since the letters are skewed, some undesired text may be cropped as well. For example, this is what one of the regions would look like if we just extract the ROI based on its given rectangle:

Fortunately, `ERFilter` provides us with an object called `ERStat`, which contains pixels inside each extremal region. With these pixels, we could use OpenCV's `floodFill` function to reconstruct each letter. This function is capable of painting similar colored pixels based on a seed point, just like the **bucket** tool of most drawing applications. This is what the function signature looks like:

```
int floodFill(InputOutputArray image, InputOutputArray mask,  Point
seedPoint, Scalar newVal,
 CV_OUT Rect* rect=0, Scalar loDiff = Scalar(), Scalar upDiff = Scalar(),
int flags = 4 );
```

Let's understand these parameters and how they will be used:

- `image`: The input image. We'll use the channel image where the extremal region was taken. This is where the function normally does the flood fill, unless `FLOODFILL_MASK_ONLY` is supplied. In this case, the image remains untouched and the drawing occurs in the mask. That's exactly what we will do.
- `mask`: The mask must be an image with two rows and two columns greater than the input image. When the flood fill draws a pixel, it verifies if the corresponding pixel in the mask is zero. In that case, it will draw and mark this pixel as one (or another value that's passed into the flags). If the pixel is not zero, the flood fill does not paint the pixel. In our case, we'll provide a blank mask so that every letter will get painted in the mask.
- `seedPoint`: The starting point. It's similar to the place you click when you want to use the **bucket** tool of a graphic application.
- `newVal`: The new value of the repainted pixels.

- loDiff and upDiff: These parameters represent the lower and upper differences between the pixel being processed and its neighbors. The neighbor will be painted if it falls into this range. If the FLOODFILL_FIXED_RANGE flag is used, the difference between the seed point and the pixels being processed will be used instead.

- rect: This is an optional parameter that limits the region where the flood fill will be applied.

- flags: This value is represented by a bit mask:
  - The least significant 8 bits of the flag contains a connectivity value. A value of 4 indicates that all four edge pixels will be used, and a value of 8 will indicate that the diagonal pixels must also be taken into account. We'll use 4 for this parameter.
  - The next 8 to 16 bits contains a value from 1 to 255, which is used to fill the mask. Since we want to fill the mask with white, we'll use 255 << 8 for this value.
  - There are two more bits that can be set by adding the FLOODFILL_FIXED_RANGE and FLOODFILL_MASK_ONLY flags, as we already described.

We'll create a function called drawER. This function will receive four parameters:

- A vector with all of the processed channels
- The ERStat region
- The group that must be drawn
- The group rectangle

This function will return an image with the word represented by this group. Let's start this function by creating the mask image and defining the flags:

```
Mat out = Mat::zeros(channels[0].rows+2, channels[0].cols+2, CV_8UC1);

int flags = 4                       //4 neighbors
    + (255 << 8)                        //paint mask in white (255)
    + FLOODFILL_FIXED_RANGE         //fixed range
    + FLOODFILL_MASK_ONLY;          //Paint just the mask
```

Then, we'll loop through each group. It's necessary to find the region index and its status. There's a chance of this extreme region being the root, which does not contain any points. In this case, we'll just ignore it:

```
for (int g=0; g < group.size(); g++)
{
    int idx = group[g][0];
    auto er = regions[idx][group[g][1]];

//Ignore root region
    if (er.parent == NULL)
        continue;
```

Now, we can read the pixel coordinate from the ERStat object. It's represented by the pixel number, counting from top to bottom, left to right. This linear index must be converted to a row (y) and column (z) notation, using a formula similar to the one we saw in Chapter 2, *An Introduction to the Basics of OpenCV*:

```
int px = er.pixel % channels[idx].cols;
int py = er.pixel / channels[idx].cols;
Point p(px, py);
```

Then, we can call the floodFill function. The ERStat object gives us the value to use in the loDiff parameter:

```
floodFill(
    channels[idx], out,          //Image and mask
    p, Scalar(255),              //Seed and color
    nullptr,                     //No rect
    Scalar(er.level),Scalar(0),  //LoDiff and upDiff
    flags                        //Flags
```

After we do this for all of the regions in the group, we'll end with an image that's a little bigger than the original one, with a black background and the word in white letters. Now, let's crop just the area of the letters. Since the region rectangle was given, we start by defining it as our region of interest:

```
out = out(rect);
```

Then, we'll find all non-zero pixels. This is the value we'll use in the `minAreaRect` function to get the rotated rectangle around the letters. Finally, we will borrow the previous chapter's `deskewAndCrop` function to crop and rotate the image for us:

```
vector<Point> points;
findNonZero(out, points);
//Use deskew and crop to crop it perfectly
return deskewAndCrop(out, minAreaRect(points));
}
```

This is the result of the process for the easel image:

Text recognition

In `Chapter 10`, *Developing Segmentation Algorithms for Text Recognition*, we used the Tesseract API directly to recognize the text regions. This time, we'll use OpenCV classes to accomplish the same goal.

In OpenCV, all OCR-specific classes derive from the **BaseOCR** virtual class. This class provides a common interface for the OCR execution method itself. Specific implementations must inherit from this class. By default, the text module provides three different implementations: **OCRTesseract**, **OCRHMMDecoder**, and **OCRBeamSearchDecoder**.

This hierarchy is depicted in the following class diagram:

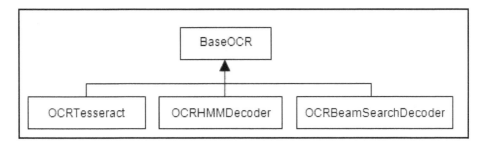

With this approach, we can separate the part of the code where the OCR mechanism is created from the execution itself. This makes it easier to change the OCR implementation in the future.

So, let's start by creating a method that decides which implementation we'll use based on a string. We currently support just Tesseract, but you may take a look in this chapter's code, where a demonstration with **HMMDecoder** is also provided. Also, we are accepting the OCR engine name in a string parameter, but we could improve our application's flexibility by reading it from an external JSON or XML configuration file:

```
cv::Ptr<BaseOCR> initOCR2(const string& ocr) { if (ocr == "tesseract") {
return OCRTesseract::create(nullptr, "eng+por"); } throw string("Invalid
OCR engine: ") + ocr; }
```

As you may have noticed, the function returns `Ptr<BaseOCR>`. Now, take a look at the highlighted code. It calls the `create` method to initialize a Tesseract OCR instance. Let's take a look at its official signature, since it allows several specific parameters:

```
Ptr<OCRTesseract> create(const char* datapath=NULL,
  const char* language=NULL,
  const char* char_whitelist=NULL,
  int oem=3, int psmode=3);
```

Let's dissect each of these parameters:

- `datapath`: This is the path to the root directory's `tessdata` files. The path must end with a backslash / character. The `tessdata` directory contains the language files you installed. Passing `nullptr` to this parameter will make Tesseract search in its installation directory, which is the location where this folder is normally present. It's common to change this value to `args[0]` when deploying an application and include the `tessdata` folder in your application path.
- `language`: This is a three letter word with the language code (for example, eng for English, por for Portuguese, or hin for Hindi). Tesseract supports the loading of multiple language codes by using the + sign. Therefore, passing `eng+por` will load both English and Portuguese languages. Of course, you can only use languages that you have previously installed, otherwise the loading will fail. A language `config` file may specify that two or more languages must be loaded together. To prevent that, you may use a tilde ~. For example, you can use `hin+~eng` to guarantee that English is not loaded with Hindi, even if it is configured to do so.

- `whitelist`: This is the character that's set to be considered for recognition. In the case that `nullptr` is passed, the characters will be `0123456789abcdefghijklmnopqrstuvwxyzABCDEFGHIJKLMNOPQRSTUVWXYZ`.
- `oem`: These are the OCR algorithms that will be used. It can have one of the following values:
    - `OEM_TESSERACT_ONLY`: Uses just Tesseract. It's the fastest method, but it also has less precision.
    - `OEM_CUBE_ONLY`: Uses Cube engine. It's slower, but more precise. This will only work if your language was trained to support this engine mode. To check if that's the case, look for `.cube` files for your language in the `tessdata` folder. The support for English language is guaranteed.
    - `OEM_TESSERACT_CUBE_COMBINED`: Combines both Tesseract and Cube to achieve the best possible OCR classification. This engine has the best accuracy and the slowest execution time.
    - `OEM_DEFAULT`: Infers the strategy based in the language config file, command-line config file or, in the absence of both, use `OEM_TESSERACT_ONLY`.
- `psmode`: This is the segmentation mode. It can be any of the following:
    - `PSM_OSD_ONLY`: Using this mode, Tesseract will just run its preprocessing algorithms to detect orientation and script detection.
    - `PSM_AUTO_OSD`: This tells Tesseract to do automatic page segmentation with orientation and script detection.
    - `PSM_AUTO_ONLY`: Does page segmentation, but avoids doing orientation, script detection, or OCR. This is the default value.
    - `PSM_AUTO`: Does page segmentation and OCR, but avoids doing orientation or script detection.
    - `PSM_SINGLE_COLUMN`: Assumes that the text of variable sizes is displayed in a single column.
    - `PSM_SINGLE_BLOCK_VERT_TEXT`: Treats the image as a single uniform block of vertically aligned text.
    - `PSM_SINGLE_BLOCK`: Assumes a single block of text. This is the default configuration. We will use this flag since our preprocessing phase guarantees this condition.

- PSM_SINGLE_LINE: Indicates that the image contains only one line of text.
- PSM_SINGLE_WORD: Indicates that the image contains just one word.
- PSM_SINGLE_WORD_CIRCLE: Indicates that the image is a just one word disposed in a circle.
- PSM_SINGLE_CHAR: Indicates that the image contains a single character.

For the last two parameters, it's recommended that you use the #include Tesseract directory to use the constant names instead of directly inserting their values. The last step is to add text detection in our main function. To do this, just add the following code to the end of the main method:

```
auto ocr = initOCR("tesseract");
for (int i = 0; i < groups.size(); i++)
{
    auto wordImage = drawER(channels, regions, groups[i],
    groupRects[i]);

    string word;
    ocr->run(wordImage, word);
    cout << word << endl;
}
```

In this code, we started by calling our initOCR method to create a Tesseract instance. Note that the remaining code will not change if we chose a different OCR engine, since the run method signature is guaranteed by the BaseOCR class. Next, we iterate over each detected ERFilter group. Since each group represents a different word, we will do the following:

1. Call the previously created drawER function to create an image with the word.
2. Create a text string called word, and call the run function to recognize the word image. The recognized word will be stored in the string.
3. Print the text string in the screen.

Let's take a look at the `run` method signature. This method is defined in the `BaseOCR` class, and will be equal for all specific OCR implementations – even the ones that might be implemented in the future:

```
virtual void run(Mat& image, std::string& output_text,
  std::vector<Rect>* component_rects=NULL,
  std::vector<std::string>* component_texts=NULL,
  std::vector<float>* component_confidences=NULL, int component_level=0) =
  0;
```

Of course, this is a pure virtual function that must be implemented by each specific class (such as the `OCRTesseract` class we just used):

- `image`: The input image. It must be a RGB or a grayscale image.
- `component_rects`: We can provide a vector to be filled with the bounding box of each component (words or text lines) that's detected by the OCR engine.
- `component_texts`: If given, this vector will be filled with the text strings of each component detected by the OCR.
- `component_confidences`: If given, the vector will be filled with floats, with the confidence values of each component.
- `component_level`: Defines what a component is. It may have the values `OCR_LEVEL_WORD` (by default), or `OCR_LEVEL_TEXT_LINE`.

> If necessary, you may prefer changing the component level to a word or line in the `run()` method instead of doing the same thing in the `psmode` parameter of the `create()` function. This is preferable since the `run` method will be supported by any OCR engine that decides to implement the `BaseOCR` class. Always remember that the `create()` method is where vendor-specific configurations are set.

This is the program's final output:

Despite a minor confusion with the & symbol, every word was perfectly recognized. You may check the entire source code in the `ocr.cpp` file, in this chapter's code file.

Summary

In this chapter, we saw that scene text recognition is a far more difficult OCR situation than working with scanned texts. We studied how the text module addresses this problem with extremal region identification using the *Newmann* and *Matas* algorithm. We also saw how to use this API with the `floodFill` function to extract the text in to an image and submit it to Tesseract OCR. Finally, we studied how the OpenCV text module integrates with Tesseract and other OCR engines, and how can we use its classes to identify what's written in an image.

In the next chapter, you will be introduced to deep learning in OpenCV. You will learn about object detection and classification by using the **you only look once** (**YOLO**) algorithm.

Deep Learning with OpenCV

12

Deep learning is a state-of-the-art form of machine learning that is reaching its best accuracy in image classification and speech recognition. Deep learning is also used in other fields, such as robotics and artificial intelligence with reinforcement learning. This is the main reason OpenCV is making significant efforts to include deep learning at its core. We are going to learn the basic use of OpenCV deep learning interfaces and look at using them in two use cases: object detection and face detection.

In this chapter, we are going to learn the basics of deep learning and see how to use it in OpenCV. To reach our objective, we are going to learn object detection and classification using the **you only look once** (**YOLO**) algorithm.

The following topics will be covered in this chapter:

- What is deep learning?
- How OpenCV works with deep learning and implementing deep learning **neural networks**(**NN**s)
- YOLO – a very fast deep learning object detection algorithm
- Face detection using Single Shot Detector

Technical requirements

To follow the chapter with ease, it is required that you install OpenCV with the deep learning module compiled. If you do not have this module, you will not be able to compile and run the sample codes.

It's very useful to have an NVIDIA GPU with CUDA support. You can enable CUDA on OpenCV to improve the speed of training and detection.

Finally, you can download the code used in this chapter from `https://github.com/PacktPublishing/Learn-OpenCV-4-By-Building-Projects-Second-Edition/tree/master/Chapter_12`.

Check out the following video to see the Code in Action:
`http://bit.ly/2SmbWf7`

Introduction to deep learning

Deep learning is most commonly written about in scientific papers nowadays with regards to image classification and speech recognition. This is a subfield of machine learning, based on traditional neural networks and inspired by the structure of the brain. To understand this technology, it is very important to understand what a neural network is and how it works.

What is a neural network and how can we learn from data?

The neural network is inspired by the structure of the brain, in which multiple neurons are interconnected, creating a network. Each neuron has multiple inputs and multiple outputs, like a biological neuron.

This network is distributed in layers, and each layer contains a number of neurons that are connected to all the previous layer's neurons. This always has an input layer, which normally consists of the features that describe the input image or data, and an output layer, which normally consists of the result of our classification. The other middle layers are called **hidden layers**. The following diagram shows a basic three-layer neural network in which the input layer contains three neurons, the output layer contains two neurons, and a hidden layer contains four neurons:

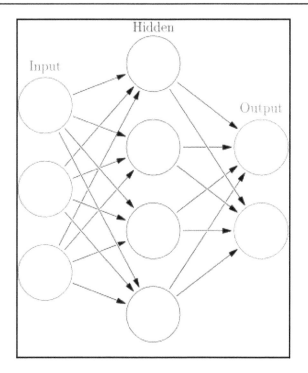

The neuron is the basic element of a neural network and it uses a simple mathematical formula that we can see in the following diagram:

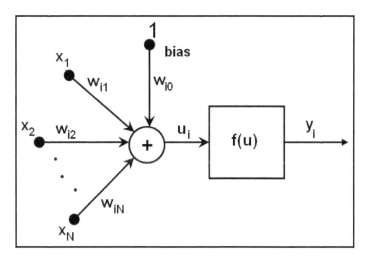

As we can see, for each neuron, **i**, we mathematically add all the previous neuron's output, which is the input of neuron **i** (**x1, x2**...), by a weight (**wi1, wi2**...) plus a bias value, and the result is the argument of an activation function, **f**. The final result is the output of **i** neuron:

$$yi = f(bias * W_{i0} + X_1 * W_{i1} + X_2 * W_{i2} + \ldots + X_n * W_{in})$$

The most common activation functions (**f**) on classical neural networks are the sigmoid function or linear functions. The sigmoid function is used most often, and it looks as follows:

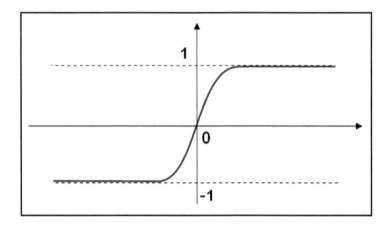

But how can we learn a neural network with this formula and these connections? How do we classify input data? The learn algorithm of neural networks can be called **supervised** if we know the desired output; while learning, the input pattern is given to the net's input layer. Initially, we set up all weights as random numbers and send the input features into the network, checking the output result. If this is wrong, we have to adjust all the weights of the network to get the correct output. This algorithm is called **backpropagation**. If you want to read more about how a neural network learns, check out http:// neuralnetworksanddeeplearning.com/chap2.html and https://youtu.be/IHZwWFHWa-w.

Now that we have a brief introduction to what a neural network is and the internal architecture of NN, we are going to explore the differences between NN and deep learning.

Convolutional neural networks

Deep learning neural networks have the same background as the classical neural network. However, in the case of image analysis, the main difference is the input layer. In a classical machine learning algorithm, the researcher has to identify the best features that define the image target to classify. For example, if we want to classify numbers, we could extract the borders and lines of numbers in each image, measure the area of an object in an image, and all of these features are the input of the neural network, or any other machine learning algorithm. However, in deep learning, you don't have to explore what the features are; instead, you use whole image as an input of the neural network directly. Deep learning can learn what the most important features are and **deep neural networks** (**DNN**) are able to detect an image or input and recognize it.

To learn what these features are, we use one of the most important layers in deep learning and neural networks: the **convolutional layer**. A convolutional layer works like a convolutional operator, where a kernel filter is applied to the whole previous layer, giving us a new filtered image, like a sobel operator:

However, in a convolutional layer we can define different parameters, and one of them is the number of filters and the sizes we want to apply to the previous layer or image. These filters are calculated in the learning step, just like the weights on a classical neural network. This is the magic of deep learning: it can extract the most significant features from labeled images.

However, these convolutional layers are the main reason behind the name **deep**, and we are going to see why in the following basic example. Imagine we have a 100 x 100 image. In a classical neural network, we will extract the most relevant features we can imagine from the input image. This will normally approximately 1,000 features, and with each hidden layer we can increase or decrease this number, but the number of neurons to calculate its weights is reasonable to compute in a normal computer. However, in deep learning, we normally start applying a convolutional layer – with a 64 filter kernels of 3 x 3 size. This will generate a new layer of 100 x 100 x 64 neurons with 3 x 3 x 64 weights to calculate. If we continue adding more and more layers, these numbers quickly increase and require huge computing power to learn the good weights and parameters of our deep learning architecture.

Convolutional layers are one of the most important aspects of the deep learning architecture, but there are also other important layers, such as **Pooling, Dropout, Flatten,** and **Softmax**. In the following diagram, we can see a basic deep learning architecture in which some convolutional and pooling layers are stacked:

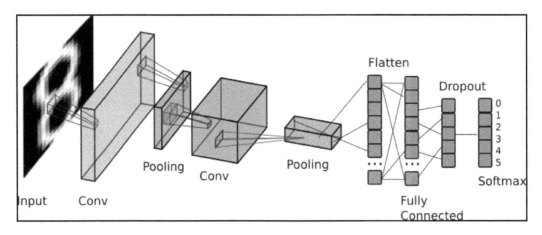

However, there is one more very important thing that makes deep learning get the best results: the amount of labeled data. If you have a small dataset, a deep learning algorithm will not help you in your classification because there is not enough data to learn the features (the weights and parameters of your deep learning architecture). However, if you have tons of data, you will get very good results. But take care, you will need a lot of time to compute and learn the weights and parameters of your architecture. This is why deep learning was not used early in the process, because computing requires a lot of time. However, thanks to new parallel architectures, such as NVIDIA GPUs, we can optimize the learning backpropagation and speed up the learning tasks.

Deep learning in OpenCV

The deep learning module was introduced to OpenCV in version 3.1 as a contribute module. This was moved to part of OpenCV in 3.3, but it was not widely adopted by developers until versions 3.4.3 and 4.

OpenCV implements deep learning only for inference, which means that you cannot create your own deep learning architecture and train in OpenCV; you can only import a pre-trained model, execute it under OpenCV library, and use it as **feedforward** (inference) to obtain the results.

The most important reason to implement the feedforward method is to optimize OpenCV to speed up computing time and performance in inference. Another reason to not implement backward methods is to avoid wasting time developing something that other libraries, such as TensorFlow or Caffe, are specialized in. OpenCV then created importers for the most important deep learning libraries and frameworks to make it possible to import pre-trained models.

Then if you wish to create a new deep learning model to use in OpenCV, you first have to create and train it using the TensorFlow, Caffe, Torch, or DarkNet frameworks or a framework that you can use to export your model in an **Open Neural Network Exchange** (**ONNX**) format. Creating a model with this framework can be easy or complex depending on the framework you use, but essentially you have to stack multiple layers like we did in the previous diagram, setting the parameters and the function required by the DNN. Nowadays there are other tools to help you to create your models without coding, such as `https://www.tensoreditor.com` or `lobe.ai`. TensorEditor allows you to download the TensorFlow code generated from a visual design architecture to train in your computer or in the cloud. In the following screenshot, we can see TensorEditor:

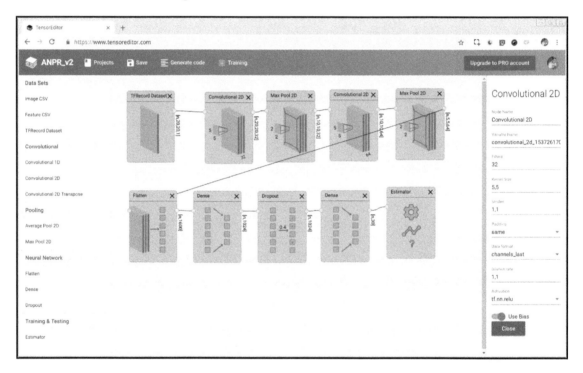

When you have your model trained and you are comfortable with the results, you can import it to OpenCV directly to predict new input images. In the next section, you will see how to import and use deep learning models in OpenCV.

YOLO – real-time object detection

To learn how to use deep learning in OpenCV, we are going to present an example of object detection and classification based on the YOLO algorithm. This is one of the fastest object detection and recognition algorithms, which can run at around 30 fps in an NVIDIA Titan X.

YOLO v3 deep learning model architecture

Common object detection in classical computer vision uses a sliding window to detect objects, scanning a whole image with different window sizes and scales. The main problem here is the huge time consumption in scanning the image several times to find objects.

YOLO uses a different approach by dividing the diagram into an S x S grid. For each grid, YOLO checks for B bounding boxes, and then the deep learning model extracts the bounding boxes for each patch, the confidence to contain a possible object, and the confidence of each category in the training dataset per each box. The following screenshot shows the S x S grid:

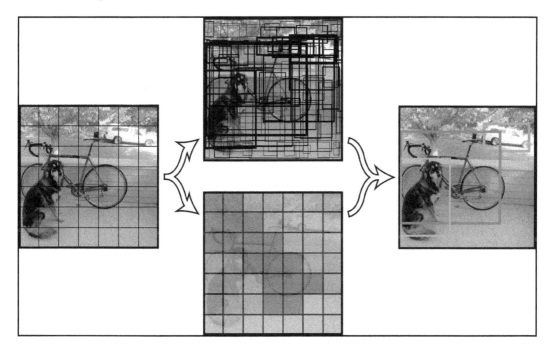

YOLO is trained with a grid of 19 and 5 bounding boxes per grid using 80 categories. Then, the output result is **19 x 19 x 425**, where 425 comes from the data of bounding box (x, y, width, height), the object confidence, and the 80 classes, confidence multiplied by the number of boxes per grid; *5_bounding boxes*(x,y,w,h,object_confidence, classify_confidence[80])=5*(4 + 1 + 80)*:

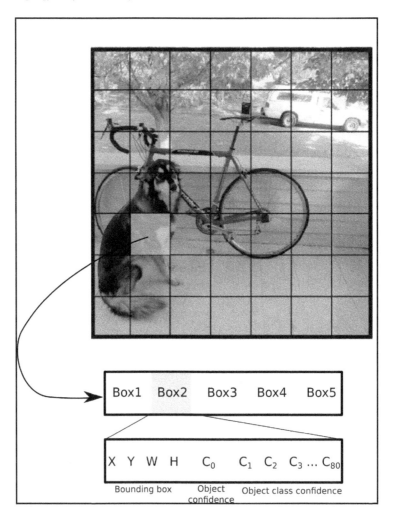

The YOLO v3 architecture is based on DarkNet, which contains 53 layer networks, and YOLO adds 53 more layers for a total of 106 network layers. If you want a faster architecture, you can check version 2 or TinyYOLO versions, which use fewer layers.

The YOLO dataset, vocabulary, and model

Before we start to import the model into our OpenCV code, we have to obtain it through the YOLO website: `https://pjreddie.com/darknet/yolo/`. This provides pre-trained model files based on the **COCO** dataset, which contains 80 object categories, such as person, umbrella, bike, motorcycle, car, apple, banana, computer, and chair.

To get all the names of categories and uses for visualization, check out `https://github.com/pjreddie/darknet/blob/master/data/coco.names?raw=true`.

The names are in the same order as the results of deep learning model confidences. If you want to see some images of the COCO dataset by category, you can explore the dataset at `http://cocodataset.org/#explore`, and download some of them to test our sample application.

To get the model configuration and pre-trained weights, you have to download the following files:

- `https://pjreddie.com/media/files/yolov3.weights`
- `https://github.com/pjreddie/darknet/blob/master/cfg/yolov3.cfg?raw=true`

Now we are ready to start to import the models into OpenCV.

Importing YOLO into OpenCV

The deep learning OpenCV module is found under the `opencv2/dnn.hpp` header, which we have to include in our source header and in `cv::dnn namespace`.

Then our header for OpenCV must look like this:

```
...
#include <opencv2/core.hpp>
#include <opencv2/dnn.hpp>
#include <opencv2/imgproc.hpp>
#include <opencv2/highgui.hpp>
using namespace cv;
using namespace dnn;
...
```

The first thing we have to do is import the COCO name's vocabulary, which is in the `coco.names` file. This file is a plaintext file that contains one class category per line, and is ordered in the same way as the confidence results. Then we are going to read each line of this file and store it in a vector of strings, called classes:

```
...
int main(int argc, char** argv)
{
    // Load names of classes
    string classesFile = "coco.names";
    ifstream ifs(classesFile.c_str());
    string line;
    while (getline(ifs, line)) classes.push_back(line);
    ...
```

Now we are going to import the deep learning model into OpenCV. OpenCV implements the most common readers/importers for deep learning frameworks, such as TensorFlow and DarkNet, and all of them have a similar syntax. In our case, we are going to import a DarkNet model using the weights, and the model using the `readNetFromDarknet` OpenCV function:

```
...
// Give the configuration and weight files for the model
String modelConfiguration = "yolov3.cfg";
String modelWeights = "yolov3.weights";
// Load the network
Net net = readNetFromDarknet(modelConfiguration, modelWeights);
...
```

Now we are in a position to read an image and send the deep neural network to inference. First we have to read an image with the `imread` function and convert it into a tensor/blob data that can read the **DotNetNuke** (**DNN**). To create the blob from an image, we are going to use the `blobFromImage` function by passing the image. This function accepts the following parameters:

- **image**: Input image (with 1, 3, or 4 channels).
- **blob**: Output `mat`.
- **scalefactor**: Multiplier for image values.
- **size**: Spatial size for output blob required as input of DNN.
- **mean**: Scalar with mean values that are subtracted from channels. Values are intended to be in (mean-R, mean-G, and mean-B) order if the image has BGR ordering and `swapRB` is true.

- **swapRB**: A flag that indicates to swap the first and last channels in a 3-channel image is necessary.
- **crop**: A flag that indicates whether the image will be cropped after resize.

You can read the full code on how to read and convert an image into a blob in the following snippet:

```
...
input= imread(argv[1]);
// Stop the program if reached end of video
if (input.empty()) {
    cout << "No input image" << endl;
    return 0;
}
// Create a 4D blob from a frame.
blobFromImage(input, blob, 1/255.0, Size(inpWidth, inpHeight),
Scalar(0,0,0), true, false);
...
```

Finally, we have to feed the blob into Deep Net and call the inference with the `forward` function, which requires two parameters: the out `mat` results, and the names of the layers that the output needs to retrieve:

```
...
//Sets the input to the network
net.setInput(blob);

// Runs the forward pass to get output of the output layers
vector<Mat> outs;
net.forward(outs, getOutputsNames(net));
// Remove the bounding boxes with low confidence
postprocess(input, outs);
...
```

In the `mat` output vector, we have all bounding boxes detected by the neural network and we have to post-process the output to get only the results that have a confidence greater than a threshold, normally 0.5, and finally apply non-maximum suppression to eliminate redundant overlapping boxes. You can get the full post-process code on GitHub.

The final result of our example is multiple-object detection and classification in deep learning that shows a window similar to the following:

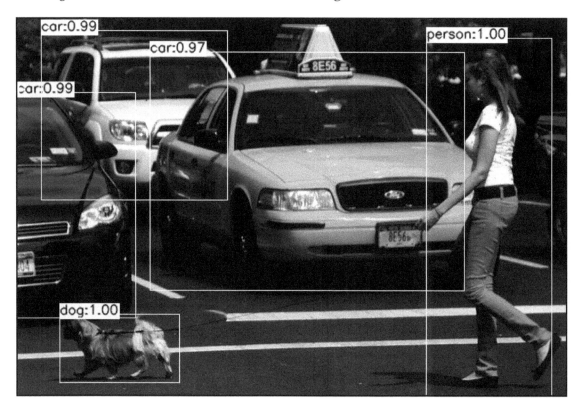

Now we are going to learn another commonly-used object detection function customized for face detection.

Face detection with SSD

Single Shot Detection (**SSD**) is another fast and accurate deep learning object-detection method with a similar concept to YOLO, in which the object and bounding box are predicted in the same architecture.

SSD model architecture

The SSD algorithm is called single shot because it predicts the bounding box and the class simultaneously as it processes the image in the same deep learning model. Basically, the architecture is summarized in the following steps:

1. A 300 x 300 image is input into the architecture.
2. The input image is passed through multiple convolutional layers, obtaining different features at different scales.
3. For each feature map obtained in 2, we use a 3 x 3 convolutional filter to evaluate small set of default bounding boxes.
4. For each default box evaluated, the bounding box offsets and class probabilities are predicted.

The model architecture looks like this:

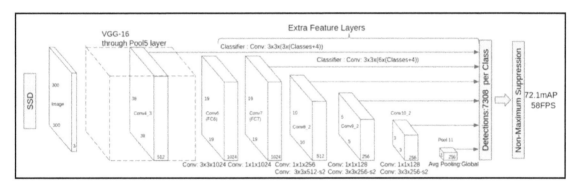

SSD is used for predicting multiple classes similar to that in YOLO, but it can be modified to detect a single object, changing the last layer and training for only one class – this is what we used in our example, a re-trained model for face detection, where only one class is predicted.

Importing SSD face detection into OpenCV

To work with deep learning in our code, we have to import the corresponding headers:

```
#include <opencv2/dnn.hpp>
#include <opencv2/imgproc.hpp>
#include <opencv2/highgui.hpp>
```

After that, we will import the required namespaces:

```
using namespace cv;
using namespace std;
using namespace cv::dnn;
```

Now we are going to define the input image size and constant that we are going to use in our code:

```
const size_t inWidth = 300;
const size_t inHeight = 300;
const double inScaleFactor = 1.0;
const Scalar meanVal(104.0, 177.0, 123.0);
```

In this example, we need a few parameters as input, such as the model configuration and pre-trained model, if we are going to process camera or video input. We also need the minimum confidence to accept a prediction as correct or not:

```
const char* params
= "{ help | false | print usage }"
"{ proto | | model configuration (deploy.prototxt) }"
"{ model | | model weights (res10_300x300_ssd_iter_140000.caffemodel) }"
"{ camera_device | 0 | camera device number }"
"{ video | | video or image for detection }"
"{ opencl | false | enable OpenCL }"
"{ min_confidence | 0.5 | min confidence }";
```

Now, we are going to start with the main function, where we are going to parse the arguments with the CommandLineParser function:

```
int main(int argc, char** argv)
{
  CommandLineParser parser(argc, argv, params);

  if (parser.get<bool>("help"))
  {
  cout << about << endl;
  parser.printMessage();
  return 0;
  }
```

We are also going to load the model architecture and pre-trained model files, and load the model in a deep learning network:

```
String modelConfiguration = parser.get<string>("proto");
String modelBinary = parser.get<string>("model");

//! [Initialize network]
```

```
dnn::Net net = readNetFromCaffe(modelConfiguration, modelBinary);
//! [Initialize network]
```

It's very important to check that we have imported the network correctly. We must also check whether the model is imported, using the `empty` function, as follows:

```
if (net.empty())
{
cerr << "Can't load network by using the following files" << endl;
exit(-1);
}
```

After loading our network, we are going to initialize our input source, a camera or video file, and load into `VideoCapture`, as follows:

```
VideoCapture cap;
if (parser.get<String>("video").empty())
{
int cameraDevice = parser.get<int>("camera_device");
cap = VideoCapture(cameraDevice);
if(!cap.isOpened())
{
cout << "Couldn't find camera: " << cameraDevice << endl;
return -1;
}
}
else
{
cap.open(parser.get<String>("video"));
if(!cap.isOpened())
{
cout << "Couldn't open image or video: " << parser.get<String>("video") <<
endl;
return -1;
}
}
```

Now we are prepared to start capturing frames and processing each one into the deep neural network to find faces.

First of all, we have to capture each frame in a loop:

```
for(;;)
{
Mat frame;
cap >> frame; // get a new frame from camera/video or read image

if (frame.empty())
```

```
{
waitKey();
break;
}
```

Next, we will put the input frame into a `Mat` blob structure that can manage the deep neural network. We have to send the image with the proper size of SSD, which is 300 x 300 (we will have initialized the `inWidth` and `inHeight` constant variables already) and we subtract from the input image a mean value, which is required in the SSD using the defined `meanVal` constant variable:

```
Mat inputBlob = blobFromImage(frame, inScaleFactor, Size(inWidth,
inHeight), meanVal, false, false);
```

Now we are ready to set the data into the network and get the predictions/detections using the `net.setInput` and `net.forward` functions, respectively. This converts the detection results into a detection `mat` that we can read, where `detection.size[2]` is the number of detected objects and `detection.size[3]` is the number of results per detection (bounding box data and confidence):

```
net.setInput(inputBlob, "data"); //set the network input
Mat detection = net.forward("detection_out"); //compute output
Mat detectionMat(detection.size[2], detection.size[3], CV_32F,
detection.ptr<float>());
```

The `Mat` detection contains the following per each row:

- **Column 0**: Confidence of object being present

- **Column 1**: Confidence of bounding box

- **Column 2**: Confidence of face detected

- **Column 3**: X bottom-left bounding box

- **Column 4**: Y bottom-left bounding box

- **Column 5**: X top-right bounding box

- **Column 6**: Y top-right bounding box

The bounding box is relative (zero to one) to the image size.

Now we have to apply the threshold to get only the desired detections based on the defined input threshold:

```
float confidenceThreshold = parser.get<float>("min_confidence");
  for(int i = 0; i < detectionMat.rows; i++)
  {
  float confidence = detectionMat.at<float>(i, 2);

  if(confidence > confidenceThreshold)
  {
```

Now we are going to extract the bounding box, draw a rectangle over each detected face, and show it as follows:

```
  int xLeftBottom = static_cast<int>(detectionMat.at<float>(i, 3) *
frame.cols);
  int yLeftBottom = static_cast<int>(detectionMat.at<float>(i, 4) *
frame.rows);
  int xRightTop = static_cast<int>(detectionMat.at<float>(i, 5) *
frame.cols);
  int yRightTop = static_cast<int>(detectionMat.at<float>(i, 6) *
frame.rows);

  Rect object((int)xLeftBottom, (int)yLeftBottom, (int)(xRightTop -
xLeftBottom), (int)(yRightTop - yLeftBottom));

  rectangle(frame, object, Scalar(0, 255, 0));
  }
  }
  imshow("detections", frame);
  if (waitKey(1) >= 0) break;
  }
```

The final result looks like this:

In this section, you learned a new deep learning architecture, SSD, and how to use it for face detection.

Summary

In this chapter, we learned what deep learning is and how to use it on OpenCV with object detection and classification. This chapter is a foundation for working with other models and deep neural networks for any purpose.

This book taught you how to obtain and compile OpenCV, how to use the basic image and `mat` operations, and how to create your own graphical user interfaces. You used basic filters and applied all of them in an industrial inspection example. We looked at how to use OpenCV for face detection and how to manipulate it to add masks. Finally, we introduced you to very complex use cases of object tracking, text segmentation, and recognition. Now you are ready to create your own applications in OpenCV, thanks to these use cases, which show you how to apply each technique or algorithm.

Further reading

To learn more about deep learning in OpenCV, check out *Object Detection and Recognition Using Deep Learning in OpenCV* by *Packt Publishing*.

Other Books You May Enjoy

If you enjoyed this book, you may be interested in these other books by Packt:

Computer Vision with OpenCV 3 and Qt5
Amin Ahmadi Tazehkandi

ISBN: 9781788472395

- Get an introduction to Qt IDE and SDK
- Be introduced to OpenCV and see how to communicate between OpenCV and Qt
- Understand how to create UI using Qt Widgets
- Know to develop cross-platform applications using OpenCV 3 and Qt 5
- Explore the multithreaded application development features of Qt5
- Improve OpenCV 3 application development using Qt5
- Build, test, and deploy Qt and OpenCV apps, either dynamically or statically
- See Computer Vision technologies such as filtering and transformation of images, detecting and matching objects, template matching, object tracking, video and motion analysis, and much more
- Be introduced to QML and Qt Quick for iOS and Android application development

OpenCV 3.x with Python By Example - Second Edition
Gabriel Garrido

ISBN: 9781788396905

- Detect shapes and edges from images and videos
- How to apply filters on images and videos
- Use different techniques to manipulate and improve images
- Extract and manipulate particular parts of images and videos
- Track objects or colors from videos
- Recognize specific object or faces from images and videos
- How to create Augmented Reality applications
- Apply artificial neural networks and machine learning to improve object recognition

Leave a review – let other readers know what you think

Please share your thoughts on this book with others by leaving a review on the site that you bought it from. If you purchased the book from Amazon, please leave us an honest review on this book's Amazon page. This is vital so that other potential readers can see and use your unbiased opinion to make purchasing decisions, we can understand what our customers think about our products, and our authors can see your feedback on the title that they have worked with Packt to create. It will only take a few minutes of your time, but is valuable to other potential customers, our authors, and Packt. Thank you!

Index